AMERICAN CAPITALISM

A Reader

Edward E. Baptist and Louis Hyman

EDITORS

SIMON & SCHUSTER PAPERBACKS

New York London Toronto Sydney New Delhi

Simon & Schuster Paperbacks
An Imprint of Simon & Schuster, Inc.
1230 Avenue of the Americas
New York, NY 10020

First Simon & Schuster trade paperback edition May 2017

For information about special discounts for bulk purchases, please contact Simon
& Schuster Special Sales at 1-866-506-1949 or business@simonandschuster.com.

The Simon & Schuster Speakers Bureau can bring authors to your live event. For
more information or to book an event, contact the Simon & Schuster Speakers
Bureau at 1-866-248-3049 or visit our website at www.simonspeakers.com.

Interior design by Ellen Sasahara

Manufactured in the United States of America

1 3 5 7 9 10 8 6 4 2

Library of Congress Cataloging-in-Publication Data is available.

ISBN 978-1-5011-7130-7
ISBN 978-1-4767-8431-1 (ebook)

Acknowledgments

We would like to thank our amazing research assistants, Ben Schneider and Jessica Stewart, for being generally swell and helping us to put together this reader. We hope that they will be teaching these documents very soon as graduate students.

Contents

-+=◎ PART I ◎=+-
CAPITALISM COMES TO AMERICA

MODULE 1: Economies Before Capitalism

MODULE 2: Mercantile World

➻➡ PART II ⬅➻

MAKING CAPITALISM AMERICAN

MODULE 6: The Haitian Revolution and the War of 1812

MODULE 7: Slavery and Industrial Demand

⊷═◉ PART III ◉═⊷
MAKING CORPORATE CAPITALISM

MODULE 12: Second Industrial Revolution

MODULE 13: Legitimating Capitalism

MODULE 14: Jim Crow Capitalism

MODULE 15: Fordism

MODULE 16: New Deal Capitalism

MODULE 17: Capitalism at War

PART IV

MAKING AMERICAN CAPITALISM GLOBAL

MODULE 18: American Superpower

MODULE 19: Postwar Capitalism

Foreword

EDWARD E. BAPTIST

Welcome to this collection of important documents and essays about the history of American capitalism. We hope you will find these to be useful supplements to courses on the history of capitalism in the United States and elsewhere. There is no one right way to read this book, and no one right way to use it as part of a course. We only hope that you will find these readings as illuminating as we have found them. Taken together, these are the bricks and mortar that allowed us to build more than a class about a specific subject, taught in a specific format. In fact, they have enabled us to shape our understandings of how capitalism has developed and changed and how it continues to change in the United States—and how those developments and changes shape lives, here and in the rest of the world.

As Louis Hyman explains in the first of the following readings, it is a strange but true fact that in the precise span of years during which the world watched the fall of North Atlantic capitalism's greatest opponent—the state-run quasi-socialist political economies of the Soviet bloc—many academic historians stopped talking about capitalism. But even if the fish is unaware of the water it breathes, the fact that it has gills shapes everything about it. The growing system of capitalism—distinctive patterns of property ownership, work, trade, and investment—is what has given shape to U.S. history over the centuries. No major institution in the United States has been untouched by that system.

And given the power of the U.S. economy to shape world markets, and the power of the American government to make the rules of international trade and finance, and the attractiveness of the U.S.

consumer market for overseas investors and manufacturers, and the attractiveness of American popular culture . . . well, you get the idea. American capitalism doesn't just shape U.S. history, it shapes world history. Although the all-powerful degree of that influence is "new"— a post–World War II phenomenon—the fact of it began even before the first bag of Georgia cotton picked by enslaved African Americans reached the Liverpool docks. So the story told in these readings is, to some extent, the story of the world as a whole since 1776, when the United States became the first postcolonial economy to launch itself into the struggle to develop and achieve prosperity. American democracy and American capitalism have grown hand-in-hand.

Here are the mosaic pieces of the vast, chaotic, astonishing story that has followed in the years since 1776. We look forward to hearing, seeing, reading about, and understanding how you fit them together into your own coherent picture.

Ithaca, NY
March 2014

Why Study the History of Capitalism?

LOUIS HYMAN

Last spring, I received a phone call from a reporter at *The New York Times*. Since I have written a couple books on the history of American personal debt, the occasional inquiry from journalists was not out of place, but usually they want to hear about the five best financial tips for success, not "real" history.

This particular journalist, Jennifer Schuessler, asked me a very odd question: What does it mean to write the history of capitalism? I was dumbfounded. I paused. I asked her where she had even heard that term. She evaded the answer—"oh, it's in the air"—but I began to tell her about where I thought the burgeoning subfield had come from, peppering my response with terms like "agency," "contingency" and other history jargon. She told me she could translate.

As I spoke, I kept wondering why she cared. After all, *The New York Times* does not usually run stories on the subfields of academic disciplines, especially history. So you can imagine my surprise when I woke up the next Sunday and saw the front-page headline: "In History Departments, It's Up With Capitalism." For days, it was the most emailed story on the *Times* web site, with hundreds of people suddenly weighing in to comment on what capitalism meant.

The discussion forums were, in many ways, more revealing than the article itself. Internet trolls had their say, but I was much more struck by the forums' threads of disagreement. Many readers pointed out what they thought all the scholars had missed or excluded, all in an effort to determine whether we were pro-corporate apologists funded by big money (no) or communist "fifth columnists" (a more interesting charge, but again, no).

For me, the *ad hominem* attacks were less telling than the fact that there was simply a fresh discussion of capitalism. For most of the readers who weighed in, capitalism is totally explained by either Karl Marx or Adam Smith (with the occasional John Maynard Keynes or Joseph Schumpeter tossed in). That is, capitalism is a system that can be universally explained through one theory or the other. Either you understand it or you do not. Either you read the right author or you are an ignoramus. In this view, the history of capitalism is simply the logical unfolding of a natural law, like an apple falling from a tree. As one reader put it, "a history of capitalism would be as revelatory as a 'history of gravity.'"

If only events befell us as predictably as Isaac Newton's proverbial apple. History is not about proving a universal theory, but seeing how change occurs over time. As a scholarly practice, history is about explaining how events actually played out, with all their attendant unruliness. The essential problem is not to primly define capitalism like a schoolmarm, but to think about why capitalism, which appears to be so simple, evades easy definitions. And in the last decade, there has been a renewed interest among historians in not only challenging existing definitions, but in historicizing that very untidiness (much to the consternation of nominalists everywhere).

As the United States emerges from the most severe financial crisis since the Great Depression, the sudden urgency is not difficult to understand. Booms and busts buffet us with alarming frequency. But it is important to note that the term "history of capitalism" began to assume a currency in the historical profession sometime in the mid-2000s, between the tech crash and the Great Recession. While the recession has sparked renewed interest from the public, the new work preceded 2008 and marked an important shift that was not just intellectual but generational.

For two generations, almost no historians who wanted to make a name for themselves worked on economic questions. New Left scholars of the 1960s and 1970s emphasized movements that fought for social change (labor, women's, and African-American rights). The postmodern shift of the 1980s and 1990s pushed traditional subjects of economic history out of the field, and with it the stillborn subfield of cliometrics—a quantitative approach to economic history. If a scholar wrote about the history of business, or even worse, businessmen, he or she seemed to betray right-wing tendencies. If you wrote about actual businesses, many on the left felt it was only to celebrate their leaders, the way that most historians wrote celebratory histories of the oppressed. Some stalwarts remained (of all political persuasions), but on the whole, they were marginalized.

By contrast, for the generation of graduate students that came of age in the late 1990s and early 2000s, the world looked very different. Social movements had either won—or lost—decades earlier. Radical reform, in the midst of seemingly unending economic stagnation, seemed a fantasy. Most importantly, American capitalism, as of 1989, had beaten Soviet communism. The either/or distinctions of the Cold War seemed less relevant. The questions that motivated so much of social history seemed naïve. The old question "Why is there no socialism in America?" became "Why do we even talk about socialism at all, since we are in America?" We knew endless amounts about deviationist Trotskyites but nothing about hegemonic bankers.

This gap came from the belief that there was very little to know. Alfred Chandler's *The Visible Hand* was the only business history book most American graduate students of history continued to read. And it reaffirmed everything that the New Left thought about capitalism: that it was inevitable, mechanical, efficient, and boring. Capitalists operated with an inexorable logic, whereas the rest of us were "contingent agents" pursuing our free will. If pressed, few scholars would have put this assumption in these words, but it colored the questions that people asked. "Hegemony," a term appropriated from Antonio Gramsci by cultural studies scholars in the 1970s, became diluted into silly analyses of advertising. In some sense, historians

believed that they "got it" when they read Marx or Smith, and there
was nothing much left to say.

My generation was shaped by all of those New Left social movement historians, taking race/gender/class as the essential lens. Business archives look very different when you are trained by reading
Judith Butler. Banks look different when you approach them like
Michel Foucault. This type of history starts by assuming that people
on the margins matter, that culture is essential, and that questions of
gender and racial power cannot be divorced from questions of class.
Capitalism must be written from margin to center, to borrow a title
from bell hooks. This history, however, must be written, even if the
people we write about are not our heroes (something my generation
never really had).

When capitalist institutions such as banks and corporations are
treated as real places filled with real people, the stories begin to
change. The imperatives of profit remain, but the choices of how to
make that profit, if at all, begin to look much less inevitable. Moreover, it becomes impossible to ignore the ways in which those choices
are shaped, not only by inter-firm competition, but also by culture and
politics. Though important, profit becomes only one factor among
many guiding the choices of executives, whose decisions matter more
than perhaps anyone's in determining our everyday lives, especially
for those on the bottom.

In short, scholars like me, who would become historians of capitalism, came to it backwards. As an undergraduate at Columbia, my
labor history class with Joshua Freeman was standing-room-only in
a large auditorium. By contrast, when I took a class on the history
of capitalism as an undergraduate with J. W. Smit, there were only
four students. He was amazing, but such courses were far outside the
norm. When my undergraduate thesis advisor, Elizabeth Blackmar,
told me I should stop studying labor and start studying capital (my
thesis was on the radical collision of syndicalism and prohibition in
the "No Beer, No Work" movement of 1919), I looked at her as if she

were an alien. She was right, but only over time, in graduate school, did I realize that to understand the history of labor, I really needed to understand the history of capital.

Nearly everyone I know who now identifies as a historian of capitalism had a similar awakening. Kim Phillips-Fein, a historian of business leaders, supply-siders and financial crises, trenchantly wrote that "in another generation we would all have been labor historians." As graduate students, we felt isolated from the normal kinds of projects that excluded business and finance. We found each other haphazardly, often in archives, when we asked each other about our work. I first met Julia Ott, now my long-term collaborator, while we were waiting out a thunderstorm at the National Archives in Washington, D.C. I had not met a self-described "financial historian" before I met her, and it sounded like the most boring thing in the world. But later, as I started to write more about bond markets, I began to think of myself as one, too (and neither of us is *that* boring). Still, when I told people in the early 2000s that I worked on the history of personal debt, the response I most often received was a glassy-eyed stare of boredom. (Before the crash, no one wanted to talk about mortgage-backed securities. Trust me.)

Friendship begot friendship, even across generations, as people who felt isolated in the 1980s and 1990s, such as Blackmar and Richard John, now found themselves serving as the bridge to older historiographies of political economy that took the power of capitalist institutions seriously. Historians who had been working on these questions for years saw a surge in interest. Conferences, small ones at first, organized by graduate students, became slowly bigger, until the 2012 national American history conference had "Frontiers of Capitalism and Democracy" as its main theme.

Simply showing that capitalism had changed over time is in itself a major shift, as the responses in the discussion forums of *The New York Times* reminded me. Capitalism is not the end of history—as Francis Fukuyama famously put it at the end of the Cold War—it *is* our history. The changes in capitalism demand explanation. Even in just our lifetimes, we have seen how basic processes of capitalism, like work and investment, have been altered by policy, culture and invention. Topics such as inequality, unemployment, and debt crowd our newspapers and blogs.

Key to all of this was the curious divide between economists and historians, who would seem to naturally share our interest in economic history. By the 1990s, economists held enormous sway in academe, with their robust models, high salaries, and public profiles. Americans, at least in elite forums, actually listened to them. We humanists ceded the public sphere, retreating to obscure journals but confident that critical theory was still much hipper than math, even if the White House did not call us.

The voices of dissent from the market orthodoxy suddenly found new opportunities after the Great Recession. After years of economic stagnation in the United States, we can no longer blindly accept the hypothesis that the free market is efficient in the long run. Opinions that flourished on the margins could now acquire a currency in the middle. As historians love to observe, most economists have failed to provide an explanation that makes sense to people. Stories, in most situations, are more powerful than regressions. Historians clearly should triumph over economists; after all, Americans hate math as much as they love the History Channel.

Yet historians have failed in their attempt to teach this lesson to a broader public. Readers love stories, but the narratives that we have provided about capitalism have been all but ignored. Some historians are still trying to impress people with clever jargon. Others cling to the puffed-up language of Marxism, or think that to discuss how the economy works is to countenance its operations, as if we become apologists whenever we discuss anything controversial. Mostly, the problem is less one of politics than imagination. We have not fully recognized that the stakes have changed. We are living in a time of tremendous possibility to fashion new ways of explaining the economy.

The history of capitalism certainly uses statistics (and well it should), but what makes it compelling are its stories of real people doing things—sometimes really risky things. Policymakers decide to change regulations. Business leaders take risks in bold ventures. Workers actually manage to resist huge corporations. Economic theory, for instance, would tell us that depressions are the worst time to strike and organize. Yet the Flint Sit-Down Strike of 1936 took place in the middle of the Great Depression. A group of auto workers took on and won a strike against General Motors, then the most powerful corporation in the world. That reality, more than any theory, is what makes the history of capitalism different from economic history. What matters most is what cannot be entirely predicted. In this sense, the most compelling history is about entrepreneurs who challenge market equilibrium and common sense.

Nearly all of our economic theories about development emerge from our histories of capitalist growth over the past five hundred years. Only by understanding capitalism's development can we hope to spur development in emerging economies and steer developed economies onto a path of sustainable growth. Above all else, historians must remind us all that things change, even capitalism. In some sense, this idea is more radical than any millenarian communist tract. While the basic rules of capitalism might appear fixed (excess profits ought to be invested, work needs to be organized, and private property needs protecting), the forms that are possible are quite endless.

Even in the last two centuries, just in our country, the varieties of capitalism reveal how truly protean even simple ideas like "investment" can be. For example, the riskiest investments of the early nineteenth century were factories, while normal investment went into merchant ventures. The trip could be insured. Multiple friends (and it was always personal) could be brought together to split a ship and a cargo, and after the trip, the ship could be sold and the profits divided. How could a factory be divided? When would its "trip" end? The longtime horizons just seemed too risky. If you wanted to invest in production, the safe bet was not factories, but slaves. Slaves could work. Slaves could have children. With the expanding frontier, slaves could be profitably sold. If one wanted to borrow money, slaves could be easily mortgaged, or even securitized. That factories, which we now think embody conservative capitalist investment, were in some sense the wild fringe of the 1820s and 1830s complicates everything we think we know about capitalism.

New Left historians knew this bit of history as well as we do. The difference is less one of fact than one of interpretation. In this sense, the "history of capitalism" is perhaps less of a break than of a continuity with the New Left historiography—as much as every new generation likes to overthrow the last. Agency still matters to us, but we confine it to the powerful few who shaped commerce and industry. We ask more questions about firms, which still have power today, than about movements, which do not. Agency, when we see it, is a problem to explain rather than an assumption.

Would we wish that modern capitalism had evolved in some other way? Of course. But the historian's task is to confront sober reality, not fashion heroic sagas. In our reality, ordinary people can make real changes only under extraordinary circumstances. The Flint Sit-down strike can happen, but rather than make it just another case of everyday agency, it should be understood as something special so that its lessons can be understood and applied. Luckily, archives always offer more instruction in the specificity of the past, even as they push us to question our assumptions about how capitalism works. Choices were and are made every day, if not by everyone, determining not only capitalism's past but its future as well. The history of capitalism is not a fad, but something that we should think about, so that we can make better choices—when we have them—in the future.

PART I

CAPITALISM COMES TO AMERICA

MODULE 1

ECONOMIES BEFORE CAPITALISM

The Wealth of Nations (1776)

ADAM SMITH

The Wealth of Nations is the origin of Western economic thought. Every thinker since Smith has been forced to engage with his foundational ideas about division of labor, productive investment, and trade. In Smith we see the roots of both Marxism and mainstream economics. Smith's belief in manufacturing broke with Continental ideas which held that value could only come from cultivating land. Instead, he distinguishes laborers who add value to a commodity from other laborers, like "menial servants," who do not. Another major insight is that productivity can be increased by either hiring more workers or providing workers with better machines. Both choices require more capital to be invested, but the possibilities for increasing the productivity of manufacturing are much greater than those for agriculture. In this way, Smith sees the future of wealth in nations that manufacture, not in ones that simply grow crops.

BOOK I: Of the Causes of Improvement in the Productive Powers of Labour, and of the Order According to which its produce is Naturally Distributed Among the Different Ranks of the People

CHAPTER I: Of the Division of Labour

The greatest improvements in the productive powers of labour, and the greater part of the skill, dexterity, and judgment, with which it is anywhere directed, or applied, seem to have been the effects of the division of labour. The effects of the division of labour, in the general business of society, will be more easily understood, by considering in what manner it operates in some particular manufactures. It is commonly supposed to be carried furthest in some very trifling ones; not perhaps that it really is carried further in them than in others of more importance: but in those trifling manufactures which are destined to supply the small wants of but a small number of people, the whole number of workmen must necessarily be small; and those employed in every different branch of the work can often be collected into the same workhouse, and placed at once under the view of the spectator.

In those great manufactures, on the contrary, which are destined to supply the great wants of the great body of the people, every different branch of the work employs so great a number of workmen, that it is impossible to collect them all into the same workhouse. We can seldom see more, at one time, than those employed in one single branch. Though in such manufactures, therefore, the work may really be divided into a much greater number of parts, than in those of a more trifling nature, the division is not near so obvious, and has accordingly been much less observed.

To take an example, therefore, from a very trifling manufacture, but one in which the division of labour has been very often taken notice of, the trade of a pin-maker: a workman not educated to this business (which the division of labour has rendered a distinct trade), nor acquainted with the use of the machinery employed in it (to the invention of which the same division of labour has probably given occasion), could scarce, perhaps, with his utmost industry, make one pin in a day, and certainly could not make twenty. But in the way in which this business is now carried on, not only the whole work is a peculiar trade, but it is divided into a number of branches, of which the greater part are likewise peculiar trades. One man draws out the wire; another straights it; a third cuts it; a fourth points it; a fifth grinds it at the top for receiving the head; to make the head requires two or three distinct operations; to put it on is a peculiar business; to whiten the pins is another; it is even a trade by itself to put them into the paper; and the important business of making a pin is, in this manner, divided into about eighteen distinct operations, which, in some manufactories, are all performed by distinct hands, though in others the same man will sometimes perform two or three of them. I have seen a small manufactory of this kind, where ten men only were employed, and where some of them consequently performed two or three distinct operations. But though they were very poor, and therefore but indifferently accommodated with the necessary machinery, they could, when they exerted themselves, make among them about twelve pounds of pins in a day. There are in a pound upwards of four thousand pins of a middling size. Those ten persons, therefore, could make among them upwards of forty-eight thousand pins in a day. Each person, therefore, making a tenth part of forty-eight thousand pins, might be considered as making four thousand eight hundred pins in a day. But if they had all wrought separately and independently, and without any of them having been educated to this peculiar business, they certainly could not each of them have made twenty, perhaps not one pin in a day; that is, certainly, not the two hundred and fortieth, perhaps not the four thousand eight hundredth, part of what they are at present capable of performing, in consequence of a proper division and combination of their different operations.

In every other art and manufacture, the effects of the division of labour are similar to what they are in this very trifling one, though, in many of them, the labour can neither be so much subdivided, nor reduced to so great a simplicity of operation. The division of labour, however, so far as it can be introduced, occasions, in every art, a proportionable increase of the productive powers of labour.

[...] It is the great multiplication of the productions of all the different arts, in consequence of the division of labour, which occasions, in a well-governed society, that universal opulence which extends itself to the lowest ranks of the people. Every workman has a great quantity of his own work to dispose of beyond what he himself has occasion for; and every other workman being exactly in the same situation, he is enabled to exchange a great quantity of his own goods for a great quantity or, what comes to the same thing, for the price of a great quantity of theirs. He supplies them abundantly with what they have occasion for, and they accommodate him as amply with what he has occasion for, and a general plenty diffuses itself through all the different ranks of the society.

Compared, indeed, with the more extravagant luxury of the great, his accommodation must no doubt appear extremely simple and easy; and yet it may be true, perhaps, that the accommodation of an European prince does not always so much exceed that of an industrious and frugal peasant, as the accommodation of the latter exceeds that of many an African king, the absolute masters of the lives and liberties of ten thousand naked savages. [. . .]

CHAPTER II: Of the Principle which gives Occasion to the Division of Labour

This division of labour, from which so many advantages are derived, is not originally the effect of any human wisdom, which foresees and intends that general opulence to which it gives occasion. It is the necessary, though very slow and gradual, consequence of a certain propensity in human nature, which has in view no such extensive utility; the propensity to truck, barter, and exchange one thing for another.

Whether this propensity be one of those original principles in human nature, of which no further account can be given, or whether, as seems more probable, it be the necessary consequence of the faculties of reason and speech, it belongs not to our present subject to inquire.

Two greyhounds, in running down the same hare, have sometimes the appearance of acting in some sort of concert. Each turns her towards his companion, or endeavours to intercept her when his companion turns her towards himself. This, however, is not the effect of any contract, but of the accidental concurrence of their passions in the same object at that particular time. Nobody ever saw a dog make a fair and deliberate exchange of one bone for another with another dog. Nobody ever saw one animal, by its gestures and natural cries signify to another, this is mine, that yours; I am willing to give this for that. Whoever offers to another a bargain of any kind, proposes to do this. Give me that which I want, and you shall have this which you want, is the meaning of every such offer; and it is in this manner that we obtain from one another the far greater part of those good offices which we stand in need of. It is not from the benevolence of the butcher, the brewer, or the baker that we expect our dinner, but from their regard to their own interest. We address ourselves, not to their humanity, but to their self-love, and never talk to them of our own necessities, but of their advantages.

The difference of natural talents in different men, is, in reality, much less than we are aware of; and the very different genius which appears to distinguish men of different professions, when grown up to maturity, is not upon many occasions so much the cause, as the effect of the division of labour. The difference between the most dissimilar characters, between a philosopher and a common street porter, for example, seems to arise not so much from nature, as from habit, custom, and education. When they came in to the world, and for the first six or eight years of their existence, they were, perhaps, very much alike, and neither their parents nor play-fellows could perceive any remarkable difference. About that age, or soon after, they come to be employed in very different occupations. The difference of talents comes then to be taken notice of, and widens by degrees, till at last the vanity of the philosopher is willing to acknowledge scarce any resemblance. But without the disposition to truck, barter, and exchange, every man must have procured to himself every necessary and conveniency of life which he wanted. All must have had the same duties to perform, and the same work to do, and there could have been no such difference of employment as could alone give occasion to any great difference of talents.

As it is this disposition which forms that difference of talents, so remarkable among men of different professions, so it is this same disposition which renders that difference useful. Those different tribes of animals, however, though all of the same species are of scarce any use to one another. The strength of the mastiff is not in the least supported either by the swiftness of the greyhound, or by the sagacity of the spaniel, or by the docility of the shepherd's dog. The effects of those different geniuses and talents, for want of the power or disposition to barter and exchange, cannot be brought into a common stock, and do not in the least contribute to the better accommodation and conveniency of the species. Each animal is still obliged to support and defend itself, separately and independently, and derives no sort of advantage from that variety of talents with which nature has distinguished its fellows. Among men, on the contrary, the most dissimilar geniuses are of use to one another; the different produces of their respective talents, by the general disposition to truck, barter, and exchange, being brought, as it were, into a common stock, where every man may purchase whatever part of the produce of other men's talents he has occasion for.

Book II: Of the Nature, Accumulation, and Employment of Stock

Chapter III: Of the Accumulation of Capital, or of Productive and Unproductive Labour

There is one sort of labour which adds to the value of the subject upon which it is bestowed: there is another which has no such effect. The former, as it produces a value, may be called productive; the latter, unproductive labour. Thus the labour of a manufacturer adds, generally, to the value of the materials which he works upon, that of his own maintenance, and of his master's profit. The labour of a menial servant, on the contrary, adds to the value of nothing.

We are more industrious than our forefathers; because in the present times the funds destined for the maintenance of industry are much greater in proportion to those which are likely to be employed in the maintenance of idleness than they were two or three centuries ago. Our ancestors were idle for want of a sufficient encouragement to industry. It is better, says the proverb, to play for nothing than to work for nothing.

The annual produce of the land and labour of any nation can be increased in its value by no other means but by increasing either the number of its productive labourers, or the productive powers of those labourers who had before been employed. The number of its productive labourers, it is evident, can never be much increased, but in consequence of an increase of capital, or of the funds destined for maintaining them. The productive powers of the same number of labourers cannot be increased, but in consequence either of some addition and improvement to those machines and instruments which facilitate and abridge labour; or of a more proper division and distribution of employment. In either case an additional capital is almost always required. It is by means of an additional capital only that the undertaker of any work can either provide his workmen with better machinery or make a more proper distribution of employment among them.

Questions

1. Why is division of labor possible?
2. What distinguishes a productive use of capital from an unproductive use of capital?
3. Why can manufacturing expand more, in Smith's mind, than agriculture?

4. Do you think you would enjoy pin making more or less if you were a pinmaker using division of labor? Would you enjoy your overall existence more or less?

5. Smith points to trade as one of the key differences between humans and animals. How does he make his argument?

6. Smith's account is largely about individual producers exchanging goods. Why do you think that his vision of the economy does not include firms? How might this story change with larger businesses?

7. Does Smith believe that talent is innate or learned? What does this mean for division of labor? What does this mean about the justice of inequality?

8. Selfishness is not usually thought of as a virtue, yet for Smith it results in virtuous outcomes. Does this imply that selfishness is not in fact unvirtuous?

9. How does Smith justify the existence of peasants in a wealthy country?

The Communist Manifesto (1848)

KARL MARX AND FRIEDRICH ENGELS

By the early 1830s, the process of industrialization, which had allowed capitalism to take hold of British society and start it on a process of continual transformation, had made Britain the wealthiest and most powerful country in the world. For some in the new working class of the factory towns and cities, life in what the poet and early critic of industrialization William Blake called "the dark Satanic mills" was indeed a process of brutalization and exploitation. The disruption of traditional agricultural society and the increasing adherence of some to the idea that the market was the measure of all things meant that community support for the poor decreased. This happened just as uncertainty and the migration to cities separated many from agricultural societies' kinship networks and other ways of cushioning economic uncertainty. Disease and malnutrition, along with child labor, persistent homelessness, and crime were thus shocking and newly prominent features of life in working places like the factory towns around Manchester, or the slums of London and Liverpool.

Many in the United States hoped that America would experience the tremendous economic growth that Britain enjoyed without the social costs. Some looked at rapidly growing urban centers like New York, or factory towns in the New England textile belt, and worried about what they saw. They perceived not only poverty and exploitation but also disquieting social changes as well: the arrival of immigrants from Europe, many of them Catholic and many non-English-speakers; the breakdown of traditional family authority as daughters and sons left the rural economy and went to earn a wage; the rise of nonmarital sexual commerce in the prostitution districts that sprang up wherever the newly wealthy bourgeoisie crossed paths with destitute women. Some of the critics of social change believed that the solution was social reform. Many believed that such reforms could be accomplished by religious conversion, which would inspire more moral behavior. A new wave of evangelization, led by both men and women, swept across the United States between the 1820s and the 1840s. From that wave grew numerous organizations designed to inspire temperance in the consumption of alcohol, to save prostitutes by giving them Bibles, and also to persuade Northerners of the evils of slavery in the South. Some among this upswelling of reformers would eventually move into still more radical orbits, becoming critics of basic social institutions like marriage, or arguing for the equality of men and women, pacifism, major dietary reforms, or immediate abolition of slavery.

Meanwhile, western European countries like France, Belgium, and the various states of Germany (which would not be fully unified under one government until 1871) were also beginning to experience industrialization. By the 1830s, textile mills and other elements of the factory system, for instance, were appearing in the cities of the Rhine Valley, where a young man from the German city of Trier named Karl Marx was attending college. Marx would be the driving intellectual force behind *The Communist Manifesto*. In the course of his law studies at the universities of Bonn and Berlin, he became embroiled in the debates of radical German political and philosophical circles. By the early 1840s, he had become fascinated with the emergence of the factory system. In some ways, studying the history and analyzing the characteristics of industrial capitalism would occupy him for the rest of his life. In 1843, he moved to Paris, where he became close friends with Friedrich Engels, the son of a wealthy German who, ironically, owned a cotton textile factory in Manchester. Engels was soon sent to Manchester to work at (and later manage) the factory. Eventually he would use some of its earnings to subsidize Marx's writing. But that would all be after 1848.

In the meantime, Engels studied conditions in the British textile mills and wrote a book called *The Condition of the English Working Class* (1845), which is still one of the best studies of life during early industrialization. After returning to Paris, he and Marx next moved to Brussels. There they began to organize what they hoped would be a radical movement to overthrow the industrial bourgeoisie and establish a new society and government all across western Europe, one led by the industrial working class and holding property in common. This "Communist" society, they hoped, would lead humanity into a new golden era that combined the hopes of political and social equality that were so important to many with egalitarian sharing of the prosperity that derived from the productive energies of industrialization. Marx and Engels published the *Manifesto*, which explained the analysis, the principles, and the hopes of radical Communists, in February 1848. Shortly afterward, a revolution broke out in France, and soon it spread to much of the rest of western Europe. Authorities were looking for Marx, along with many other radicals. He eventually found asylum in London, where he spent most of the rest of his life. Over the next thirty-odd years he would write many things, including journalistic commentary on the American Civil War, and volumes of analysis of economics and history that we now know by the titles *Grundrisse* and *Capital*, volumes 1–3.

Marx and Engels probably hoped that the 1848 uprisings against traditional rulers, which anyone could have seen were on the horizon during the months when the two of them were writing the *Manifesto*, would become a class revolution in which the industrial workers would rise up and take the reins of western European societies. That did not happen, and even the defenders of Communism as an idea and an intellectual tradition would probably concede that in some ways it has never happened. So, why should you read *The Communist Manifesto*? Well, for one thing, it is one of the most important documents in human history. It helped launch the movement that became capitalism's biggest challenger and most serious alternative. And although the Marxism-Leninism of the old Soviet bloc now appears to be dead and buried, the *Manifesto* also contains some powerfully accurate criticisms of industrial capitalism. Marx and Engels were probably right to argue that crises of overproduction, driven by the enhanced technological capacity of the factory system (and the workers who toiled to supply it with raw materials, in the case of the American South's cotton-making slave-labor camps), were in turn driving a series of historical crises. The *Manifesto* was also on target when it argued that the emergence of industrial production was one of the most profound transformations in human history.

Although not everyone would agree with the criticisms the *Manifesto* offered, much less the solutions it proposed, many others agreed with at least some portion of it. Much of its proposed program has been adopted at one point or another by various societies and governments around the globe. Alexander Hamilton and Henry Clay, for instance, had already built their political careers in the United States on the advocacy of central banks and government support of internal improvements that would facilitate commerce and communication. By the early twentieth century, most Western governments had adopted some kind of inheritance tax—as the *Manifesto* suggests—in order to keep capital from stagnating in the hands of a few families who would have no incentive to invest it in truly entrepreneurial or socially beneficial ways. And many people have begun to think about human history along some of the lines proposed by Marx and Engels. Like it or not, the way that the *Manifesto* proposes we view human social, cultural, economic, and political development has shaped us all. Thinking about the human past as a series of struggles over economic resources, and thinking about processes of production as generators of particular forms of social and cultural order—these are things we now do "naturally," whether we are leftist, rightist, or somewhere in between. In fact, it was not until the *Manifesto* was published that people began to call the massive economic forces that were reshaping human history by the one name "capitalism." So in some ways, *The Communist Manifesto* is the earliest history of capitalism.

The history of all hitherto existing society is the history of class struggles.

Freeman and slave, patrician and plebeian, lord and serf, guild-master and journeyman, in a word, oppressor and oppressed, stood in constant opposition to one another, carried on an uninterrupted, now hidden, now open fight, a fight that each time ended, either in a revolutionary reconstitution of society at large, or in the common ruin of the contending classes.

In the earlier epochs of history, we find almost everywhere a complicated arrangement of society into various orders, a manifold gradation of social rank. In ancient Rome we have patricians, knights, plebeians, slaves; in the Middle Ages, feudal lords, vassals, guild-masters, journeymen, apprentices, serfs; in almost all of these classes, again, subordinate gradations.

The modern bourgeois society that has sprouted from the ruins of feudal society has not done away with class antagonisms. It has but established new classes, new conditions of oppression, new forms of struggle in place of the old ones.

Our epoch, the epoch of the bourgeoisie, possesses, however, this distinct feature: it has simplified class antagonisms. Society as a whole is more and more splitting up into two great hostile camps, into two great classes directly facing each other—Bourgeoisie and Proletariat.

From the serfs of the Middle Ages sprang the chartered burghers of the earliest towns. From these burgesses the first elements of the bourgeoisie were developed.

The discovery of America, the rounding of the Cape, opened up fresh ground for the rising bourgeoisie. The East-Indian and Chinese markets, the colonisation of America, trade with the colonies, the increase in the means of exchange and in commodities generally, gave to commerce, to navigation, to industry, an impulse never before known, and thereby, to the revolutionary element in the tottering feudal society, a rapid development.

The feudal system of industry, in which industrial production was monopolised by closed guilds, now no longer sufficed for the growing wants of the new markets. The manufacturing system took its place. [...]

Meantime the markets kept ever growing, the demand ever rising. Even manufacture no longer sufficed. Thereupon, steam and machinery revolutionised industrial production. The place of manufacture was taken by the giant, Modern Industry; the place of the industrial middle class by industrial millionaires, the leaders of the whole industrial armies, the modern bourgeois.

Modern industry has established the world market, for which the discovery of America paved the way. This market has given an immense development to commerce, to navigation, to communication by land. This development has, in its turn, reacted on the extension of industry; and in proportion as industry, commerce, navigation, railways extended, in the same proportion the bourgeoisie developed, increased its capital, and pushed into the background every class handed down from the Middle Ages.

We see, therefore, how the modern bourgeoisie is itself the product of a long course of development, of a series of revolutions in the modes of production and of exchange. [...]

The bourgeoisie, wherever it has got the upper hand, has put an end to all feudal, patriarchal, idyllic relations. It has pitilessly torn asunder the motley feudal ties that bound man to his "natural superiors," and has left remaining no other nexus between man and man than naked self-interest, than callous "cash payment." It has drowned the most heavenly ecstasies of religious fervour, of chivalrous enthusiasm, of philistine sentimentalism, in the icy water of egotistical calculation. It has resolved personal worth into exchange value, and in place of the numberless indefeasible chartered freedoms, has set up that single, unconscionable freedom—Free Trade. In one word, for exploitation, veiled by religious and political illusions, it has substituted naked, shameless, direct, brutal exploitation.

The bourgeoisie has stripped of its halo every occupation hitherto honoured and looked up to with reverent awe. It has converted the physician, the lawyer, the priest, the poet, the man of science, into its paid wage labourers.

The bourgeoisie has torn away from the family its sentimental veil, and has reduced the family relation to a mere money relation.

[. . .] It has been the first to show what man's activity can bring about. It has accomplished wonders far surpassing Egyptian pyramids, Roman aqueducts, and Gothic cathedrals; it has conducted expeditions that put in the shade all former Exoduses of nations and crusades.

The bourgeoisie cannot exist without constantly revolutionising the instruments of production, and thereby the relations of production, and with them the whole relations of society. Conservation of the old modes of production in unaltered form, was, on the contrary, the first condition of existence for all earlier industrial classes. Constant revolutionising of production, uninterrupted disturbance of all social conditions, everlasting uncertainty and agitation distinguish the bourgeois epoch from all earlier ones. All fixed, fast-frozen relations, with their train of ancient and venerable prejudices and opinions, are swept away, all new-formed ones become antiquated before they can ossify. All that is solid melts into air, all that is holy is profaned, and man is at last compelled to face with sober senses his real conditions of life, and his relations with his kind. The need of a constantly expanding market for its products chases the bourgeoisie over the entire surface of the globe. It must nestle everywhere, settle everywhere, establish connexions everywhere.

The bourgeoisie has through its exploitation of the world market given a cosmopolitan character to production and consumption in every country. To the great chagrin of Reactionists, it has drawn from under the feet of industry the national ground on which it stood. All old-established national industries have been destroyed or are daily being destroyed. They are dislodged by new industries, whose introduction becomes a life and death question for all civilised nations, by industries that no longer work up indigenous raw material, but raw material drawn from the remotest zones; industries whose products are consumed, not only at home, but in every quarter of the globe. In place of the old wants, satisfied by the production of the country, we find new wants, requiring for their satisfaction the products of distant lands and climes. In place of the old local and national seclusion and self-sufficiency, we have intercourse in every direction, universal inter-dependence of nations. And as in material, so also in intellectual production. The intellectual creations of individual nations become common property. National one-sidedness and narrow-mindedness become more and more impossible, and from the numerous national and local literatures, there arises a world literature.

[. . .] In one word, it creates a world after its own image.

The bourgeoisie, during its rule of scarce one hundred years, has created more massive and more colossal productive forces than have all preceding generations together. [. . .]

Modern bourgeois society, with its relations of production, of exchange and of property, a society that has conjured up such gigantic means of production and of exchange, is like the sorcerer who is no longer able to control the powers of the nether world whom he has called up by his spells. [. . .] The conditions of bourgeois society are too narrow to comprise the wealth created by them. And how does the bourgeoisie get over these crises? On the one hand by enforced destruction of a mass of productive forces; on the other, by the conquest of new markets, and by the more thorough exploitation of the old ones. That is to say, by paving the way for more extensive and more destructive crises, and by diminishing the means whereby crises are prevented. [. . .]

In proportion as the bourgeoisie, i.e., capital, is developed, in the same proportion is the proletariat, the modern working class, developed—a class of labourers, who live only so long as they find work, and who find work only so long as their labour increases capital. These labourers, who must sell themselves piecemeal, are a commodity, like every other article of commerce, and are consequently exposed to all the vicissitudes of competition, to all the fluctuations of the market.

Owing to the extensive use of machinery, and to the division of labour, the work of the proletarians has lost all individual character, and, consequently, all charm for the workman. He becomes an appendage of the machine, and it is only the most simple, most monotonous, and most easily acquired knack, that is required of him. Hence, the cost of production of a workman is restricted, almost entirely, to the means of subsistence that he requires for maintenance, and for the propagation of his race. But the price of a commodity, and therefore also of labour, is equal to its cost of production. In proportion, therefore, as the repulsiveness of the work increases, the wage decreases. Nay more, in proportion as the use of machinery and division of labour increases, in the same proportion the burden of toil also increases, whether by prolongation of the working hours, by the increase of the work exacted in a given time or by increased speed of machinery, etc.

Modern Industry has converted the little workshop of the patriarchal master into the great factory of the industrial capitalist. Masses of labourers, crowded into the factory, are organised like soldiers.

As privates of the industrial army they are placed under the command of a perfect hierarchy of officers and sergeants. Not only are they slaves of the bourgeois class, and of the bourgeois State [. . .] The less the skill and exertion of strength implied in manual labour, in other words, the more modern industry becomes developed, the more is the labour of men superseded by that of women. Differences of age and sex have no longer any distinctive social validity for the working class. All are instruments of labour, more or less expensive to use, according to their age and sex.

[. . .] But with the development of industry, the proletariat not only increases in number; it becomes concentrated in greater masses, its strength grows, and it feels that strength more. The various interests and conditions of life within the ranks of the proletariat are more and more equalised, in proportion as machinery obliterates all distinctions of labour, and nearly everywhere reduces wages to the same low level. The growing competition among the bourgeois, and the resulting commercial crises, make the wages of the workers ever more fluctuating. The increasing improvement of machinery, ever more rapidly developing, makes their livelihood more and more precarious; the collisions between individual workmen and individual bourgeois take more and more the character of collisions between two classes. Thereupon, the workers begin to form combinations (Trades' Unions) against the bourgeois; they club together in order to keep up the rate of wages; they found permanent associations in order to make provision beforehand for these occasional revolts. Here and there, the contest breaks out into riots.

Now and then the workers are victorious, but only for a time. The real fruit of their battles lies, not in the immediate result, but in the ever expanding union of the workers. This union is helped on by the improved means of communication that are created by modern industry, and that place the workers of different localities in contact with one another. It was just this contact that was needed to centralise the numerous local struggles, all of the same character, into one national struggle between classes. But every class struggle is a political struggle. [...]

Altogether collisions between the classes of the old society further, in many ways, the course of development of the proletariat. The bourgeoisie finds itself involved in a constant battle. At first with the aristocracy; later on, with those portions of the bourgeoisie itself, whose interests have become antagonistic to the progress of industry; at all time with the bourgeoisie of foreign countries. In all these battles, it sees itself compelled to appeal to the proletariat, to ask for help, and thus, to drag it into the political arena. The bourgeoisie itself, therefore, supplies the proletariat with its own elements of political and general education, in other words, it furnishes the proletariat with weapons for fighting the bourgeoisie.

[...]The essential conditions for the existence and for the sway of the bourgeois class is the formation and augmentation of capital; the condition for capital is wage-labour. Wage-labour rests exclusively on competition between the labourers. The advance of industry, whose involuntary promoter is the bourgeoisie, replaces the isolation of the labourers, due to competition, by the revolutionary combination, due to association. The development of Modern Industry, therefore, cuts from under its feet the very foundation on which the bourgeoisie produces and appropriates products. What the bourgeoisie therefore produces, above all, are its own gravediggers. Its fall and the victory of the proletariat are equally inevitable. [...]

The proletariat will use its political supremacy to wrest, by degree, all capital from the bourgeoisie, to centralise all instruments of production in the hands of the State, i.e., of the proletariat organised as the ruling class; and to increase the total productive forces as rapidly as possible.

Of course, in the beginning, this cannot be effected except by means of despotic inroads on the rights of property, and on the conditions of bourgeois production; by means of measures, therefore, which appear economically insufficient and untenable, but which, in the course of the movement, outstrip themselves, necessitate further inroads upon the old social order, and are unavoidable as a means of entirely revolutionising the mode of production.

These measures will, of course, be different in different countries.

Nevertheless, in most advanced countries, the following will be pretty generally applicable.

1. Abolition of property in land and application of all rents of land to public purposes.

2. A heavy progressive or graduated income tax.

3. Abolition of all rights of inheritance.

4. Confiscation of the property of all emigrants and rebels.

5. Centralisation of credit in the hands of the state, by means of a national bank with State capital and an exclusive monopoly.

6. Centralisation of the means of communication and transport in the hands of the State.

7. Extension of factories and instruments of production owned by the State; the bringing into cultivation of waste-lands, and the improvement of the soil generally in accordance with a common plan.

8. Equal liability of all to work. Establishment of industrial armies, especially for agriculture.

9. Combination of agriculture with manufacturing industries; gradual abolition of all the distinction between town and country by a more equable distribution of the populace over the country.

10. Free education for all children in public schools. Abolition of children's factory labour in its present form. Combination of education with industrial production, &c, &c.

[. . .] Political power, properly so called, is merely the organised power of one class for oppressing another. If the proletariat during its contest with the bourgeoisie is compelled, by the force of circumstances, to organise itself as a class, if, by means of a revolution, it makes itself the ruling class, and, as such, sweeps away by force the old conditions of production, then it will, along with these conditions, have swept away the conditions for the existence of class antagonisms and of classes generally, and will thereby have abolished its own supremacy as a class.

In place of the old bourgeois society, with its classes and class antagonisms, we shall have an association, in which the free development of each is the condition for the free development of all.

Questions

1. Sketch out the path of economic development under capitalism, according to Marx and Engels.
2. Consider the first line from the *Manifesto*: "The history of all hitherto existing society is the history of class struggles." To what extent do you agree or disagree, and why?
3. Who are the classes in industrial capitalism, how did they originate, and what is their supposed future?
4. *The Communist Manifesto* has a special place and special praise for those "elements" of the ruling class who come over to the side of the revolutionary proletariat. Who are Marx and Engels talking about when they write that?
5. What is the role of America, whether the United States or the Americas in general, in the argument made by *The Communist Manifesto*?

6. Are historical events inevitable? What about broad structural shifts and movements?

7. How would Marx interpret globalization today? Does globalization fit with his schema for the future of capitalism?

8. Would Marx have been surprised that the "Communist" revolutions ultimately took place outside of Europe and the U.S., in predominantly peasant economies (e.g., Russia and China)?

A Farewell to Alms: A Brief Economic
History of the World (2007)

GREGORY CLARK

Gregory Clark's very controversial *A Farewell to Alms* received extensive criticism because it seems to depict the Industrial Revolution as something produced by a behavioral change. The section we excerpt here is on the pre-industrial world, however. It begins from the basic fact that for most human beings, life after the beginning of the age of agriculture was actually worse than life in the Stone Age. But it also suggests that while the change in (some) human economies after 1800 is dramatic, the roots of the change originate long before, in the slow, barely observed processes of change in human attitudes that provided the setup for innovation and the investment to make innovation tell in the years of the Industrial Revolution.

The basic outline of world economic history is surprisingly simple. Indeed it can be summarized in one diagram: Figure 1.1. Before 1800 income per person—the food, clothing, heat, light, and housing available per head—varied across societies and epochs. But there was no upward trend. A simple but powerful mechanism, [. . .] the Malthusian Trap, ensured that short-term gains in income through technological advances were inevitably lost through population growth.

Thus the average person in the world of 1800 was no better off than the average person of 100,000 BC. Indeed in 1800 the bulk of the world's population was poorer than their remote ancestors.

The lucky denizens of wealthy societies such as eighteenth-century England or the Netherlands managed a material lifestyle equivalent to that of the Stone Age. But the vast swath of humanity in East and South Asia, particularly in China and Japan, eked out a living under conditions probably significantly poorer than those of cavemen.

The quality of life also failed to improve on any other observable dimension. Life expectancy was no higher in 1800 than for hunter-gatherers: thirty to thirty-five years. Stature, a measure both of the quality of diet and of children's exposure to disease, was higher in the Stone Age than in 1800. And while foragers satisfy their material wants with small amounts of work, the modest comforts of the English in 1800 were purchased only through a life of unrelenting drudgery. Nor did the variety of material consumption improve. The average forager had a diet, and a work life, much more varied than the typical English worker of 1800, even though the English table by then included such exotics as tea, pepper, and sugar.

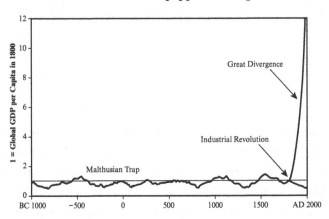

Figure 1.1: World economic history in one picture. Incomes rose sharply in many countries after 1800 but declined in others.

[. . .] The Industrial Revolution, a mere two hundred years ago, changed forever the possibilities for material consumption. Incomes per person began to undergo sustained growth in a favored group of countries. The richest modern economies are now ten to twenty times wealthier than the 1800 average. Moreover the biggest beneficiary of the Industrial Revolution has so far been the unskilled. There have been benefits aplenty for the typically wealthy owners of land or capital, and for the educated. But industrialized economies saved their best gifts for the poorest.

Prosperity, however, has not come to all societies. Material consumption in some countries, mainly in sub-Saharan Africa, is now well below the preindustrial norm. Countries such as Malawi or Tanzania would be better off in material terms had they never had contact with the industrialized world and instead continued in their preindustrial state. Modern medicine, airplanes, gasoline, computers—the whole technological cornucopia of the past two hundred years—have succeeded there in producing among the lowest material living standards ever experienced. These African societies have remained trapped in the Malthusian era, where technological advances merely produce more people and living standards are driven down to subsistence. But modern medicine has reduced the material minimum required for subsistence to a level far below that of the Stone Age. Just as the Industrial Revolution reduced income inequalities within societies, it has increased them between societies, in a process recently labeled the Great Divergence. The gap in incomes between countries is of the order of 50:1. There walk the earth now both the richest people who ever lived and the poorest.

Thus world economic history poses three interconnected problems: Why did the Malthusian Trap persist for so long? Why did the initial escape from that trap in the Industrial Revolution occur on one tiny island, England, in 1800? Why was there the consequent Great Divergence?

[The origin of the] Great Divergence, lies in processes that began thousands of years ago, deep in the Malthusian era. The dead hand of the past still exerts a powerful grip on the economies of the present. The recent demise first of the American farmer and then of the manufacturing worker were already preordained when income began its upward march during the Industrial Revolution. Had we been more clear-sighted, we could have foreseen in 1800 our world of walk-in closets, his-and-her bathrooms, caramel macchiatos, balsamic reductions, boutique wines, liberal arts colleges, personal trainers, and $50 entrees.

There are surely many surprises ahead for mankind in the centuries to come, but for the most part the economic future is not an alien and exotic land. We already see how the rich live, and their current lifestyle predicts powerfully how we will all eventually live if economic growth continues. Just as we can see the future through the lives of the rich, so the small wealthy elite of the preindustrial world led lives that prefigured our own. The delight of the modern American suburbanite in his or her first SUV echoes precisely that of Samuel Pepys, the wealthy London civil servant, on acquiring his first coach in 1668. A walk through the reconstructed villas of Pompeii and Herculaneum, frozen in time on the day of the eruption of Vesuvius in AD 79, reveals homes that suburban Americans would happily move into: "Charming home with high ceilings, central courtyard, great room, finely detailed mosaics, and garden water feature—unobstructed Vesuvian views."

[. . .] The economy of humans in the years before 1800 turns out to be just the natural economy of all animal species, with the same kinds of factors determining the living conditions of animals and humans. It is called the Malthusian Trap because the vital insight underlying the model was that of the Reverend Thomas Robert Malthus, who in 1798 in *An Essay on the Principle of Population* took the initial steps toward understanding the logic of this economy [. . .] [in which] economic policy was turned on its head: vice now was virtue then, and virtue vice. Those scourges of failed modern states—war, violence, disorder, harvest failures, collapsed public infrastructures, bad sanitation—were the friends of mankind before 1800. They reduced population pressures and increased material living standards. [. . .]

[This reveals] the crucial importance of fertility control to material conditions before 1800. [. . .] Mortality conditions also mattered, and here Europeans were lucky to be a filthy people who squatted happily above their own feces, stored in basement cesspits, in cities such as London. Poor hygiene, combined with high urbanization rates with their attendant health issues, meant incomes had to be high to maintain the population in eighteenth-century England and the Netherlands. The Japanese, with a more highly developed sense of cleanliness, could maintain the level of population at miserable levels of material comforts, and they were accordingly condemned to subsist on a much more limited income.

Since the economic laws governing human society were those that govern all animal societies, mankind was subject to natural selection throughout the Malthusian era, even after the arrival of settled agrarian societies with the Neolithic Revolution of 8000 BC, which transformed hunters into settled agriculturalists. The Darwinian struggle that shaped human nature did not end with the Neolithic Revolution but continued right up until the Industrial Revolution.

For England [. . .] in the years 1250–1800 [. . .] economic success translated powerfully into reproductive success. The richest men had twice as many surviving children at death as the poorest. The poorest individuals in Malthusian England had so few surviving children that their families were dying out. Preindustrial England was thus a world of constant downward mobility. Given the static nature of the Malthusian economy, the superabundant children of the rich had to, on average, move down the social hierarchy in order to find work. Craftsmen's sons became laborers, merchants' sons petty traders, large landowners' sons smallholders. [. . .] The economy of the preindustrial era was shaping people, at least culturally and perhaps also genetically. The Neolithic Revolution created agrarian societies that were just as capital intensive as the modern world. At least in England, the emergence of such an institutionally stable, capital-intensive economic system created a society that rewarded middle-class values with reproductive success, generation after generation. This selection process was accompanied by changes in the characteristics of the preindustrial economy, due largely to the population's adoption of more middle-class preferences. Interest rates fell, murder rates declined, work hours increased, the taste for violence declined, and numeracy and literacy spread even to the lower reaches of society. The stasis of the preindustrial world [. . .] was shattered by two seemingly unprecedented events in European society in the years 1760–1900. The first was the Industrial Revolution, the appearance for the first time of rapid economic growth fueled by increasing production efficiency made possible by advances in knowledge. The second was the demographic transition, a decline in fertility which started with the upper classes and gradually encompassed all of society. The demographic transition allowed the efficiency advance of the Industrial Revolution to translate not into an endless supply of impoverished people but into the astonishing rise of income per person that we have seen since 1800. [. . .] The Industrial Revolution and the associated demographic transition constitute the great questions of economic history.

Questions

1. Clark claims that the poorest have benefited the most from industrialization. Given the massive wealth of the top tier of current income distribution, how can this claim possibly be true?

2. Do the lifestyles of the rich and famous of today predict the ordinary lives of the future? Can that be possible, or are there major constraints that will reverse the rapid economic growth of the last two hundred and fifty years?

3. Would you place as much emphasis as Clark on natural selection as a cause of the Industrial Revolution? If so, then why did those who were exiled to North America as indentured servants, slaves, or convicts play such a big role in forming one of the most successful of all industrial economies?

MODULE 2

MERCANTILE WORLD

The First Charter of Virginia (1606)

KING JAMES I

Between 1492 and the early 1600s, Spanish adventurers conquered huge swaths of the New World. Their incursion into the Americas led to the deaths of millions of native people by violence, forced labor, starvation, and, above all, the introduction of Old World diseases. Meanwhile, conquistadors and their successors, who established plantations and mines operated with forced Indian labor, sent huge quantities of gold and silver back to the Old World. The influx of New World bullion helped finance Spain's imperial ambitions in Europe, and made the Spanish Crown the envy of other ambitious ruling factions.

Especially after the English Crown pushed the English people through a transition from Catholicism to Protestantism, England and aggressively Catholic Spain became rivals. Spain claimed the right to exclusive control over the New World, except for Portuguese Brazil. But English policymakers and rulers were increasingly determined to establish their own American colonies, which would enable them to obtain a share of the riches that were making Spain so powerful. In addition to the goals of gaining wealth and national glory, English writers also claimed Spanish colonization was particularly murderous. English expansion, they promised, would convert Native Americans to Protestant Christianity peacefully, and would incorporate them as partners in the larger project of national expansion without genocide or forced labor. And the process of converting part of the English rural countryside from communally controlled land, farmed by peasants using age-old subsistence methods, to "enclosed" private property farmed commercially by a new class of increasingly wealthy gentry, had produced a lot of "surplus" population.

Spanish exploration had often taken a quasi-military form. English colonization in the early 1600s was usually built on a somewhat different structure that would eventually become a crucial component of American capitalism: the joint-stock corporation. In such an organization, multiple investors pool their resources, creating a corporate entity. Their investments are reflected in shares of stock, which typically give them the right to dividends (shares of corporate profit) and a vote in corporate decision making as well. Typically, shares can be sold to others who want to become investors. The English Crown oversaw the creation of multiple joint-stock corporations. In addition to the Virginia and the Plymouth Companies, created in this charter, the East India Company had received its charter in 1600 from Queen Elizabeth I. The most successful joint-stock corporation in the world in the seventeenth century, however, was probably the massive Dutch East India Company. It dominated trade in the spices and other products of what is today Indonesia, paid annual dividends of about 20 percent, and helped seventeenth-century Amsterdam become the banking center of the Western world.

The two East India Companies were designed to gain access to the world's best-established circuits of trade—trading Asia's best-known commodities—for the merchants of upstart Protestant nations. But the Virginia Company didn't really know what it was going to trade, or whom it would find to trade with. The Native Americans who lived around Chesapeake Bay would turn out to be reluctant participants in English colonization, especially in terms of converting to Protestant Christianity. Readers should think about the obvious naïveté in the Virginia Company's plan, and they should look for it in this document. But they should also read carefully in order to discover what kind of government the document creates.

J AMES, by the Grace of God, King of England, Scotland, France and Ireland, Defender of the Faith, &c. WHEREAS our loving and well-disposed Subjects, Sir Thorn as Gales, and Sir George Somers, Knights, Richard Hackluit, Clerk, Prebendary of Westminster, and Edward-Maria Wingfield, Thomas Hanharm and Ralegh Gilbert, Esqrs. William Parker, and George Popham, Gentlemen, and divers others of our loving Subjects, have been humble Suitors unto us, that We would vouchsafe unto them our Licence, to make Habitation, Plantation, and to deduce a colony of sundry of our People into that part of America commonly called VIRGINIA, and other parts and Territories in America, either appertaining unto us, or which are not now actually possessed by any Christian Prince or People, situate, lying, and being all along the Sea Coasts, between four and thirty Degrees of Northerly Latitude from the Equinoctial Line, and five and forty Degrees of the same Latitude, and in the main Land between the same four and thirty and five and forty Degrees, and the Islands hereunto adjacent, or within one hundred Miles of the Coast thereof;

And to that End, and for the more speedy Accomplishment of their said intended Plantation and Habitation there, are desirous to divide themselves into two several Colonies and Companies; the one consisting of certain Knights, Gentlemen, Merchants, and other Adventurers, of our City of London and elsewhere, which are, and from time to time shall be, joined unto them, which do desire to begin their Plantation and Habitation in some fit and convenient Place, between four and thirty and one and forty Degrees of the said Latitude, alongst the Coasts of Virginia, and the Coasts of America aforesaid. [. . .]

We, greatly commending, and graciously accepting of, their Desires for the Furtherance of so noble a Work, which may, by the Providence of Almighty God, hereafter tend to the Glory of his Divine Majesty, in propagating of Christian Religion to such People, as yet live in Darkness and miserable Ignorance of the true Knowledge and Worship of God, and may in time bring the Infidels and Savages, living in those parts, to human Civility, and to a settled and quiet Government: DO, by these our Letters Patents, graciously accept of, and agree to, their humble and well-intended Desires;

And do therefore, for Us, our Heirs, and Successors, GRANT and agree, that the said Sir Thomas Gates, Sir George Somers, Richard Hackluit, and Edward-Maria Wingfield, Adventurers of and for our City of London, and all such others, as are, or shall be, joined unto them of that Colony, shall be called the first Colony; And they shall and may begin their said first Plantation and Habitation, at any Place upon the said-Coast of Virginia or America, where they shall think fit and convenient, between the said four and thirty and one and forty Degrees of the said Latitude; And that they shall have all the Lands, Woods, Soil, Grounds, Havens, Ports, Rivers, Mines, Minerals, Marshes, Waters, Fishings, Commodities, and Hereditaments, whatsoever, from the said first Seat of their Plantation and Habitation by the Space of fifty Miles of English Statute Measure, all along the said Coast of Virginia and America, towards the West and Southwest, as the Coast lyeth, with all the Islands within one hundred Miles directly over against the same Sea Coast; And also all the Lands, Soil, Grounds, Havens, Ports, Rivers, Mines, Minerals, Woods, Waters, Marshes, Fishings, Commodities, and Hereditaments, whatsoever, from the said Place of their first Plantation and Habitation for the space of fifty like English Miles, all alongst the said Coasts of Virginia and America, towards the East and Northeast, or towards the North, as the Coast lyeth, together with all the Islands within one hundred Miles, directly over against the said Sea Coast, And also all the Lands, Woods, Soil, Grounds, Havens, Ports,

Rivers, Mines, Minerals, Marshes, Waters, Fishings, Commodities, and Hereditaments, whatsoever, from the same fifty Miles every way on the Sea Coast, directly into the main Land by the Space of one hundred like English Miles; And shall and may inhabit and remain there; and shall and may also build and fortify within any the same, for their better Safeguard and Defense, according to their best Discretion, and the Discretion of the Council of that Colony; And that no other of our Subjects shall be permitted, or suffered, to plant or inhabit behind, or on the Backside of them, towards the main Land, without the Express License or Consent of the Council of that Colony, thereunto in Writing; first had and obtained. [. . .]

And we do also ordain, establish, and agree, for Us, our Heirs, and Successors, that each of the said Colonies shall have a Council, which shall govern and order all Matters and Causes, which shall arise, grow, or happen, to or within the same several Colonies, according to such Laws, Ordinances, and Instructions, as shall be, in that behalf, given and signed with Our Hand or Sign Manual, and pass under the Privy Seal of our Realm of England; Each of which Councils shall consist of thirteen Persons, to be ordained, made, and removed, from time to time, according as shall be directed and comprised in the same instructions. [. . .] And moreover, we do GRANT [. . .] that the said several Councils of and for the said several Colonies, shall and lawfully may, by Virtue hereof, from time to time, without any Interruption of Us, our Heirs or Successors, give and take Order, to dig, mine, and search for all Manner of Mines of Gold, Silver, and Copper, as well within any Part of their said several Colonies, as of the said main Lands on the Backside of the same Colonies; And to HAVE and enjoy the Gold, Silver, and Copper, to be gotten thereof, to the Use and Behoof of the same Colonies, and the Plantations thereof; YIELDING therefore to Us, our Heirs and Successors, the fifth Part only of all the same Gold and Silver, and the fifteenth Part of all the same Copper. [. . .] Also we do [. . .] DECLARE, by these Presents, that all and every the Persons being our Subjects, which shall dwell and inhabit within every or any of the said several Colonies and Plantations, and every of their children, which shall happen to be born within any of the Limits and Precincts of the said several Colonies and Plantations, shall HAVE and enjoy all Liberties, Franchises, and Immunities, within any of our other Dominions, to all Intents and Purposes, as if they had been abiding and born, within this our Realm of England, or any other of our said Dominions.

Moreover, our gracious Will and Pleasure is, and we do, by these Presents, for Us, our Heirs, and Successors, declare and set forth, that if any Person or Persons, which shall be of any of the said Colonies and Plantations, or any other, which shall trick to the said Colonies and Plantations, or any of them, shall, at any time or times hereafter, transport any Wares, Merchandises, or Commodities, out of any of our Dominions, with a Pretence to land, sell, or otherwise dispose of the same, within any the Limits and Precincts of any of the said Colonies and Plantations, and yet nevertheless, being at Sea, or after he hath landed the same within any of the said Colonies and Plantations, shall carry the same into any other Foreign Country, with a Purpose there to sell or dispose of the same, without the Licence of Us, our Heirs, and Successors, in that Behalf first had and obtained; That then, all the Goods and Chattels of such Person or Persons, so offending and transporting together with the said Ship or Vessel, wherein such Transportation was made, shall be forfeited to Us, our Heirs, and Successors. [. . .]

IN Witness whereof, we have caused these our Letters to be made Patent; Witness Ourself at Westminster, the tenth Day of April, in the fourth Year of our Reign of England, France, and Ireland, and of Scotland the nine and thirtieth.

Questions

1. What is the purpose of English colonization, judging from this document?

2. If this was a business plan, how would you evaluate it? Does it look like the revenue is likely to exceed the capital invested? Are there good reasons to choose this investment over another possible one?

3. What kind of government is being created here? What kinds of expectations—for policymakers, for investors, and for potential colonists—are being created here?

4. The Virginia Company, like most corporations, never turned a real profit, and failed. By the mid-1620s, the English Crown was directly administering the colony. But perhaps the way this Virginia colonization project was mapped out at its very inception set the stage for other phases of New World colonization and then expansion of the United States. Can you think of any continuities that might first be seen in the seed, here? Are those elements of American government or culture, or of American capitalism?

The Mayflower Compact, 1620: Agreement Between the Settlers at New Plymouth (1620)

By the time King James I succeeded Queen Elizabeth and became the ruler of Britain (England, Wales, and Scotland, all under one crown) in 1603, England had become a Protestant society. The question was what kind of Protestantism would dominate. Numerous groups—collectively called "Puritans"—argued that the Anglican Church was not "pure" enough in its rejection of Catholicism and what they viewed as its corrupting influences on the essential messages of Christianity. Puritans usually followed some version of Calvinist theology, which means that, like the sixteenth-century Swiss religious reformer John Calvin, they believed that God had predestined some people for salvation, but not others. Religious institutions should be led by the godly "elect," and perhaps those leaders should also run entire societies. Calvin had tried to institute such a theocracy in his hometown of Geneva, for instance. Some among the English Puritans were "non-separatist," meaning that they hoped to reform and remake the Church of England from within. These would be the source of both the Puritans who came to found the Massachusetts Bay Colony in 1629, and of much of the opposition to James I's son Charles I. In 1642 a Puritanism-influenced Parliament would emerge victorious in the English Civil War, execute Charles I, and install Oliver Cromwell as the "Lord Protector" of an English Commonwealth that for nearly two decades would go without a king.

Many people who have searched for the cultural origins of capitalist attitudes and ideas have looked to the Puritans and other

Calvinist Protestants as a source of capitalism's process of constant questioning of old ways. The Pilgrims, however—a group of "separatist" English Puritans who came to what is today Massachusetts in 1620—were not particularly successful in economic terms. And in demographic terms they would be overshadowed by the waves of "non-separatist" Puritans who fled the Crown-versus-Parliament conflicts of 1630s England and settled in the Massachusetts Bay colony. But they were the first English settlers north of Virginia, and in the form of their Mayflower Compact they created a kind of contract that would govern them for years to come. This was important as a precedent for political constitutions created by later American societies, but also because the Plymouth colony became a kind of joint-stock corporation that might be a foreshadowing of later styles of American economic organization.

IN THE NAME OF GOD, AMEN. We, whose names are underwritten, the Loyal Subjects of our dread Sovereign Lord King *James*, by the Grace of God, of *Great Britain*, *France*, and *Ireland*, King, *Defender of the Faith*, &c. Having undertaken for the Glory of God, and Advancement of the Christian Faith, and the Honour of our King and Country, a Voyage to plant the first Colony in the northern Parts of *Virginia*; Do by these Presents, solemnly and mutually, in the Presence of God and one another, covenant and combine ourselves together into a civil Body Politick, for our better Ordering and Preservation, and Furtherance of the Ends aforesaid: And by Virtue hereof do enact, constitute, and frame, such just and equal Laws, Ordinances, Acts, Constitutions, and Officers, from time to time, as shall be thought most meet and convenient for the general Good of the Colony; unto which we promise all due Submission and Obedience. IN WITNESS whereof we have hereunto subscribed our names at *Cape-Cod* the eleventh of November, in the Reign of our Sovereign

Lord King *James*, of *England*, *France*, and *Ireland*, the eighteenth, and of *Scotland* the fifty-fourth, *Anno Domini*, 1620.

Questions

1. What do the settlers claim as their purpose(s) in establishing this colony?
2. Aside from creating a legal underpinning for the colony, what do you think was the purpose of the Mayflower Compact?
3. This is a short document. Can it really have the kind of historical influence that we often ascribe to it?
4. What would be more influential over time: The Virginia colony's model of a joint-stock corporation formed in order to exploit the natural (and later, human) resources of the colony? Or the Mayflower Compact's model of a settlement that was supposed to provide a space where people could live out their own unique aspirations and dreams—in this case, as separatist Puritans?

Second Treatise of Civil Government (1690)

JOHN LOCKE

In late medieval England, a vast array of rules governed the ownership of land. Much of it was was owned in common, by villages or
other groups of people. A significant portion of it—maybe more
than a quarter—was owned by the Catholic Church, whether by
monasteries, bishops, or local churches. Other land was owned by
the Crown, or by nobles—or was it held by the Crown and perpetually granted to a noble family? It could be hard to tell. Even
when land seemed to be clearly owned by one family, it could still
be "encumbered." Readers of Jane Austen's *Pride and Prejudice* will
remember that one of the central forces driving the plot was the
fact that the Bennet family property was held under an "entail." This
meant that the land had to pass after Mr. Bennet's male heir, but as
he had only daughters, the entail would therefore give the land to
the unctuous Mr. Collins. The land couldn't be sold, or willed, as
the owner desired. Did Mr. Bennet really own the land?

   In the 1500s, during the long reigns of King Henry VIII and
his daughter Elizabeth I, two important developments took place
that would shape both John Locke's writings and the emergence
of American capitalism. The first was the creation of the Church of
England, a Protestant institution that rejected the authority of the
pope in Rome. Instead, the monarch of England became the head of
the Church of England, and Henry VIII saw this as the occasion for
seizing the Catholic Church's lands. Much of it was distributed to
his followers and henchmen. As the Catholic Church disappeared
from the scene as an English landowner, another simplification of

England's complex landholding laws and practices also began. Well-capitalized gentry began to convince local villages to sell or give up their common lands, which the gentry then "enclosed" with the hedgerows that now dominate the landscape of much of England. But these grants and purchases and deals also changed the status of a huge amount of land to "fee simple" ownership—landholdings unencumbered by restrictions on selling, transferring, using, and developing; in other words, property ownership as we now understand it. Though much land was still held in common until the late eighteenth century, enclosure made possible Locke's concepts of property, moved hundreds of thousands of people off the land, and led to a new kind of profitable commercial farming.

The philosopher John Locke, born in rural England in 1632, grew up in a world shaped by enclosure, and by Puritanism. He created a philosophy that focused on first principles. He argued that people come into the world as blank slates. These can be filled up with ideas about property and rights from existing cultural inheritances, but sound reasoning could instead lead people to the conclusion that all human beings have certain inalienable rights. These include life, liberty, and the right to own property. And what is property? Here, he argues that property is goods from the world that humans mix with their labor through processes like growing, digging up, cutting down, harvesting, collecting—and thus making their property their own, which can only be taken from them by injustice.

Locke helped draw up a set of "Fundamental Constitutions" for the Carolina colony, but he also influenced the United States in much deeper and broader ways. As you read this, think about the implications of his idea that property is a natural right. If property seems like something natural, then perhaps telling me what to do with my property is an invasion of natural rights, and must be resisted. And once people's use of property was unbound by, for instance, regulations that imposed slow growth because of community concerns like environmental damage, then the pace of economic change might accelerate. We can see the influence of Locke in many areas of American political and economic life.

Chapter V: Of Property

Sect. 25. Whether we consider natural *reason*, which tells us, that men, being once born, have a right to their preservation, and consequently to meat and drink, and such other things as nature affords for their subsistence: or *revelation*, which gives us an account of those grants God made of the world to *Adam*, and to *Noah*, and his sons, it is very clear, that God [. . .] *has given the earth to the children of men;* given it to mankind in common. But this being supposed, it seems to some a very great difficulty, how any one should ever come to have a *property* in any thing. [. . .] I shall endeavour to shew, how men might come to have a *property* in several parts of that which God gave to mankind in common, and that without any express compact of all the commoners.

Sect. 26. God, who hath given the world to men in common, hath also given them reason to make use of it to the best advantage of life, and convenience. The earth, and all that is therein, is given to men for the support and comfort of their being. And tho' all the fruits it naturally produces, and beasts it feeds, belong to mankind in common, as they are produced by the spontaneous hand of nature; and no body has originally a private dominion, exclusive of the rest of mankind, in any of them, as they are thus in their natural state: yet being given for the use of men, there must of necessity be *a means to appropriate* them some way or other, before they can be of any use, or at all beneficial to any particular man. The fruit, or venison, which nourishes the *wild Indian*, who knows no enclosure, and is still a tenant in common, must be his, and so his, i.e. a part of him, that another can no longer have any right to it, before it can do him any good for the support of his life.

Sect. 27. Though the earth, and all inferior creatures, be common to all men, yet every man has a *property* in his own *person:* this no body has any right to but himself. The *labour* of his body, and the *work* of his hands, we may say, are properly his. Whatsoever then he removes out of the state that nature hath provided, and left it in, he hath mixed his *labour* with, and joined to it something that is his own, and thereby makes it his *property. [. . .]*

Sect. 28. He that is nourished by the acorns he picked up under an oak, or the apples he gathered from the trees in the wood, has certainly appropriated them to himself. No body can deny but the nourishment is his. I ask then, when did they begin to be his? when he digested? or when he eat? or when he boiled? or when he brought them home? or when he picked them up? and it is plain, if the first gathering made them not his, nothing else could. That *labour* put a distinction between them and common: that added something to them more than nature, the common mother of all, had done; and so they became his private right. And will any one say, he had no right to those acorns or apples, he thus appropriated, because he had not the consent of all mankind to make them his? Was it a robbery thus to assume to himself what belonged to all in common? If such a consent as that was necessary, man had starved, notwithstanding the plenty God had given him. We see in *commons,* which remain so by compact, that it is the taking any part of what is common, and removing it out of the state nature leaves it in, which *begins the property;* without which the common is of no use. And the taking of this or that part, does not depend on the express consent of all the commoners. Thus the grass my horse has bit; the turfs my servant has cut; and the ore I have digged in any place, where I have a right to them in common with others, become my *property,* without the as-signation or consent of any body. The *labour* that was mine, removing them out of that common state they were in, hath *fixed my property* in them. [. . .]

Sect. 32. But the *chief matter of property. [. . .]* As *much land* as a man tills, plants, improves, cultivates, and can use the product of, so much is his *property*. He by his labour does, as it were, inclose it from the common. Nor will it invalidate his right, to say every body else has an equal title to it; and therefore he cannot appropriate, he cannot inclose, without the consent of all his fellow-commoners, all mankind. God, when he gave the world in common to all mankind, commanded man also to labour, and the penury of his condition required it of him. God and his reason commanded him to subdue the earth, i.e. improve it for the benefit of life, and therein lay out something upon it that was his own, his labour. He that in obedience to this command of God, subdued, tilled and sowed any part of it, thereby annexed to it something that was his *property*, which another had no title to, nor could without injury take from him.

Sect. 33. Nor was this *appropriation* of any parcel of land, by improving it, any prejudice to any other man, since there was still enough, and as good left; and more than the yet unprovided could use. [. . .] No body could think himself injured by the drinking of another man, though he took a good draught, who had a whole river of the same water left him to quench his thirst: and the case of land and water, where there is enough of both, is perfectly the same.

Sect. 34. God gave the world to men in common; but since he gave it them for their benefit, and the greatest conveniencies of life they were capable to draw from it, it cannot be supposed he meant it should always remain common and uncultivated. He gave it to the use of the industrious and rational, (and *labour* was to be his *title* to it;) not to the fancy or covetousness of the quarrelsome and contentious. [. . .]

Sect. 36. [. . .] Supposing a man, or family, in the state they were at first peopling of the world by the children of *Adam*, or *Noah*; let him plant in some inland, vacant places of *America*, we shall find that the *possessions* he could make himself, upon the *measures* we have given, would not be very large, nor, even to this day, prejudice the rest of mankind, or give them reason to complain, or think themselves injured by this man's incroachment, though the race of men have now spread themselves to all the corners of the world, and do infinitely exceed the small number was at the beginning. [. . .] There is land enough in the world to suffice double the inhabitants, had not the invention of money, and the tacit agreement of men to put a value on it, introduced (by consent) larger possessions, and a right to them. [. . .]

Sect. 37. This is certain, that in the beginning, before the desire of having more than man needed had altered the intrinsic value of things, which depends only on their usefulness to the life of man; or had *agreed, that a little piece of yellow metal,* which would keep without wasting or decay, should be worth a great piece of flesh, or a whole heap of corn. [. . .]

Sect. 38. [. . .] But as families increased, and industry inlarged their stocks, their *possessions inlarged* with the need of them; but yet it was commonly *without any fixed property in the ground* they made use of, till they incorporated, settled themselves together, and built cities; and then, by consent, they came in time, to set out the *bounds of their distinct territories,* and agree on limits between them and their neighbours; and by laws within themselves, settled the *properties* of those of the same society. [. . .]

Sect. 40. [. . .] Let any one consider what the difference is between an acre of land planted with tobacco or sugar, sown with wheat or barley, and an acre of the same land lying in common, without any husbandry upon it, and he will find, that the improvement of *labour makes* the far greater part of the value.

Sect. 41. There cannot be a clearer demonstration of any thing, than several nations of the *Americans* are of this, who are rich in land, and poor in all the comforts of life; whom nature having furnished as liberally as any other people, with the materials of plenty, *i.e.* a fruitful soil, apt to produce in abundance, what might serve for food, raiment, and delight; yet for *want of improving it by labour,* have not one hundredth part of the conveniencies we enjoy: and a king of a large and fruitful territory there, feeds, lodges, and is clad worse than a day-labourer in *England.* [. . .]

Sect. 46. [...] He that *gathered* a hundred bushels of acorns or apples, had thereby a *property* in them, they were his goods as soon as gathered. He was only to look, that he used them before they spoiled, else he took more than his share, and robbed others. [...] And if he also bartered away plums, that would have rotted in a week, for nuts that would last good for his eating a whole year, he did no injury; he wasted not the common stock; destroyed no part of the portion of goods that belonged to others, so long as nothing perished uselesly in his hands. Again, if he would give his nuts for a piece of metal, pleased with its colour; or exchange his sheep for shells, or wool for a sparkling pebble or a diamond, and keep those by him all his life he invaded not the right of others, he might heap up as much of these durable things as he pleased; the *exceeding of the bounds of* his *just property* not lying in the largeness of his possession, but the perishing of any thing uselessly in it.

Sect. 47. And thus *came in the use of money*, some lasting thing that men might keep without spoiling, and that by mutual consent men would take in exchange for the truly useful, but perishable supports of life.

Sect. 48. And as different degrees of industry were apt to give men possessions in different proportions, so this invention of money gave them the opportunity to continue and enlarge them. [...]

Sect. 49. Thus in the beginning all the world was *America*, and more so than that is now; for no such thing as *money* was any where known. Find out something that hath the *use and value of money* amongst his neighbours, you shall see the same man will begin presently to enlarge his possessions.

Questions

1. Locke refers to "the commons." What does he mean by this? And what does he mean when he says that someone who has the use of the commons does not have to obtain all the other

users' permission when he takes hay from it to feed his horse, or perhaps hunts or fishes there? What kind of outcome could that have?

2. "In the beginning all the world was America." What does Locke mean by this? How could settlers use his ideas about property to denigrate the claims of Native Americans to their ancestral lands? And what influence might Locke's idea that America was in a kind of state of nature have on American capitalists' ideas?

3. Which comes first for Locke: money, or the accumulation of wealth and property? Do people have a right to accumulate as much property as they can, even if they can't use it all? Why or why not?

4. What is the difference, then, between private property and common property? How do those two things become separate things, according to Locke?

MODULE 3

PLANTATIONS

Virginia Slavery Laws (1630–1670)

WILLIAM WALLER HENING

The first Africans were brought to Virginia in 1619, and almost certainly sold as slaves. Africans remained a tiny minority throughout the colony's first fifty years, numbering perhaps no more than a few hundred as late as 1650. The colony boomed during many of those years, and it did so because of the rapidly expanding European demand for tobacco. But the merchant adventurers who had formed the Virginia Company, and its earliest emissaries, were certainly not interested in the extraordinarily difficult labor of working in tobacco fields all summer long under the hot Southern sun. Even though African slavery was becoming a crucial component of European economic expansion in other parts of the New World, from the sugar plantations of Brazil to the silver mines of Peru to the cattle ranches of Hispaniola, most early Virginia labor came from indentured European servants. These were people who, in return for passage to the new World, signed a contract to toil without pay for the next term of years (usually five to seven). Many were "masterless men and women" forced out of rural England by the enclosure of much of the common land in the previous century, or people fleeing the growing Crown-versus-Parliament crisis.

Despite the fantasies of some historians, the few Africans in the Virginia colony before the 1660s were not treated as the equals of Englishmen—even though those Englishmen who toiled as indentured servants in the tobacco fields of the Chesapeake's nouveau riche were also not free. Still, the law of slavery was still undefined enough that some Africans and some children of Africans managed to achieve freedom through various means. Some converted to Christianity, and convinced court authorities that this should lead to emancipation. Some had half-white children, and the children were accounted by many as free. Others earned money and purchased their freedom.

But after the 1650s, the number of British people willing to sign away the next five to seven years of their lives in order to get to the New World began to decline. The number of enslaved Africans being brought to the Chesapeake started to increase, as English traders began to participate more heavily in the transatlantic slave trade. The legislature of the Virginia colony, the instrument of governance controlled by the most successful people in the colony, started to make and codify formal rules that would draw lines between slavery and freedom. The result was a set of codes and practices that ensured that people born of a slave mother would be slaves. The laws established the patterns of slavery in North America: that enslaved people would be fully "chattel"—property— virtually in "fee simple," tradeable, sellable, heritable and so on. And the laws drew sharp lines between the colony's poor and often less-than-free whites and its now completely unfree Africans. These lines would help to ensure a divide-and-conquer strategy that helped keep slavery around in Virginia for another two hundred years. They also ensured that, just as in other New World colonies, slavery would be a sound financial strategy for Virginia's individual entrepreneurs.

September 17, 1630. [From the Minutes of the Judicial proceedings of the Governor and Council of Virginia.]

Hugh Davis to be soundly whipped, before an assembly of Negroes and others for abusing himself to the dishonor of God and shame of Christians, by defiling his body in lying with a negro; which fault he is to acknowledge next Sabbath day.

December 1662 (Statutes):

Whereas some doubts have arisen whether children got by any Englishman upon a Negro woman should be slave or free, be it therefore enacted and declared by this present Grand Assembly, that all children born in this country shall be held bond or free only according to the condition of the mother; and that if any Christian shall commit fornication with a Negro man or woman, he or she so offending shall pay double the fines imposed by the former act.

September 1667 (Statutes)

Whereas some doubts have arisen whether children that are slaves by birth, and by the charity and piety of their owners made partakers of the blessed sacrament of baptism, should by virtue of their baptism be made free, it is enacted and declared by this Grand Assembly, and the authority thereof, that the conferring of baptism does not alter the condition of the person as to his bondage or freedom; that diverse masters, freed from this doubt may more carefully endeavor the propagation of Christianity by permitting children, through slaves, or those of greater growth if capable, to be admitted to that sacrament.

September 1668 (Statutes)

Whereas it has been questioned whether servants running away may be punished with corporal punishment by their master or magistrate, since the act already made gives the master satisfaction by prolonging their time by service, it is declared and enacted by this Assembly that moderate corporal punishment inflicted by master or magistrate upon a runaway servant shall not deprivate the master of the satisfaction allowed by the law, the one being as necessary to reclaim them from persisting in that idle course as the other is just to repair the damages sustained by the master.

October 1669 (Statutes)

Whereas the only law in force for the punishment of refractory servants resisting their master, mistress, or overseer cannot be inflicted upon Negroes, nor the obstinacy of many of them be suppressed by other than violent means, be it enacted and declared by this Grand Assembly if any slave resists his master (or other by his master's order correcting him) and by the extremity of the correction should chance to die, that his death shall not be accounted a felony, but the master (or that other person appointed by the master to punish him) be acquitted from molestation, since it cannot be presumed that premeditated malice (which alone makes murder a felony) should induce any man to destroy his own estate.

Questions

1. How would the law of October 1669 suggest that Europeans and Africans were inherently different?
2. Do these laws build upon existing racial prejudice, or do they create it?
3. What made slavery in Virginia different than in other places where it also existed, like Brazil?
4. Why was controlling and regulating interracial sex important to those who wanted to maintain slavery?
5. Why would a slaveowner, whose main capital investment was an enslaved human being, kill or destroy that "property"? Wouldn't indentured servitude have been just as violent as slavery, or even more so, considering the incentives of the enslavers?

Sweetness and Power: The Place of Sugar in Modern History (1985)

SIDNEY MINTZ

Sugar plantations might seem old-fashioned, part of the "Third World." They appeared, in fact, in parts of the world that are advertised to potential tourists today as being populated by people who supposedly aren't too worried about rushing around doing modern capitalist things. Sugar—which as we know is now being put into almost every food in some way or another—seems almost too ordinary and basic to be a key part of the transformation of an old world based on subsistence agriculture into one characterized by commodification and capitalism and industry. Sugar was also usually, at least before the late 1800s, made by slaves, and slavery is also not usually part of our stories about how the world became capitalist.

Sidney Mintz's fantastic book *Sweetness and Power*, however, shows that almost all of those ideas and suppositions are just wrong. Sugar and slavery were key parts of the emergence of the modern world. Not only were sugar plantations in the New World essentially the first modern factories, but sugar itself was the first modern commodity. Mintz's work explores the economic process and the cultural meanings of sugar, showing how something that started as a luxury in European cultural life became an avidly acquired signal of middle-class refinement. Eventually, the refinement of the production process became so complete that sugar emerged as the first industrial food.

* * *

During the Mediterranean epoch, western Europe very slowly became accustomed to sugar. From the Mediterranean, the industry then shifted to the Atlantic islands of Spain and Portugal, including Madeira, the Canaries, and São Tomé; but this relatively brief phase came to an end when the American industries began to grow. [...] [W]herever they went, the Arabs [had] brought with them sugar, the product and the technology of its production; sugar, we are told, followed the Koran.

[...] The spread of sugar cane and the technology required for its cultivation and conversion encountered obstacles—mostly rain and seasonal temperature fluctuations. As we have seen, sugar cane is a tropical and subtropical crop with a growing season that may be in excess of twelve months; it requires large amounts of water and labor. Though it can flourish without irrigation, it does far better (and increases its sugar content) when it is watered regularly and when its growing season is not subject to sharp and sudden declines in temperature. [...]

Sugar cane—if the crop is to be used to make sugar and not just for the extraction of juice, so that proper cultivation, prompt cutting and grinding, and skilled processing are involved—has always been a labor-intensive crop, at least until well into the twentieth century. Sugar production was a challenge not only in technical and political (administrative) terms, but also in regard to the securing and use of labor. [...] Slavery played a part in the Moroccan sugar industry and probably elsewhere; a slave revolt involving thousands of East African agricultural laborers took place in the Tigris-Euphrates delta in the mid-ninth century, and they may even have been sugar-cane-plantation workers. [S]lavery did grow more important as the European Crusaders seized the sugar plantations of the eastern Mediterranean from their predecessors; and its importance for sugar production did not diminish significantly until the Haitian Revolution, at the close of the eighteenth century. [...] Portugal was not content to experiment with sugar-cane cultivation at home in the Algarve when better opportunities beckoned elsewhere, and Spain was not far behind. [. . .] The eastern Mediterranean [. . .] became less and less important as a source of sugar; and it was the development of the industry by the Portuguese and Spaniards on the Atlantic islands that changed forever the character of European sugar consumption. These were the stepping stones by which the industry would move from the Old World to the New; it was in the form perfected on them that the New World industry was to find its prototype.

At the time that the Portuguese and the Spaniards set out to establish a sugar industry on the Atlantic islands they controlled, sugar was still a luxury, a medicine, and a spice in western Europe. [. . .] In [. . .] a series of experiments, the plantation system, now combining African slaves under the authority of European settlers in a racially mixed society, producing sugar cane and other commercial crops, spread as island after island (the Madeira Islands [. . .] the Canary Islands [. . .] the nine widely scattered islands that compose the Azores; the Cape Verde Islands) was integrated as part of the expanding kingdom. [. . .] There were intimate links between the Atlantic-island experiments of the Portuguese, especially São Tomé, and west European centers of commercial and technical power, especially Antwerp. [. . .] Sugar itself was now known throughout western Europe, even though it was still a product *de luxe*, rather than a common commodity or necessity. No longer so precious a good as musk or pearls [. . .] sugar was becoming a raw material whose supply and refining were managed more and more by European powers, as European populations consumed it in larger and larger quantities. [. . .]

Sugar cane was first carried to the New World by Columbus on his second voyage, in 1493; he brought it there from the Spanish Canary Islands. Cane was first grown in the New World in Spanish Santo Domingo; it was from that point that sugar was first shipped back to Europe, beginning around 1516. Santo Domingo's pristine sugar industry was worked by enslaved Africans, the first slaves having been imported there soon after the sugar cane. Hence it was Spain that pioneered sugar cane, sugar making, African slave labor, and the plantation form in the Americas. Some scholars agree with Fernando Ortiz that these plantations were "the favored child of capitalism." [. . .] By 1526, Brazil was shipping sugar to Lisbon in commercial quantities, and soon the sixteenth century was the Brazilian century for sugar [. . .] The first African slaves were imported [to Santo Domingo] before 1503. [. . .] When the surgeon Gonzalo de Vellosa—perhaps taking note of the rising prices of sugar in Europe—imported skilled sugar masters from the Canary Islands in 1515, he took the first step toward creating an authentic sugar industry in the Caribbean. With the Canary Island technicians, he (and his new partners, the Tapia brothers) imported a mill with two vertical rollers, usable with either animal or water power. [. . .] By the 1530s, [Santo Domingo] had a "fairly stable total" of thirty-four mills; and by 1568, "plantations owning a hundred-fifty to two hundred slaves were not uncommon. A few of the more magnificent estates possessed up to five hundred slaves, with production figures correspondingly high."

[. . .] The Portuguese planters in Brazil [soon surpassed] the Spaniards in the Antilles, then within only a century, the French, and even more the British (though with Dutch help from the outset), became the western world's great sugar makers and exporters. [. . .] Englishmen understood well the benefits of having their own sugar-producing colonies, and they also understood better and better the growth potential of the British market for sugar. Hence it is no surprise that later centuries saw the production of tropical commodities in the colonies tied ever more closely to British consumption—and to the production of British shops and factories. Production and consumption—at least with regard to the product we are considering here—were not simply opposite sides of the same coin, but neatly interdigitated; it is difficult to imagine one without the other.

[By the 1800s, one] Englishman commented on the colonies and their products in illuminating fashion. "There is a class of trading and exporting communities," John Stuart Mill wrote, "on which a few words of explanation seem to be required: These are hardly to be looked upon as countries, carrying on an exchange of commodities with other countries, but more properly as outlying agricultural or manufacturing estates belonging to a larger community. Our West Indian colonies, for example, cannot be regarded as countries with a productive capital of their own [. . .] [but are, rather,] the place where England finds it convenient to carry on the production of sugar, coffee and a few other tropical commodities. All the capital employed is English capital; almost all the industry is carried on for English uses; there is little production of anything except for staple commodities, and these are sent to England, not to be exchanged for things exported to the colony and consumed by its inhabitants, but to be sold in England for the benefit of the proprietors there. The trade with the West Indies is hardly to be considered an external trade, but more resembles the traffic between town and country."

[. . .] There grew up, in effect, two so-called triangles of trade, both of which arose in the seventeenth century and matured in the eighteenth. The first and most famous triangle linked Britain to Africa and to the New World: finished goods were sold to Africa, African slaves to the Americas, and American tropical commodities (especially sugar) to the mother country and her importing neighbors. The second triangle functioned in a manner contradictory to the mercantilist ideal. From New England went rum to Africa, whence slaves to the West Indies, whence molasses back to New England (with which to make rum). The maturation of this second triangle put the New England colonies on a political collision course with Britain, but the underlying problems were economic, taking on political import precisely because they brought divergent economic interests into confrontation.

The important feature of these triangles is that human cargoes figured vitally in their operation [. . .] millions of human beings were treated as commodities. To obtain them, products were shipped to Africa; by their labor power, wealth was created in the Americas. The wealth they created mostly returned to Britain; the products they made were consumed in Britain; and the products made by Britons—cloth, tools, torture instruments—were consumed by slaves who were themselves consumed in the creation of wealth.

In the seventeenth century, English society was very slowly evolving toward a system of free labor, by which I mean the creation of a labor force that, lacking any access to productive property such as land, would have to sell its labor to the owners of the means of production. Yet in that same century, England was adapting a system of mostly coerced labor in her colonies to satisfy her needs there. These two radically different patterns of labor exaction were growing in two ecologically different settings and were critically different in form. Yet they served the same overarching economic goals, and were created—albeit in such different form—by the evolution of a single economic and political system.

[. . .] The qualitative changes that mark the differences between the Spanish plantation experiments of the late sixteenth century and the English achievements of the mid-seventeenth and eighteenth centuries [. . .] have to do with changes in the scale not only of plantation operations, but also of the market. [. . .] Plantations were highly speculative enterprises. While they eventuated in enormous profits for fortunate investors, bankruptcies were common; some of the most daring plantation entrepreneurs ended their days in debtors' prison. Sugar was never a sure thing, despite the unfailingly optimistic predictions of its protagonists. But the risks taken by individual investors and planters in particular colonies were counterbalanced, over time, by the unceasing increases in demand. Those who foresaw the increases included, as always, both eventual winners and losers. Overall, the British imperial system was able to gorge itself on an ever-growing demand for sugar that accompanied both a declining unit price for sugar and increases in worker productivity at home.

[. . .] Until the eighteenth century, sugar was really the monopoly of a privileged minority, and its uses were still primarily as a medicine, as a spice, or as a decorative (display) substance. "An entirely new taste for sweetness manifested itself," Davis declares, "as soon as the means to satisfy it became available [. . .] by 1750 the poorest English farm labourer's wife took sugar in her tea." [. . .] the masses of English people were now steadily consuming more of it, and desiring more of it than they could afford. [. . .]

Eventually the mercantilist viewpoint embodied in the imperial sugar trade was crushed by an aggressive new economic philosophy labeled "free trade." But the importance of the mercantilist dogma to Britain's development was at least threefold: it guaranteed her supply of sugar (and other tropical commodities) and the profits made from processing and re-exporting them; it secured a large overseas market for finished British goods; and it supported the growth of the civil (and military) marine. [. . .] Overall, however, the two hundred years during which mercantilism persisted were marked by a gradual decline in the position of the planter classes, after their swift and early rise to power within the national state—and a more or less steady improvement in the position of the industrial capitalists and their interests at home. Mercantilism was finally dealt its quietus in the mid-nineteenth century, and the sugar market and its potential played a part. By then, sugar and consumer items like it had become too important to permit an archaic protectionism to jeopardize future metropolitan supplies. Sugar surrendered its place as luxury and rarity and became the first mass-produced exotic necessity of a proletarian working class.

Before turning to the last period in the history of sugar production, it might be useful to look more intently at the plantations, those tropical enterprises that were the seats of sugar production. These were, of course, agricultural undertakings, but because so much of the industrial processing of the cane was also carried out on the plantations, it makes good sense to view the plantations as a synthesis of

field and factory. Thus approached, they were really quite unlike anything known in mainland Europe at the time.

[. . .] Sugar cane must be cut when it is ripe, and ground as soon
as it is cut. These simple facts give a special character to any enterprise
dedicated to the production of sugar, as opposed to the simple expression of cane juice. The history of sugar making and refining has been
one of irregular improvement of the level of chemical purity, with
many consumers (in different cultures, and in different historical periods) developing preferences for one or another degree of purity, color,
form, granule size, and so on. But without boiling and skimming and
reducing juice there is no way to make granular sugar. It cannot be
done without solid technical mastery, particularly in the control of
heat. Just as factory and field are wedded in sugar making, brute field
labor and skilled artisanal knowledge are both necessary. [. . .] Perhaps only a tenth of the labor force was required in the mill and the
boiling house, but their operations and those of the cutting crews had
to be coordinated, while the field labor had to be divided not only
seasonally but also between the cane and the subsistence crops. The
specialization by skill and jobs, and the division of labor by age, gender, and condition into crews, shifts, and "gangs," together with the
stress upon punctuality and discipline, are features associated more
with industry than with agriculture. [. . .] Most like a factory was the
boiling house, where the juice from the crushed cane was transferred
for reduction, clarification, and crystallization. The Barbadian colo-
nist Thomas Tryon—whose complaints must be viewed with some
skepticism, since he was a planter himself—nonetheless conveys well
the modern-sounding quality of the mill in this seventeenth-century
description: "In short, 'tis to live in a perpetual Noise and Hurry."

Questions

1. If a commodity is a kind of product of which one can say that one
   unit of the product is virtually identical to the next unit of the

product, can it be that the product also has a cultural "meaning"?
If so, what is sugar's meaning today?

2. Critics of slavery in late eighteenth-century Britain and France
   sometimes tried to get consumers to stop using sugar, saying
   things like "sugar is made with blood"? Do you think that this
   worked, at least as a strategy to reduce the consumption of sugar?
   Why or why not?

3. Mintz's book was the first of what are now dozens of commodity
   histories—books that look at one product and try to use that as
   a "lens" for telling a story about history, society, and culture. Can
   you think of other such books? Have you read any of them, and if
   so, what did you think about the approach?

MODULE 4

THE TEA PARTY

The Autobiography of Benjamin Franklin (1791)

BENJAMIN FRANKLIN

When the great German social scientist Max Weber tried to figure out why capitalism had by the late nineteenth century become the dominant way of organizing societies and economies in the Western world, he thought about *The Autobiography of Benjamin Franklin*. By 1777, when he arrived in France as the ambassador of the postrevolutionary United States, Franklin was unquestionably the most famous American in the world. His fame came partly from his political activities. Franklin signed both the Declaration of Independence in 1776 and the Constitution in 1787, and also served as governor of Pennsylvania. His fame also came from his scientific activities. He did not discover electricity, but he helped create the lightning rod, charted the Gulf Stream current of the Atlantic Ocean, and measured the rate of natural increase of the population of the British colonies in North America.

Above all, however, Franklin was famous because he was American capitalism's first celebrity entrepreneur. Running away from apprenticeship in his brother's Boston printing shop, he arrived in Philadelphia at the age of fifteen. Within a few years, he had established himself as the proprietor of one of North America's first newspapers, the *Pennsylvania Gazette*. The paper offered political news, and it helped create a market by advertising ship arrivals and goods for sale, as well as publishing notices of runaway slaves and apprentices. But what made the *Gazette* so popular was Franklin's careful cultivation of his own image as a humble, hardworking, self-made man who was also a down-to-earth source of folksy wisdom—a well that would be tapped by many American entrepreneurs interested in selling the idea of themselves. Franklin employed this persona for the rest of his life.

Max Weber believed that the idea of capitalism grew from Puritanism: that entrepreneurs like Franklin turned away from repressing their sinful thoughts or anxiously contemplating their salvation, and put the same energies into their "calling" by God to the realm of business. They focused on repressing the behaviors that might keep them from working hard. The section of Franklin's *Autobiography* we have here reports on Franklin's account of his self-improvement process—how he graded his behavior every day, rewarding himself with higher marks when he was diligent, chaste, or moderate in his speech. Both the virtues and the process of constant self-evaluation and improvement, Weber and Franklin both believed, served businessmen well.

But there are other ways to look at Franklin, and other ways to see his influence on American capitalism. Although Weber saw capitalism as the transmutation of religious energies, it wasn't just salvation that Franklin was after. He also loved to measure things and make decisions based upon that accounting. He believed in a process of social reform and improvement—he supported colonial Pennsylvania's unique laws governing religious freedom, which allowed an unprecedented diversity of belief and practice. He helped found the American colonies' first lending library. By the end of his life, this slaveholder came to oppose slavery, freeing his slaves and arguing for state-sponsored emancipation in Pennsylvania. And Franklin in private was no abstemious Puritan—he fathered an illegitimate son, flirted endlessly with the women of Paris, and wrote a pamphlet entitled *Fart Freely*. Depicting Franklin as a black-suited Puritan, and claiming that capitalists succeed because of hard work and self-denial, is too simplistic. Risk taking, creativity, and re-creating your own image in a market-friendly way—these are all things that Franklin did, and all things that became crucial to capitalism in the country that he helped to invent.

At the time I establish'd myself in Pennsylvania, there was not a good bookseller's shop in any of the colonies to the southward of Boston. Those who lov'd reading were oblig'd to send for their books from England. I propos'd that we should all of us bring our books to that room, where they would not only be ready to consult in our conferences, but become a common benefit, each of us being at liberty to borrow such as he wish'd to read at home. Finding the advantage of this little collection, I propos'd to render the benefit from books more common, by commencing a public subscription library. So few were the readers at that time in Philadelphia, and the majority of us so poor, that I was not able, with great industry, to find more than fifty persons, mostly young tradesmen, willing to pay down for this purpose forty shillings each, and ten shillings per annum. On this little fund we began. The books were imported; the library was opened one day in the week for lending to the subscribers, on their promissory notes to pay double the value if not duly returned. The institution soon manifested its utility, was imitated by other towns, and in other provinces. The libraries were augmented by donations; reading became fashionable; and our people, having no publick amusements to divert their attention from study, became better acquainted with books, and in a few years were observ'd by strangers to be better instructed and more intelligent than people of the same rank generally are in other countries. [. . .]

My original habits of frugality continuing, and my father having, among his instructions to me when a boy, frequently repeated a proverb of Solomon, "Seest thou a man diligent in his calling, he shall stand before kings, he shall not stand before mean men," I from thence considered industry as a means of obtaining wealth and distinction, which encourag'd me, tho' I did not think that I should ever literally stand before kings, which, however, has since happened; for I have stood before five, and even had the honor of sitting down with one, the King of Denmark, to dinner. [. . .]

It was about this time I conceiv'd the bold and arduous project of arriving at moral perfection. I wish'd to live without committing any fault at any time; I would conquer all that either natural inclination, custom, or company might lead me into. As I knew, or thought I knew, what was right and wrong, I did not see why I might not always do the one and avoid the other. But I soon found I had undertaken a task of more difficulty than I had imagined. While my care was employ'd in guarding against one fault, I was often surprised by another; habit took the advantage of inattention; inclination was sometimes too strong for reason. I concluded, at length, that the mere speculative conviction that it was our interest to be completely virtuous, was not sufficient to prevent our slipping; and that the contrary habits must be broken, and good ones acquired and established, before we can have any dependence on a steady, uniform rectitude of conduct. For this purpose I therefore contrived the following method. [. . .] I included under thirteen names of virtues all that at that time occurr'd to me as necessary or desirable, and annexed to each a short precept, which fully express'd the extent I gave to its meaning.

These names of virtues, with their precepts, were:

1. TEMPERANCE. Eat not to dullness; drink not to elevation.

2. SILENCE. Speak not but what may benefit others or yourself; avoid trifling conversation.

3. ORDER. Let all your things have their places; let each part of your business have its time.

4 RESOLUTION. Resolve to perform what you ought; perform without fail what you resolve.

5. FRUGALITY. Make no expense but to do good to others or yourself; i.e., waste nothing.

6. INDUSTRY. Lose no time; be always employ'd in something useful; cut off all unnecessary actions.

7. SINCERITY. Use no hurtful deceit; think innocently and justly, and, if you speak, speak accordingly.

8. JUSTICE. Wrong none by doing injuries, or omitting the benefits that are your duty.

9. MODERATION. Avoid extreams; forbear resenting injuries so much as you think they deserve.

10. CLEANLINESS. Tolerate no uncleanliness in body, cloaths, or habitation.

11. TRANQUILLITY. Be not disturbed at trifles, or at accidents common or unavoidable.

12. CHASTITY. Rarely use venery but for health or offspring, never to dulness, weakness, or the injury of your own or another's peace or reputation.

13. HUMILITY. Imitate Jesus and Socrates.

My intention being to acquire the habitude of all these virtues, I judg'd it would be well not to distract my attention by attempting the whole at once, but to fix it on one of them at a time; and, when I should be master of that, then to proceed to another, and so on, till I should have gone thro' the thirteen; and, as the previous acquisition of some might facilitate the acquisition of certain others, I arrang'd them with that view, as they stand above. Temperance first, as it tends to procure that coolness and clearness of head, which is so necessary where constant vigilance was to be kept up, and guard maintained against the unremitting attraction of ancient habits, and the force of perpetual temptations. This being acquir'd and establish'd, Silence would be more easy; and my desire being to gain knowledge at the same time that I improv'd in virtue, and considering that in conversation it was obtain'd rather by the use of the ears than of the tongue, and therefore wishing to break a habit I was getting into of prattling, punning, and joking, which only made me acceptable to trifling company, I gave Silence the second place. This and the next, Order, I expected would allow me more time for attending to my project and my studies. Resolution, once become habitual, would keep me firm in my endeavors to obtain all the subsequent virtues; Frugality and Industry freeing me from my remaining debt, and producing affluence and independence, would make more easy the practice of Sincerity and Justice, etc., etc. Conceiving then, that, agreeably to the advice of Pythagoras in his Golden Verses, daily examination would be necessary, I contrived the following method for conducting that examination.

I made a little book, in which I allotted a page for each of the virtues. [. . .] I might mark, by a little black spot, every fault I found upon examination to have been committed respecting that virtue upon that day.

	Sunday	Monday	Tuesday	Wednes-day	Thursday	Friday	Saturday
Temperance							
Silence	*	*		*		*	
Order	**	*	*		*	*	*
Resolution			*			*	
Frugality		*			*		
Industry			*				
Sincerity							
Justice							
Moderation							

Cleanliness							
Tranquility							
Chastity							
Humility							

I determined to give a week's strict attention to each of the virtues successively. Thus, in the first week, my great guard was to avoid every the least offence against Temperance, leaving the other virtues to their ordinary chance, only marking every evening the faults of the day. Thus, if in the first week I could keep my first line, marked T, clear of spots, I suppos'd the habit of that virtue so much strengthen'd and its opposite weaken'd, that I might venture extending my attention to include the next, and for the following week keep both lines clear of spots. Proceeding thus to the last, I could go thro' a course compleat in thirteen weeks, and four courses in a year. And like him who, having a garden to weed, does not attempt to eradicate all the bad herbs at once, which would exceed his reach and his strength, but works on one of the beds at a time, and, having accomplish'd the first, proceeds to a second, so I should have, I hoped, the encouraging pleasure of seeing on my pages the progress I made in virtue, by clearing successively my lines of their spots, till in the end, by a number of courses, I should be happy in viewing a clean book, after a thirteen weeks' daily examination.

[. . .] The precept of Order requiring that every part of my business should have its allotted time, one page in my little book contain'd the following scheme of employment for the twenty-four hours of a natural day:

THE MORNING 5 [AM]: Rise, wash, and address. Powerful Goodness! Contrive day's business, and take the resolution of the day; prosecute the present study, and breakfast. Question: What good shall I do this day?

9 Work.

NOON   12 [PM] Read, or overlook my accounts, and dine.

          3 Work.

EVENING   6 Put things in their places.

          7 Supper. Music or diversion, or conversation. Examination of the day. Question: What good have I done to-day?

NIGHT   1 [AM] Sleep

I enter'd upon the execution of this plan for self-examination, and continu'd it with occasional intermissions for some time. I was surpris'd to find myself so much fuller of faults than I had imagined; but I had the satisfaction of seeing them diminish. To avoid the trouble of renewing now and then my little book, which, by scraping out the marks on the paper of old faults to make room for new ones in a new course, became full of holes, I transferr'd my tables and precepts to the ivory leaves of a memorandum book, on which the lines were drawn with red ink, that made a durable stain, and on those lines I mark'd my faults with a black-lead pencil, which marks I could easily wipe out with a wet sponge. After a while I went thro' one course only in a year, and afterward only one in several years, till at length I omitted them entirely, being employ'd in voyages and business abroad, with a multiplicity of affairs that interfered; but I always carried my little book with me. [. . .]

It may be well my posterity should be informed that to this little artifice, with the blessing of God, their ancestor ow'd the constant felicity of his life, down to his 79th year, in which this is written. What reverses may attend the remainder is in the hand of Providence; but, if they arrive, the reflection on past happiness enjoy'd ought to help his bearing them with more resignation. To Temperance he ascribes his long-continued health, and what is still left to him of a good constitution; to Industry and Frugality, the early easiness of his circumstances and acquisition of his fortune, with all that knowledge that enabled him to be a useful citizen, and obtained for him some degree of reputation among the learned; to Sincerity and Justice, the confidence of his country, and the honorable employs it conferred upon him; and to the joint influence of the whole mass of the virtues, even in the imperfect state he was able to acquire them, all that evenness of temper, and that cheerfulness in conversation, which makes his company still sought for, and agreeable even to his younger acquaintance. I hope, therefore, that some of my descendants may follow the example and reap the benefit.

It will be remark'd that, tho' my scheme was not wholly without religion, there was in it no mark of any of the distinguishing tenets of any particular sect. I had purposely avoided them; for, being fully persuaded of the utility and excellency of my method, and that it might be serviceable to people in all religions, and intending some time or other to publish it, I would not have any thing in it that should prejudice any one, of any sect, against it. [. . .]

My list of virtues contain'd at first but twelve; but a Quaker friend having kindly informed me that I was generally thought proud; that my pride show'd itself frequently in conversation; that I was not content with being in the right when discussing any point, but was overbearing, and rather insolent . . . and I added Humility to my list, giving an extensive meaning to the word.

I cannot boast of much success in acquiring the reality of this virtue, but I had a good deal with regard to the appearance of it. I made it a rule to forbear all direct contradiction to the sentiments of others, and all positive assertion of my own. I even forbid myself . . . the use of every word or expression in the language that imported a fix'd opinion, such as certainly, undoubtedly, etc., and I adopted, instead of them, I conceive, I apprehend, or I imagine a thing to be so or so; or it so appears to me at present. When another asserted something that I thought an error, I deny'd myself the pleasure of contradicting him abruptly, and of showing immediately some absurdity in his proposition; and in answering I began by observing that in certain cases or circumstances his opinion would be right, but in the present case there appear'd or seem'd to me some difference, etc. I soon found the advantage of this change in my manner; the conversations I engag'd in went on more pleasantly. The modest way in which I propos'd my opinions procur'd them a readier reception and less contradiction; I had less mortification when I was found to be in the wrong, and I more easily prevail'd with others to give up their mistakes and join with me when I happened to be in the right.

And this mode, which I at first put on with some violence to natural inclination, became at length so easy, and so habitual to me, that perhaps for these fifty years past no one has ever heard a dogmatical expression escape me. And to this habit (after my character of integrity) I think it principally owing that I had early so much weight with my fellow-citizens when I proposed new institutions, or alterations in the old, and so much influence in public councils when I became a member; for I was but a bad speaker, never eloquent, subject to much hesitation in my choice of words, hardly correct in language, and yet I generally carried my points.

In reality, there is, perhaps, no one of our natural passions so hard to subdue as pride. Disguise it, struggle with it, beat it down, stifle it, mortify it as much as one pleases, it is still alive, and will every now and then peep out and show itself; you will see it, perhaps, often in this history; for, even if I could conceive that I had compleatly overcome it, I should probably be proud of my humility.

Questions

1. What are the implications of Franklin's moral precepts for economic behavior? More generally, how does morality affect capitalism?
2. To what extent are self-improvement principles a part of American identity? If so, why does this matter?
3. What is the utility of institutions like Franklin's lending library? Do they serve an economic purpose as well as a social purpose?

MODULE 5

THE CAPITALIST CONSTITUTION

Federalist Paper No. 10 (1787)

JAMES MADISON

After the writing of the Constitution by the Philadelphia Convention in the summer of 1787, the advocates of this new framework of government hoped to convince the individual states to ratify it as soon as possible. But they found that in virtually every state, opponents—who were soon called "Antifederalists" for their opposition to the federal government proposed in the Constitution—launched vehement rhetorical attacks against ratification. The Antifederalists' opposition derived from many causes. Some disliked the Constitution because it seemed to take away power from the individual states, while others sought an even more centralized government with a single popularly elected legislature. Some wished for a Bill of Rights to protect individual liberties, while others worried that the Constitution would undermine the claims of slaveholders or other property owners. In order to get control of the debate, which was leading up to elections for delegates to ratification conventions in the different states, John Jay, James Madison, and Alexander Hamilton published eighty-five pro-Constitution essays under pseudonyms. Appearing in important newspapers, these essays were soon published under one cover and dubbed "the Federalist papers." They contain rhetoric intended to convince voters not only to support "Federalist" candidates for the ratification conventions—at this point, "Federalist" meant someone who supported ratification—but also to "buy into" a set of theories of government.

James Madison's first goal in Federalist Paper No. 10 was to demolish the commonly held belief that republican governments were uniquely subject to destabilizing factionalism, and that the larger the government, the more factionalized and more unstable it would be. Madison dismissed the claim that what was needed was more virtuous politicians, whose selfless morality would keep them clear of the temptations of factionalism. Prefiguring one of Hamilton's tactics in Federalist Paper No. 51, Madison here points out that human beings are not and cannot be angels, so a properly designed government will find a way to use humans' divergent interests so that one group will restrain another's selfishness. This argument parallels Adam Smith's argument that in the free market, individual actors' pursuit of their own good can (with a properly constructed market) lead to the greatest possible benefit for the greatest possible number. And this is just the first element in a larger proof that Madison is attempting to construct, for here he goes on to explain how a larger republic actually makes a structure built on the principle of balancing contending interests more likely to succeed. Indeed, a large republic emerges from this discussion as being equally as significant as the formal checks and balances built into the Constitution. And one might think, along those lines, that a larger market with more buyers and sellers would likewise be more likely to lead to a more equitable or at least beneficial outcome for all producers and consumers.

What is at stake for Madison is the need for a more centralized government that can bring order to the chaos of the state legislatures. This centralized federal government would in turn prove essential to the development of American capitalism. Its ability to regulate both international and interstate commerce would give the federal government the policy to make a national market, one without substantial barriers to efficient production and consumption. Of course, actualizing that potential would take decades, and the differences between Northern and Southern laws on the matter of slavery would shape the national economy in ways that still persist.

In part because of that, and in part because of other causes, different laws about labor, wages, social security mechanisms, licensing, and so on persist to this day. This can allow those with friends in state governments, for instance, to capture or control markets despite the fact that they might not necessarily be producing the greatest amount of possible benefit for their overworked, underpaid, unsafe employees or their overcharged customers. What would happen with greater federal power to control commerce? This has been an active debate for centuries now.

The Same Subject Continued: The Union as a Safeguard Against Domestic Faction and Insurrection

To the People of the State of New York:

AMONG the numerous advantages promised by a well constructed Union, none deserves to be more accurately developed than its tendency to break and control the violence of faction. The friend of popular governments never finds himself so much alarmed for their character and fate, as when he contemplates their propensity to this dangerous vice. He will not fail, therefore, to set a due value on any plan which, without violating the principles to which he is attached, provides a proper cure for it. The instability, injustice, and confusion introduced into the public councils, have, in truth, been the mortal diseases under which popular governments have everywhere perished; as they continue to be the favorite and fruitful topics from which the adversaries to liberty derive their most specious declamations. . . . Complaints are everywhere heard from our most considerate and virtuous citizens, equally the friends of public and private faith, and of public and personal liberty, that our governments are too unstable, that the public good is disregarded in the conflicts of rival parties, and that measures are too often decided, not according to the rules of justice and the rights of the minor party, but by the superior force of an interested and overbearing majority. However anxiously we may wish that these complaints had no foundation, the evidence, of known facts will not permit us to deny that they are in some degree true. [. . .] [And] these must be chiefly, if not wholly, effects of the unsteadiness and injustice with which a factious spirit has tainted our public administrations.

By a faction, I understand a number of citizens, whether amounting to a majority or a minority of the whole, who are united and actuated by some common impulse of passion, or of interest, adverse to the rights of other citizens, or to the permanent and aggregate interests of the community.

There are two methods of curing the mischiefs of faction: the one, by removing its causes; the other, by controlling its effects.

There are again two methods of removing the causes of faction: the one, by destroying the liberty which is essential to its existence; the other, by giving to every citizen the same opinions, the same passions, and the same interests.

It could never be more truly said than of the first remedy, that it was worse than the disease. Liberty is to faction what air is to fire, an aliment without which it instantly expires. But it could not be less folly to abolish liberty, which is essential to political life, because it nourishes faction, than it would be to wish the annihilation of air, which is essential to animal life, because it imparts to fire its destructive agency.

The second expedient is as impracticable as the first would be unwise. As long as the reason of man continues fallible, and he is at liberty to exercise it, different opinions will be formed. As long as the connection subsists between his reason and his self-love, his opinions and his passions will have a reciprocal influence on each other; and the former will be objects to which the latter will attach themselves. The diversity in the faculties of men, from which the rights of property originate, is not less an insuperable obstacle to a uniformity of interests. The protection of these faculties is the first object of government. From the protection of different and unequal faculties of acquiring property, the possession of different degrees and kinds of property immediately results; and from the influence of these on the sentiments and views of the respective proprietors, ensues a division of the society into different interests and parties.

The latent causes of faction are thus sown in the nature of man; and we see them everywhere brought into different degrees of activity, according to the different circumstances of civil society. A zeal for different opinions concerning religion, concerning government, and many other points, as well of speculation as of practice; an attachment to different leaders ambitiously contending for preeminence and power; or to persons of other descriptions whose fortunes have been interesting to the human passions, have, in turn, divided mankind into parties, inflamed them with mutual animosity, and rendered them much more disposed to vex and oppress each other than to co-operate for their common good. So strong is this propensity of mankind to fall into mutual animosities, that where no substantial occasion presents itself, the most frivolous and fanciful distinctions have been sufficient to kindle their unfriendly passions and excite their most violent conflicts. But the most common and durable source of factions has been the various and unequal distribution of property. Those who hold and those who are without property have ever formed distinct interests in society. Those who are creditors, and those who are debtors, fall under a like discrimination. A landed interest, a manufacturing interest, a mercantile interest, a moneyed interest, with many lesser interests, grow up of necessity in civilized nations, and divide them into different classes, actuated by different sentiments and views. The regulation of these various and interfering interests forms the principal task of modern legislation, and involves the spirit of party and faction in the necessary and ordinary operations of the government.

No man is allowed to be a judge in his own cause, because his interest would certainly bias his judgment, and, not improbably, corrupt his integrity. With equal, nay with greater reason, a body of men are unfit to be both judges and parties at the same time; yet what are many of the most important acts of legislation, but so many judicial determinations, not indeed concerning the rights of single persons, but concerning the rights of large bodies of citizens? And what are the different classes of legislators but advocates and parties to the causes which they determine? Is a law proposed concerning private debts? It is a question to which the creditors are parties on one side and the debtors on the other. Justice ought to hold the balance between them. Yet the parties are, and must be, themselves the judges; and the most numerous party, or, in other words, the most powerful faction must be expected to prevail. Shall domestic manufactures be encouraged, and in what degree, by restrictions on foreign manufactures? are questions which would be differently decided by the landed and the manufacturing classes, and probably by neither with a sole regard to justice and the public good. The apportionment of taxes on the various descriptions of property is an act which seems to require the most exact impartiality; yet there is, perhaps, no legislative act in which greater opportunity and temptation are given to a predominant party to trample on the rules of justice. Every shilling with which they overburden the inferior number, is a shilling saved to their own pockets.

It is in vain to say that enlightened statesmen will be able to adjust these clashing interests, and render them all subservient to the public good. Enlightened statesmen will not always be at the helm. [. . .] The inference to which we are brought is, that the CAUSES of faction cannot be removed, and that relief is only to be sought in the means of controlling its EFFECTS.

If a faction consists of less than a majority, relief is supplied by the republican principle, which enables the majority to defeat its sinister views by regular vote. It may clog the administration, it may convulse the society; but it will be unable to execute and mask its violence under the forms of the Constitution. When a majority is included in a faction, the form of popular government, on the other hand, enables it to sacrifice to its ruling passion or interest both the public good and the rights of other citizens. To secure the public good and private rights against the danger of such a faction, and at the same time to preserve the spirit and the form of popular government, is then the great object to which our inquiries are directed. [. . .]

By what means is this object attainable? Evidently by one of two only. Either the existence of the same passion or interest in a majority at the same time must be prevented, or the majority, having such coexistent passion or interest, must be rendered, by their number and local situation, unable to concert and carry into effect schemes of oppression. If the impulse and the opportunity be suffered to coincide, we well know that neither moral nor religious motives can be relied on as an adequate control. [. . .]

A chosen body of citizens, whose wisdom may best discern the true interest of their country, and whose patriotism and love of justice will be least likely to sacrifice it to temporary or partial considerations [. . .] [might] be more consonant to the public good than [. . .] the people themselves, convened for the purpose. On the other hand, the effect may be inverted. Men of factious tempers, of local prejudices, or of sinister designs, may, by intrigue, by corruption, or by other means, first obtain the suffrages, and then betray the interests, of the people. The question resulting is, whether small or extensive republics are more favorable to the election of proper guardians of the public weal; and it is clearly decided in favor of the latter by two obvious considerations:

In the first place [. . .] however small the republic may be, the representatives must be raised to a certain number, in order to guard against the cabals of a few; and that, however large it may be, they must be limited to a certain number, in order to guard against the confusion of a multitude. Hence, the number of representatives in the two cases not being in proportion to that of the two constituents, and being proportionally greater in the small republic, it follows that, if the proportion of fit characters be not less in the large than in the small republic, the former will present a greater option, and consequently a greater probability of a fit choice.

In the next place, as each representative will be chosen by a greater number of citizens in the large than in the small republic, it will be more difficult for unworthy candidates to practice with success the vicious arts by which elections are too often carried; and the suffrages of the people being more free, will be more likely to centre in men who possess the most attractive merit and the most diffusive and established characters.

[. . .] The greater number of citizens and extent of territory [. . .] brought within the compass of republican [. . .] government [. . .] renders factious combinations less to be dreaded. [. . .] The smaller the society, the fewer probably will be the distinct parties and interests composing it; the fewer the distinct parties and interests, the more frequently will a majority be found of the same party; and the smaller the number of individuals composing a majority, and the smaller the compass within which they are placed, the more easily will they concert and execute their plans of oppression. Extend the sphere, and you take in a greater variety of parties and interests; you make it less probable that a majority of the whole will have a common motive to invade the rights of other citizens; or if such a common motive exists, it will be more difficult for all who feel it to discover their own strength, and to act in unison with each other. Besides other impediments, it may be remarked that, where there is a consciousness of unjust or dishonorable purposes, communication is always checked by distrust in proportion to the number whose concurrence is necessary.

Hence, it clearly appears, that the same advantage which a republic has over a democracy, in controlling the effects of faction, is enjoyed by a large over a small republic,—is enjoyed by the Union over the States composing it. Does the advantage consist in the substitution of representatives whose enlightened views and virtuous sentiments render them superior to local prejudices and schemes of injustice? It will not be denied that the representation of the Union will be most likely to possess these requisite endowments. Does it consist in the greater security afforded by a greater variety of parties, against the event of any one party being able to outnumber and oppress the rest? In an equal degree does the increased variety of parties comprised within the Union, increase this security. Does it, in fine, consist in the greater obstacles opposed to the concert and accomplishment of the secret wishes of an unjust and interested majority? Here, again, the extent of the Union gives it the most palpable advantage.

The influence of factious leaders may kindle a flame within their particular States, but will be unable to spread a general conflagration through the other States. A religious sect may degenerate into a political faction in a part of the Confederacy; but the variety of sects dispersed over the entire face of it must secure the national councils against any danger from that source. A rage for paper money, for an abolition of debts, for an equal division of property, or for any other improper or wicked project, will be less apt to pervade the whole body of the Union than a particular member of it; in the same proportion as such a malady is more likely to taint a particular county or district, than an entire State.

In the extent and proper structure of the Union, therefore, we behold a republican remedy for the diseases most incident to republican government. [. . .]

PUBLIUS. [James Madison]

Questions

1. Madison assumes that a minority will not be able to oppress a majority under the system of Constitutional government, but is it possible that he is wrong?
2. How important is "property" to Madison's thinking here? What does he mean by that? What role does "property" play in the politics of the present?

3. Madison thinks that "the influence of factious leaders may kindle a flame within their particular States, but will be unable to spread a general conflagration through the other States." Is this true? What kinds of mechanisms might undermine his assumption that greater size means a healthy diversity of interest?

Federalist Paper No. 51 (1787)

JAMES MADISON

After the writing of the Constitution by the Philadelphia Convention in the summer of 1787, the advocates of this new framework of government hoped to convince the individual states to ratify it as soon as possible. But they found that in virtually every state, opponents who were soon called "Antifederalists" for their opposition to the federal government proposed in the Constitution launched vehement rhetorical attacks against ratification. The Antifederalists' opposition derived from many causes. Some disliked the Constitution because it seemed to take away power from the individual states, while others sought an even more centralized government with a single popularly elected legislature. Some wished for a Bill of Rights to protect individual liberties, while others worried that a Constitution would undermine the claims of slaveholders or other property owners. In order to get control of the debate, which was leading up to elections for delegates to ratification conventions in the different states, John Jay, James Madison, and Alexander Hamilton published eighty-five pro-Constitution essays under pseudonyms. Appearing in important newspapers, these essays were soon published under one cover and dubbed "the Federalist papers." They contain rhetoric intended to convince voters not only to support "Federalist" candidates for the ratification conventions—at this point, "Federalist" meant someone who supported ratification—but also to "buy into" a set of theories of government.

The theories embedded in the Federalist papers have profound implications, whether as abstract arguments about the nature of government or as clues suggesting the ideas that important early leaders held about whether and how the new federal government could make the United States strong, prosperous, and republican. Popular governments, in which the decisions were made by representatives selected by a broad electorate, were thought to be vulnerable to factional discord that led to internal war, or to single dictators who took over and became tyrants, or to the whims of a majority who seized the property of a wealthier minority. All of these fears are still present, you'll surely notice, in the way that the American media discuss U.S. politics. But what Madison and the other writers did so successfully was to argue that the Constitution actually turned the alleged flaws of popular government into strengths. No, men were not angels, and some would be elected who could not be trusted. They would misuse power for personal gain, try to manipulate the people, and divide into factions. But the large size of the United States, Madison argued, would actually make it difficult for such concentrated attempts to undermine justice to prevail. And the division of the government into three wings—executive, legislative, and judicial—along with the division of legislative powers between the House and the Senate would further cushion against misuses of power. The opposing interests and counterbalancing powers of fallible human beings would enable them to keep each other from suborning the government.

Yet the theories in the Federalist Papers also suggest ideas and assumptions that would profoundly shape the development of capitalism in the United States. Madison's argument here also implies that property-owners—a minority in the new United States, perhaps even among white male adults—would be able to resist the dangers of property confiscation feared by many of those who had examined the previous history of representative, popular governments. Enslavers took the idea that state governments could counterbalance the power of the federal government and made that into one more bulwark for the defense of slavery. The division of powers has also, over time, made it more difficult for the federal government, or Presidents (who are after all but one branch of three, the Executive branch), to set fundamental economic policy. In some cases this might enable capitalism to function more efficiently, and to grow more freely, or even more justly. But, others might argue, the policy inertia can also prevent regulation needed to curb destructive speculation, unjust economic practices, or the "regulatory capture" of one or more states by specific and selfish economic interests. As you read, think about which of these concerns, if any, were on Madison's mind. And think also about the fact that in just a few years, Madison would lead a political party that had nearly eliminated its Federalist competitors, and he would then eliminate the national bank, which helped regulate the young American financial economy.

The Structure of the Government Must Furnish the Proper Checks and Balances Between the Different Departments

[. . .] The great security against a gradual concentration of the several powers in the same department, consists in giving to those who administer each department the necessary constitutional means and personal motives to resist encroachments of the others. [. . .] Ambition must be made to counteract ambition. The interest of the man must be connected with the constitutional rights of the place. It may be a reflection on human nature, that such devices should be necessary to control the abuses of government. But what is government itself, but the greatest of all reflections on human nature? If men were angels, no government would be necessary. If angels were to govern men, neither external nor internal controls on government would be necessary. In framing a government which is to be administered by men over men, the great difficulty lies in this: you must first enable the government to control the governed; and in the next place oblige it to control itself.

A dependence on the people is, no doubt, the primary control on the government; but experience has taught mankind the necessity of auxiliary precautions. This policy of supplying, by opposite and rival interests, the defect of better motives, might be traced through the whole system of human affairs, private as well as public. We see it particularly displayed in all the subordinate distributions of power, where the constant aim is to divide and arrange the several offices in such a manner as that each may be a check on the other that the private interest of every individual may be a sentinel over the public rights. These inventions of prudence cannot be less requisite in the distribution of the supreme powers of the State. But it is not possible to give to each department an equal power of self-defense. In republican government, the legislative authority necessarily predominates. The remedy for this inconveniency is to divide the legislature into different branches; and to render them, by different modes of election and different principles of action, as little connected with each other as the nature of their common functions and their common dependence on the society will admit. It may even be necessary to guard against dangerous encroachments by still further precautions. As the weight of the legislative authority requires that it should be thus divided, the weakness of the executive may require, on the other hand, that it should be fortified. [. . .]

There are, moreover, two considerations particularly applicable to the federal system of America, which place that system in a very interesting point of view. First. In a single republic, all the power surrendered by the people is submitted to the administration of a single government; and the usurpations are guarded against by a division of the government into distinct and separate departments. In the compound republic of America, the power surrendered by the people is first divided between two distinct governments, and then the portion allotted to each subdivided among distinct and separate departments. Hence a double security arises to the rights of the people. The different governments will control each other, at the same time that each will be controlled by itself. Second. It is of great importance in a republic not only to guard the society against the oppression of its rulers, but to guard one part of the society against the injustice of the other part. Different interests necessarily exist in different classes of citizens. If a majority be united by a common interest, the rights of the minority will be insecure.

There are but two methods of providing against this evil: the one by creating a will in the community independent of the majority that is, of the society itself; the other, by comprehending in the society so many separate descriptions of citizens as will render an unjust combination of a majority of the whole very improbable, if not impracticable. [. . .] The second method will be exemplified in the federal republic of the United States. Whilst all authority in it will be derived from and dependent on the society, the society itself will be broken into so many parts, interests, and classes of citizens, that the rights of individuals, or of the minority, will be in little danger from interested combinations of the majority.

In a free government the security for civil rights must be the same as that for religious rights. It consists in the one case in the multiplicity of interests, and in the other in the multiplicity of sects. The degree of security in both cases will depend on the number of interests and sects; and this may be presumed to depend on the extent of country and number of people comprehended under the same government. [. . .] Justice is the end of government. It is the end of civil society. It ever has been and ever will be pursued until it be obtained, or until liberty be lost in the pursuit. In a society under the forms of which the stronger faction can readily unite and oppress the weaker, anarchy may as truly be said to reign as in a state of nature, where the weaker individual is not secured against the violence of the stronger; and as, in the latter state, even the stronger individuals are prompted, by the uncertainty of their condition, to submit to a government which may protect the weak as well as themselves; so, in the former state, will the more powerful factions or parties be gradually induced, by a like motive, to wish for a government which will protect all parties, the weaker as well as the more powerful. [. . .] In the extended republic of the United States, and among the great variety of interests, parties, and sects which it embraces, a coalition of a majority of the whole society could seldom take place on any other principles than those of justice and the general good.

PUBLIUS. [James Madison]

Questions

1. Madison's colleague Alexander Hamilton was attracted to the idea of a monarchy, and even suggested at one point that the Constitution should incorporate the idea of a President-for-Life, who would be almost a king. So why doesn't he suggest the idea of one central sovereign in the government—someone to stand above the different interests and referee between the factions?

2. Madison writes that "in a free government the security for civil rights must be the same as that for religious rights. It consists in the one case in the multiplicity of interests, and in the other in the multiplicity of sects." What about in the economy? What do we call the situation in which a multiplicity of interests are all trying to sell what they need to sell and buy what they need to buy? What economic thinker's ideas most resemble Madison's argument that the division of powers leads to the greatest amount of good for the greatest number of people?

Sections from the Constitution
of the United States

The thirteen states that declared themselves united and independent in July 1776 fought the Revolution and achieved victory over Great Britain while working together under the framework of a document called the Articles of Confederation. The government this produced might have been adequate when all those who desired independence saw in front of them a single, all-encompassing goal—that of defeating the British Empire and its invading armies. But after the British surrender at Yorktown, the last major battle of the war, and the signing of the Treaty of Paris in 1783, the weaknesses of the Articles became much more apparent. No state could be required to do anything important by either Congress—the only branch of the federal government that existed under the Articles—or by other states. States refused to contribute to the common treasury. They disputed ownership of the western lands with each other. They did not pay the debts owed to citizens and foreign investors who had bought bonds to support the American war effort. They created competing trade regulations to take away business from each other's ports. And since Congress had so little power or money, it could not evict the British from the forts they still occupied in the western territories, could not force open foreign markets, and could not impose order on the economic chaos created by the fact that every state issued its own currency. The economic chaos, meanwhile, was causing social unrest in places like western Massachusetts, where farmers occupied courthouses in which judges were trying to foreclose on families' lands. All the farmers had was the paper currency that they had received for crops or for service in the Revolutionary armies, and creditors refused to accept paper currency as payment.

In the summer of 1787, representatives from almost all of the states descended on Philadelphia to try to create a strong federal government that would establish order. The result of a summer of deliberation in Independence Hall was, of course, the Constitution. This document was full of compromises, including political ones over the balance of power between big states and small states, between those who wanted a more democratic legislature and those who wanted one more insulated from the people, and between the power of the central government and of the state governments. But some things are clear. First, the Constitution provided for a much more orderly and centralized system of national government than had been created under the old Articles. Second, the Constitution gave the new federal Congress—and perhaps the other branches of the federal government as well—tools to use in shaping a national economic policy. And third, the convention's debates produced a set of compromises that, at least for the foreseeable future, would enable slavery to persist as a significant component of production, consumption, and wealth accumulation in the new national economy. Even though the export crops slaves produced in the 1780s—tobacco, rice, wheat, and indigo—were selling for low prices, and many doubted whether slavery could persist at such low levels of profitability, those crops were still collectively the biggest source of the national economy's all-important export earnings. As South Carolina delegate John Rutledge, who would eventually become Chief Justice of the U.S. Supreme Court, put it: "Interest alone is the governing principle with nations. The true question at present is whether the Southern States shall or shall not be parties to the Union. If the Northern States consult their interest, they will not oppose the increase of Slaves which will increase the commodities of which they will become the carriers." The Northern states did not oppose. The Constitution protected their economic interests, and those of the South.

Article I

Section 2
Representatives and direct Taxes shall be apportioned among the several States which may be included within this Union, according to their respective Numbers, which shall be determined by adding to the whole Number of free Persons, including those bound to Service for a Term of Years, and excluding Indians not taxed, three fifths of all other Persons.

Section 7
All Bills for raising Revenue shall originate in the House of Representatives; but the Senate may propose or concur with Amendments as on other Bills.

Section 8
The Congress shall have Power To lay and collect Taxes, Duties, Imposts and Excises, to pay the Debts and provide for the common Defence and general Welfare of the United States; but all Duties, Imposts and Excises shall be uniform throughout the United States;

To borrow Money on the credit of the United States;

To regulate Commerce with foreign Nations, and among the several States, and with the Indian Tribes;

To establish an uniform Rule of Naturalization, and uniform Laws on the subject of Bankruptcies throughout the United States;

To coin Money, regulate the Value thereof, and of foreign Coin, and fix the Standard of Weights and Measures;

To provide for the Punishment of counterfeiting the Securities and current Coin of the United States;

To establish Post Offices and post Roads;

To promote the Progress of Science and useful Arts, by securing for limited Times to Authors and Inventors the exclusive Right to their respective Writings and Discoveries;

To make all Laws which shall be necessary and proper for carrying into Execution the foregoing Powers, and all other Powers vested by this Constitution in the Government of the United States, or in any Department or Officer thereof.

Section 9

The Migration or Importation of such Persons as any of the States now existing shall think proper to admit, shall not be prohibited by the Congress prior to the Year one thousand eight hundred and eight, but a Tax or duty may be imposed on such Importation, not exceeding ten dollars for each Person.

No Capitation, or other direct, Tax shall be laid, unless in Proportion to the Census or enumeration herein before directed to be taken.

No Tax or Duty shall be laid on Articles exported from any State.

No Preference shall be given by any Regulation of Commerce or Revenue to the Ports of one State over those of another; nor shall Vessels bound to, or from, one State, be obliged to enter, clear, or pay Duties in another.

Section 10

No State shall, without the Consent of the Congress, lay any Imposts or Duties on Imports or Exports, except what may be absolutely necessary for executing its inspection Laws: and the net Produce of all Duties and Imposts, laid by any State on Imports or Exports, shall be for the Use of the Treasury of the United States.

Article IV

Section 2

No Person held to Service or Labour in one State, under the Laws thereof, escaping into another, shall, in Consequence of any Law or Regulation therein, be discharged from such Service or Labour, but shall be delivered up on Claim of the Party to whom such Service or Labour may be due.

Article VI

All Debts contracted and Engagements entered into, before the Adoption of this Constitution, shall be as valid against the United States under this Constitution, as under the Confederation.

Amendments to the Constitution

Amendment V (1791)

No person shall be held to answer for a capital, or otherwise infamous crime, unless on a presentment or indictment of a Grand Jury, except in cases arising in the land or naval forces, or in the Militia, when in actual service in time of War or public danger; nor shall any person be subject for the same offense to be twice put in jeopardy of life or limb; nor shall be compelled in any criminal case to be a witness against himself, nor be deprived of life, liberty, or property, without due process of law; nor shall private property be taken for public use, without just compensation

Amendment XIII (1865)

Section 1
Neither slavery nor involuntary servitude, except as a punishment for crime whereof the party shall have been duly convicted, shall exist within the United States, or any place subject to their jurisdiction.

Amendment XIV (1868)

Section 1
All persons born or naturalized in the United States and subject to the jurisdiction thereof, are citizens of the United States and of the

State wherein they reside. No State shall make or enforce any law which shall abridge the privileges or immunities of citizens of the United States; nor shall any State deprive any person of life, liberty, or property, without due process of law; nor deny to any person within its jurisdiction the equal protection of the laws.

Section 2

Representatives shall be apportioned among the several States according to their respective numbers, counting the whole number of persons in each State, excluding Indians not taxed. But when the right to vote at any election for the choice of electors for President and Vice President of the United States, Representatives in Congress, the Executive and Judicial officers of a State, or the members of the Legislature thereof, is denied to any of the male inhabitants of such State, being *twenty-one* years of age, and citizens of the United States, or in any way abridged, except for participation in rebellion, or other crime, the basis of representation therein shall be reduced in the proportion which the number of such male citizens shall bear to the whole number of male citizens twenty-one years of age in such State.

Section 4

The validity of the public debt of the United States, authorized by law, including debts incurred for payment of pensions and bounties for services in suppressing insurrection or rebellion, shall not be questioned. But neither the United States nor any State shall assume or pay any debt or obligation incurred in aid of insurrection or rebellion against the United States, or any claim for the loss or emancipation of any slave; but all such debts, obligations and claims shall be held illegal and void.

Amendment XVI (1913)

The Congress shall have power to lay and collect taxes on incomes, from whatever source derived, without apportionment among the several States, and without regard to any census or enumeration.

Questions

1. Did the Constitution anticipate federal government intervention in the economy? Did it suggest ways in which the government could or should stimulate economic growth, guide that growth, or organize the economy on a more fundamental basis?
2. Is either of these statements true?

    (a) "Free trade between states is the most important aspect of the Constitution for the American economy."

    (b) "The Framers envisioned America as primarily a customs union."

3. Where does slavery fit into the American economy according to the Constitution? What was its legal status?
4. How do the principles of the Constitution (not the Amendments) reflect the theories of economics that you have seen in previous documents? Who seemed to be winning the ideological struggle over the role of the state in the economy?
5. How do the Amendments affect your answers to questions 1 and 4? How did they change the government's place in the American economy?

First Report on the Public Credit (1790)

ALEXANDER HAMILTON

Wars are expensive, and governments that indulge in them almost always have to borrow money in order to run them. Governments that are engaged in a war of independence face the additional burden of trying to borrow money when their future existence—and future ability to repay those debts—might seem especially questionable. In the course of the American Revolution, both the continental government and the thirteen state governments were able to borrow from both their citizens and from overseas lenders (especially in France and the Netherlands), and debt financing was essential to securing the independence of the United States. But the Articles of Confederation created a national state that was not really worthy of the name, as it had little power to regulate trade or levy taxes that might enable it to begin to repay its outstanding debts. And they were massive debts: from his research in the late 1780s, Alexander Hamilton concluded that the national government owed $40 million in bonds held by its citizens and $12 million held overseas, while the individual states owed $25 million. In many cases, interest payments were in default and not being paid, adding to the total burden with the power of compound interest. The combined debt of $77 million was almost half the size of the GDP, or gross domestic product—the sum value of all goods and services produced by all economic activity in the United States, which in 1790 came to $190 million. And in a primarily agricultural economy in which most farmers produced little above subsistence, the capacity of an economy to absorb massive debt payments was inherently small.

One main impetus for the Constitutional Convention was the desire to create a strong federal government that could bring order to financial chaos, create a stable currency, and tax effectively in order to promote national objectives like a strong defense, infrastructure improvements, and a coherent trade policy. The Constitution as written and ratified gave the federal government the power to tax, to create debt, and to redeem debt. But how would it use that power? When Alexander Hamilton became the first secretary of the Treasury in 1789, he wrote this report, which addressed the problem of the national debt. Many economic thinkers—then and now—saw debt as a negative, especially for a national state, an impediment to growth and a source of weakness. Yet in his first Report on the Public Credit, Hamilton advocated the creation of a strong federal state that was—seemingly paradoxically—deeply indebted.

To understand the quandaries Hamilton faced, but also the opportunities that he perceived, one needs to understand the history of the debts incurred during the war. Most were issued in the form of bonds, for which the initial creditor gave value in the form of coins or goods to the revolutionary government. Those bonds, like most bonds, could be sold to other people, who would then hold the claim for repayment. But by the mid-1780s, the market value of bonds issued by the wartime Continental Congress and state legislatures had plunged, because most people did not believe that they would ever be paid back. This plunge in value created several dynamics. First of all, original bondholders who paid full value but then sold their paper at cents on the dollar had lost money on their investment, and many were already in dire straits because of other disruptions in the post-revolutionary economy—disrupted foreign trade, falling crop prices, and so on. Thus those who had sacrificed for the revolution were suffering, even though their financial support had helped to achieve independence.

Yet at the same time, those who bought the bonds at cents on the dollar would receive a massive speculative windfall if the debts were redeemed at full value. For this reason, many of the pamphlet writers and newspaper editors and politicians who wrote about the debt problem in the 1780s suggested that any debt-redemption plan had to "discriminate" between original holders (who were good) and "speculators," who were bad. Finally, one more effect of the plunge in confidence that the United States would pay its debts was the failure of anything like a financial market to develop in the 1780s. Without reliable debt in which people could invest, banks could not open for business, meaning that entrepreneurs could not secure loans, meaning in turn that the entire economy limped along on life-support. And at the same time, the federal government also couldn't borrow at anything less than a ruinously high rate of interest, whether at home or abroad. This limited its ability—even in peacetime—to carry out any of the functions with which the Constitutional Convention had sought to task it: national defense, enhancing economic stability, and so on.

Many in the United States suggested that the government needed to repay only the federal debt, and leave the states to pay off their own commitments. Others suggested that all the debt should be "repudiated"—that the new federal government should refuse to pay old debts and ask creditors to start over, as it were. Many repudiators actually wanted the U.S. government to operate with a purely balanced budget, in which outlays never exceeded intakes. But drawing on his study of the British system of government-issued debt which that empire had used to fund its wars, colonial expansions, and rise to superpower status in the 1700s, Hamilton argued for a revolutionary and sweeping plan that seemed to expand U.S. debt and reward speculators. This plan, he argued, would create a thriving economy with a stable currency, ready availability of loans for those who wanted to create or expand entrepreneurial activities, and a strong federal government that could borrow at low cost, and would bind the wealthiest people in the United States to support and invest in the new nation.

Hamilton's plan had three main components. The first was assumption. The federal government would assume the states' debts. To some this seemed unfair, because while certain states had been paying their bond interest in the 1780s, others had been irresponsible by not taxing their citizens to pay their debts. But Hamilton wasn't concerned with that issue. The second component was redemption. The federal government would repay all bonds at full face value—whether or not they were still in the hands of the original purchaser. Although James Madison, for instance, supported paying current holders the amount that they had paid to purchase the bond, and paying original holders the difference between that price and the face value of the security in question, Hamilton rejected that plan. And thirdly, having promised to take on the burden of paying back the full $77 million in outstanding debt—far more than it could pay in any short time frame—the federal government, Hamilton proposed, would reissue the debt in the form of fifteen or twenty-year bonds. In many cases they would bear slightly less interest than the original bonds, but Hamilton believed—correctly, as it turned out—that the holders of the securities would be happy to accept a lower yield from the bond in return for the greater security created by the promises of assumption and redemption.

Here's the historical outcome of the first Report on the Public Credit: Hamilton's proposals were ultimately accepted by Congress and became federal policy. The government committed itself to paying off the bonds over time, using excise taxes and revenues from import tariffs. For the first ten years, interest payments comprised about forty percent of all federal expenditures. The high costs limited America's ability to build a military that would deter European bullies from harassing American trade, and fiscal pressure also helped push the federal government into some unwise decisions—like imposing the excise tax that led to the so-called

Whiskey Rebellion of 1796. And yet, as Hamilton predicted, economic growth soon shrank the relative size of the federal debt. In Boston, New York, and Philadelphia in particular, thriving markets in government securities developed, and banks began to appear. Borrowing costs for the government shrank, ironically enabling Hamilton's political rival Jefferson to become one of the most successful empire-building American presidents of all time. By 1803, U.S. credit on European markets was so good that Jefferson could borrow nearly $80 million to finance the Louisiana Purchase, in which the United States bought from France nearly 828,000 square miles of land in the heart of the North American continent. The First Report on the Public Credit was a key component in establishing a federal state that could do big things, and the creation of a massive federal debt helped create a dynamic capitalist economy in the United States.

As you read the text, pay attention to how Hamilton argues for each of his plan's elements—How does he anticipate and knock down the arguments of those who complain that assumption and redemption reward speculators? What does he claim will be the benefits for the nation as a whole?—and think about how similar arguments reappear in more recent debates about national debts, the role of the financial economy in capitalism more broadly, and the ways in which government policies can enhance or detract from the economic power of particular groups in a capitalist society.

Treasury Department, January 9, 1790.

[To the Speaker of the House of Representatives]

[...] Exigencies are to be expected to occur, in the affairs of nations, in which there will be a necessity for borrowing; [...] loans in times of public danger, especially from foreign war, are found an indispensable resource, even to the wealthiest of them; And [...] in a country which, like this, is possessed of [. . .] little monied capital, the necessity for that resource, must, in such emergencies, be proportionably urgent. And as, on the one hand, the necessity for borrowing in particular emergencies cannot be doubted, so on the other, it is equally evident, that to be able to borrow upon *good terms*, it is essential that the credit of a nation should be well established. For, when the credit of a country is in any degree questionable, it never fails to give an extravagant premium, in one shape or another, upon all the loans it has occasion to make. [. . .]

If the maintenance of public credit, then, be truly so important, the next enquiry which suggests itself is, by what means it is to be effected? The ready answer to which question is, by good faith, by a punctual performance of contracts. States, like individuals, who observe their engagements, are respected and trusted: while the reverse is the fate of those, who pursue an opposite conduct. [. . .]

This reflection derives additional strength from the nature of the debt of the United States. It was the price of liberty. The faith of America has been repeatedly pledged for it, and with solemnities that give peculiar force to the obligation. There is indeed reason to regret that it has not hitherto been kept; that the necessities of the war, conspiring with inexperience in the subjects of finance, produced direct infractions: and that the subsequent period has been a continued scene of negative violation, or non-compliance. But a diminution of this regret arises from the reflection, that the last seven years have exhibited an earnest and uniform effort, on the part of the government of the union, to retrieve the national credit, by doing justice to the creditors of the nation; and that the embarrassments of a defective constitution, which defeated this laudable effort, have ceased.

From this evidence of a favorable disposition given by the former government, the institution of a new one, clothed with powers competent to calling forth the resources of the community, has excited correspondent expectations. A general belief accordingly prevails, that the credit of the United States will quickly be established on the firm foundation of an effectual provision for the existing debt. [. . .]

To justify and preserve their confidence; to promote the encreasing respectability of the American name; to answer the calls of justice; to restore landed property to its due value; to furnish new resources both to agriculture and commerce; to cement more closely the union of the states; to add to their security against foreign attack; to establish public order on the basis of an upright and liberal policy—These are the great and invaluable ends to be secured, by a proper and adequate provision, at the present period, for the support of public credit. [. . .]

It is a well known fact, that in countries in which the national debt is properly funded, and an object of established confidence, it answers most of the purposes of money. Transfers of stock or public debt are there equivalent to payments in specie; or in other words, stock, in the principal transactions of business, passes current as specie. The same thing would, in all probability happen here, under the like circumstances. [. . .]

First. Trade is extended by it; because there is a larger capital to carry it on, and the merchant can at the same time, afford to trade for smaller profits; as his stock, which, when unemployed, brings him in an interest from the government, serves him also as money, when he has a call for it in his commercial operations. Secondly. Agriculture and manufactures are also promoted by it: For the like reason, that more capital can be commanded to be employed in both; and because the merchant, whose enterprize in foreign trade, gives to them activity and extension, has greater means for enterprize. Thirdly. The interest of money will be lowered by it; for this is always in a ratio, to the quantity of money, and to the quickness of circulation. This circumstance will enable both the public and individuals to borrow on easier and cheaper terms.

And from the combination of these effects, additional aids will be furnished to labour, to industry, and to arts of every kind. But these good effects of a public debt are only to be looked for, when, by being well funded, it has acquired an adequate and stable value; [. . .] [whereas] one serious inconvenience of an unfunded debt is, that it contributes to the scarcity of money. [. . .]

The effect which the funding of the public debt, on right principles, would have upon landed property, is one of the circumstances attending such an arrangement, which has been least adverted to, though it deserves the most particular attention. The present depreciated state of that species of property is a serious calamity. The value of cultivated lands in most of the States, has fallen, since the revolution, from twenty-five to fifty per cent. In those furthest South, the decrease is still more considerable. [. . .] This decrease in the value of lands, ought, in a great measure, to be attributed to the scarcity of money; consequently, whatever produces an augmentation of the monied capital of the country, must have a proportional effect in raising that value. The beneficial tendency of a funded debt, in this respect, has been manifested by the most decisive experience in Great Britain. [. . .]

It is agreed on all hands, that that part of the debt which has been contracted abroad, and is denominated the foreign debt, ought to be provided for, according to the precise terms of the contracts relating to it. The discussions which can arise, therefore, will have reference essentially to the domestic part of it, or to that which has been contracted at home.

[. . .] [Let us consider] this question, whether a discrimination ought not to be made between original holders of the public securities, and present possessors, by purchase. Those who advocate a discrimination are for making a full provision for the securities of the former, at their nominal value; but contend, that the latter ought to receive no more than the cost to them, and the interest. [. . .]

The Secretary, after the most mature reflection on the force of this argument, is induced to reject the doctrine it contains, as equally unjust and impolitic, as highly injurious, even to the original holders of public securities; as ruinous to public credit. It is inconsistent with justice, because in the first place, it is a breach of contract; in violation of the rights of a fair purchaser. The nature of the contract in its origin, is, that the public will pay the sum expressed in the security, to the first holder, or his *assignee*. The intent, in making the security assignable, is, that the proprietor may be able to make use of his property, by selling it for as much as it *may be worth in the market*, and that the buyer may be *safe* in the purchase.

Every buyer, therefore, stands exactly in the place of the seller, has the same right with him to the identical sum expressed in the security, and having acquired that right, by fair purchase, and in conformity to the original agreement and intention of the government, his claim cannot be disputed, without manifest injustice. That he is to be considered as a fair purchaser, results from this: whatever necessity the seller may have been under, was occasioned by the government, in not making a proper provision for its debts. The buyer had no agency in it, and therefore ought not to suffer. He is not even chargeable with having taken an undue advantage. He paid what the commodity was worth in the market, and took the risks of reimbursement upon himself. He of course gave a fair equivalent, and ought to reap the benefit of his hazard; a hazard which was far from inconsiderable, and which, perhaps, turned on little less than a revolution in government. [...]

The impolicy of a discrimination results from two considerations; one, that it proceeds upon a principle destructive of that *quality* of the public debt, or the stock of the nation, which is essential to its capacity for answering the purposes of money—that is the *security* of *transfer*; the other, that as well on this account, as because it includes a breach of faith, it renders property in the funds less valuable; consequently induces lenders to demand a higher premium for what they lend, and produces every other inconvenience of a bad state of public credit.

It will be perceived at first sight, that the transferable quality of stock is essential to its operation as money, and that this depends on the idea of complete security to the transferree, and a firm persuasion, that no distinction can in any circumstances be made between him and the original proprietor. The precedent of an invasion of this fundamental principle, would, of course, tend to deprive the community of an advantage with which no temporary saving could bear the least comparison. [. . .]

The Secretary, concluding that a discrimination, between the different classes of creditors of the United States, cannot with propriety be made, proceeds to examine whether a difference ought to be permitted to remain between them, and another description of public creditors—Those of the states individually. The Secretary, after mature reflection on this point, entertains a full conviction, that an assumption of the debts of the particular states by the union, and a like provision for them, as for those of the union, will be a measure of sound policy and substantial justice. [. . .] [Otherwise] different plans originating in different authorities [. . .] [would lead to] interfering regulations, and thence collision and confusion. [. . .]

If all the public creditors receive their dues from one source, distributed with an equal hand, their interest will be the same. And, having the same interests, they will unite in the support of the fiscal arrangements of the government: as these, too, can be made with more convenience where there is no competition. These circumstances combined, will ensure to the revenue laws a more ready and more satisfactory execution. If, on the contrary, there are distinct provisions, there will be distinct interests, drawing different ways. That union and concert of views, among the creditors, which in every government is of great importance to their security, and to that of public credit, will not only not exist, but will be likely to give place to mutual jealousy and opposition. [. . .]

[. . .] Neither would it be just, that one class of the public creditors should be more favored than the other. The objects for which both descriptions of the debt were contracted, are in the main the same. Indeed a great part of the particular debts of the States has arisen from assumptions by them on account of the Union. And it is most equitable, that there should be the same measure of retribution for all. [...]

The result of the foregoing discussions is this. That there ought to be no discrimination between the original holders of the debt, and present possessors by purchase. That it is expedient there should be an assumption of the State debts by the Union, and that the arrears of interest should be provided for on an equal footing with the principal. [...]

Persuaded, as the Secretary is, that the proper funding of the present debt, will render it a national blessing, yet he is so far from acceding to the position in the latitude in which it is sometimes laid down, that "public debts are public benefits," a position inviting to prodigality, and liable to dangerous abuse, that he ardently wishes to see it incorporated, as a fundamental maxim, in the system of public credit of the United States, that the creation of debt should always be accompanied with the means of extinguishment. [...]

Under this impression, the Secretary proposes that the net product of the Post Office, to a sum not exceeding one million of dollars, be vested in Commissioners, to consist of the Vice-President of the United States, or President of the Senate, the Speaker of the House of Representatives, the Chief Justice, Secretary of the Treasury, and Attorney General of the United States, for the time being, in trust; to be applied by them, or any three of them, to the discharge of the existing public debt, either by purchase of stock in the market, or by payments on account of the principal, as shall appear to them most adviseable, in conformity to public engagements; to continue so vested, until the whole of the debt shall be discharged.

As an additional expedient for effecting a reduction of the debt, and for other purposes which will be mentioned, the Secretary would further propose, that the same Commissioners be authorized, with the approbation of the President of the United States, to borrow, on their credit, a sum not exceeding twelve millions of dollars, to be applied—

First. To the payments of the interest and instalments of the foreign debt, to the end of the present year. [. . .]

Secondly. To the payment of any deficiency which may happen in the product of the funds provided for paying the interest of the domestic debt.

Thirdly. To the effecting a change in the form of such part of the foreign debt, as bears an interest of five per cent. It is conceived that, for this purpose, a new loan, at a lower interest, may be combined with other expedients. [. . .]

The Secretary contemplates the application of this money through the medium of a national bank, for which, with the permission of the House, he will submit a plan in the course of the session.

The Secretary now proceeds, in the last place, to offer to the consideration of the House, his ideas of the steps which ought, at the present session, to be taken towards the assumption of the State debts. These are, briefly, that concurrent resolutions of the two Houses, with the approbation of the President, be entered into, declaring in substance—

That the United States do assume, and will, at the first session in the year 1791, provide, on the same terms with the present debt of the United States, for all such part of the debts of the respective States, or any of them, as shall, prior to the first day of January, in the said year, 1791, be subscribed towards a loan to the United States, upon the principles of either of the plans, which shall have been adopted by them, for obtaining a re-loan of their present debt.

Provided, that the provision to be made as aforesaid, shall be suspended, with respect to the debt of any State, which my have changed the securities of the United States for others issued by itself, until the whole of said securities shall either be re-exchanged or surrendered to the United States. [. . .]

That the amount of the debt of each State so assumed and provided for, be charged to such State in account with the United States, upon the same principles which it shall be lent to the United States.

That subscriptions be opened for receiving loans of the said debts, at the same times and places, and under the like regulation, as shall have been prescribed in relation to the debt of the United States. [. . .]

He is fully convinced, that it is of the greatest importance, that no further delay should attend the making of the requisite provision: not only because it will give a better impression of the good faith of the country, and will bring earlier relief to the creditors—both which circumstances are of great moment to public credit—but because the advantages to the community, from raising stock, as speedily as possible, to its natural value, will be incomparably greater, than any that can result from its continuance below that standard. No profit which could be derived from purchases in the market, on account of the government, to an practicable extent, would be an equivalent for the loss which would be sustained by the purchases of foreigners at a low value. Not to repeat, that governmental purchases, to be honorable, ought to be preceded by a provision. Delay, by disseminating doubt, would sink the price of stock; and as the temptation to foreign speculations, from the lowness of the price, would be too great to be neglected, millions would probably be lost to the United States.

All which is humbly submitted.
Alexander Hamilton,
Secretary of the Treasury

Questions

1. What were Hamilton's key arguments in favor of his plan for the national debt?

2. What sort of "fiscal state" was Hamilton trying to create? How would the plan of assuming and redeeming (and incurring still

more) debt set the pattern for the behavior of the federal state? What possibilities and what limits would be created?

3. What was Hamilton's goal for the broader economy in this plan?

4. Why did Hamilton insist on the assumption of state debts? What implications would this have had, and how might the political debates on this issue have played out?

5. Hamilton was insistent on the importance of circulating notes as a substitute for specie. Why did he take this view, and how might his opponents have responded to this argument?

6. How does Hamilton's message to the House of Representatives fit into current debates about the size and importance of the national debt? Do any of his arguments have relevance for modern policymakers?

Report on a National Bank (1790)

ALEXANDER HAMILTON

As the first Treasury secretary of the United States, Alexander Hamilton had a tremendous influence in determining the new federal government's economic policy. His actions would help to shape the development of capitalism in the United States. But his policies also generated a lot of opposition, and the assumptions and arguments of his opponents still find supporters today.

Nowhere was the gap between Hamiltonian policies and their opponents more persistent than in the areas of monetary and credit policies. In his Report on a National Bank, Hamilton argued for an institution that would steer credit into the U.S. economy, decide who received it, support federal-government growth policies, and control the amount of money in the economy. That's exactly what he got with the First Bank of the United States. The bank, based in Philadelphia and chartered for twenty years, helped the federal government bring control to an unruly financial system, establish a common currency, and support the expansion of trade.

Hamilton's understanding of finance was far in advance of that of most of his peers, and his interventions were perfectly timed for shaping the development of capitalism in the young United States. He understood that banks can create money by lending to those who patronize them. By doing so, as long as they retain the public's confidence, banks' credit creation can spur wider investment and economic growth. And the world of trade with which he was familiar from his own days as a merchant was starting to grow hotter. But banks that behave irresponsibly can create financial disasters, sending trade into a deep freeze and blocking growth. Making one responsible bank the focus of the financial economy would provide a sort of regulation to the economy, since smaller banks would inevitably owe money to the central bank. It could require immediate repayment, even in scarce gold and silver, from those institutions which behaved irresponsibly. And, by serving as the conduit of lending to the federal government, Hamilton believed that (just like the Bank of England, after which it was in part modeled), the First Bank of the United States would create a creditor class that was not only patriotically but financially interested in the nation's long-term success and continued independence.

It was difficult for Hamilton to explain to people who were used to thinking of money as, ideally, gold or silver, with paper as a poor substitute, that a well-run bank could multiply the usefulness of money deposited in its vaults many, many times over and make paper just as sure a store of value as gold. And even as Hamilton proposed it, the Bank drew intense political opposition from the Treasury Secretary's onetime ally James Madison. The Virginian and future president Madison believed that the Constitution did not permit the federal government to create a credit-granting institution that would by its nature set policy for state economies, choose winners and losers in the economy, and make it possible for the Executive Branch—and even the unelected wealthy creditors and officials of the Bank—to use their leverage as lenders to dictate policy to the federal government. Madison, and later Jefferson, scoffed at Hamilton's claim that the "necessary and proper" clause of the Constitution permitted a Bank, pointing out that anyone could say that any institution or project was "necessary and proper." And this institution, they feared, meant that Hamilton would be able to oversee the transition of the United States from an agricultural commodity-exporting society dominated by Virginia planters like themselves into one dominated by New York and Pennsylvania bankers and merchants—like Hamilton.

The Bank, whose charter the by-then President Madison allowed to expire in 1811 at the end of its twenty years, helped establish a coherent financial system in the United States. The propensity of politicians to remove controls over the banking system, however, helped lead to episodes of financial chaos. The War of 1812 revealed the inability of a Bank-less banking system to mobilize financing for the federal government's war effort. The yo-yo movement between centralized regulation of American financial networks and deregulated chaos has persisted to the present day.

Treasury Department, December 13th, 1790.

In obedience to the order of the House of Representatives, of the ninth day of August last, requiring the Secretary of the Treasury to prepare and report, on this day, such further provision as may, in his opinion, be necessary for establishing the Public Credit; the said Secretary further respectfully reports:

That a National Bank is an institution of primary importance to the prosperous administration of the Finances, and would be of the greatest utility in the operations connected with the support of the Public Credit, his attention has been drawn to devising the plan of such an institution, upon a scale which will entitle it to the confidence, and be likely to render it equal to the exigencies, of the public. [. . .] It is a fact, well understood, that public banks have found admission and patronage among the principal and most enlightened commercial nations. They have successively obtained in Italy, Germany, Holland, England and France, as well as in the United States. [. . .] Theorists and men of business unite in the acknowledgment of it. Trade and industry [. . .] have been indebted to them for important aid. [. . .] The following are among the principal advantages of a Bank:

First. The augmentation of the active or productive capital of a country. Gold and silver, where they are employed merely as the instruments of exchange and alienation, have been [. . .] denominated dead stock; but when deposited in banks, to become the basis of a paper circulation, which takes their character and place, as the signs or representatives of value, they then acquire life, or, in other words, an active and productive quality. [. . .] It is a well established fact, that banks in good credit can circulate a far greater sum than the actual quantum of their capital in gold and silver. The extent of the possible excess [. . .] has been conjecturally stated at the proportions of two and three to one. This faculty is produced in various ways.

First—A great proportion of the notes which are issued and pass current as cash, are indefinitely suspended in circulation, from the confidence which each holder has, that he can at any moment turn them into gold and silver.

Secondly—Every loan which a bank makes, is, in its first shape, a credit given to the borrower on its books, the amount of which it stands ready to pay, either in its own notes, or in gold or silver, at his option. But, in a great number of cases, no actual payment is made in either. The borrower frequently, by a check or order, transfers his credit to some other person, to whom he has a payment to make; who, in his turn, is as often content with a similar credit, because he is satisfied that he can, whenever he pleases, either convert it into cash, or pass it to some other hand, as an equivalent for it. And in this manner the credit keeps circulating, performing in every stage the office of money, till it is extinguished by a discount with some person who has a payment to make to the bank, to an equal or greater amount. Thus large sums are lent and paid, frequently through a variety of hands, without the intervention of a single piece of coin. [. . .] These different circumstances explain the manner in which the ability of a bank to circulate a greater sum than its actual capital in coin is acquired. [. . .] The same circumstances illustrate the truth of the position, that it is one of the properties of banks to increase the active capital of a country. [. . .]

Secondly. Greater facility to the government, in obtaining pecuniary aids, especially in sudden emergencies. [. . .] The reason is obvious: the capitals of a great number of individuals are, by this operation, collected to a point, and placed under one direction. The mass formed by this union, is, in a certain sense, magnified by the credit attached to it; and while this mass is always ready, and can at once be put in motion, in aid of the government. [. . .] There is, in the nature of things, as will be more particularly noticed in another place, an intimate connexion of interest between the government and the bank of a nation.

Thirdly. The facilitating of the payment of taxes. [. . .] It is evident, that whatever enhances the quantity of circulating money, adds to the ease with which every industrious member of the community may acquire that portion of it of which he stands in need, and enables him the better to pay his taxes, as well as to supply his other wants. [. . .]

[. . .] [The] disadvantages [of banks] real or supposed are now to be reviewed. The most serious of the charges which have been, brought against them, are, [. . .] That they furnish temptations to overtrading; [. . .] That they have a tendency to banish gold and silver from the country.

There is great reason to believe, that on a close and candid survey, it will be discovered, that these charges are either without foundation, or that, [. . .] they have proceeded from other, or partial, or temporary causes; are not inherent in the nature and permanent tendency of such institutions; or are more than counterbalanced by opposite advantages. [. . .]

The directors of a bank, too, though in order to extend its business and its popularity in the infancy of an institution, they may be tempted to go further in accommodation than the strict rules of prudence will warrant, [. . .] [but], in the course of practice, from the very nature of things, the interest will make it the policy of a bank to succor the wary and industrious; to discredit the rash and unthrifty; to discountenance both usurious lenders and usurious borrowers. [Thus] in every case the evil is to be compared with the good; and in the present case, such a comparison will issue in this, that the new and increased energies derived to commercial enterprise, from the aid of banks, are a source of general profit and advantage, which greatly outweigh the partial ills of the overtrading of a few individuals at particular times, or of numbers in particular conjunctures.

[. . .] The last and heaviest charge is still to be examined: this is, that banks tend to banish the gold and silver out of the country.

The force of this objection rests upon their being an engine of paper credit, which, by furnishing a substitute for the metals, is supposed to promote their exportation. It is an objection, which, if it has any foundation, lies not against banks peculiarly, but against every species of paper credit. [. . .] It is immaterial what serves the purpose of money, whether paper or gold and silver; that the effect of both upon industry is the same; and that the intrinsic wealth of a nation is to be measured, not by the abundance of the precious metals contained in it, but by the quantity of the productions of its labor and industry. [. . .] A nation that has no mines of its own must derive the precious metals from others; generally speaking, in exchange for the products of its labor and industry. The quantity it will possess, will, therefore, in the ordinary course of things, be regulated by the favorable or unfavorable balance of its trade; that is, by the proportion between its abilities to supply foreigners, and its wants of them; between the amount of its exportations and that of its importations. Hence, the state of its agriculture and manufactures, the quantity and quality of its labor and industry, must in the main, influence and determine the increase or decrease of its gold and silver.

If this be true, the inference seems to be, that well constituted banks favor the increase of the precious metals. It has been shown that they augment, in different ways, the active capital of a country. This it is which generates employment; which animates and expands labor and industry. Every addition which is made to it, by contributing to put in motion a greater quantity of both, tends to create a greater quantity of the products of both; and, by furnishing more materials for exportation, conduces to a favorable balance of trade, and, consequently, to the introduction and increase of gold and silver. [. . .] The support of industry is, probably, in every case, of more consequence towards correcting a wrong balance of trade, than any practicable retrenchments in the expenses of families or individuals; and the stagnation of it would be likely to have more effect in prolonging, than any such savings in shortening, its continuance. That stagnation is a natural consequence of an inadequate medium, which, without the aid of bank circulation, would, in the cases supposed, be severely felt.

[. . .] There is one thing, however, which the government owes to itself and to the community—at least to all that part of it who are not stockholders—which is, to reserve to itself a right of ascertaining, as often as may be necessary, the state of the bank—excluding, however, all pretension to control. This right forms an article in the primitive constitution of the bank of North America; and its propriety stands upon the clearest reasons. If the paper of a bank is to be permitted to insinuate itself into all the revenues and receipts of a country; if it is even to be tolerated as the substitute for gold and silver in all the transactions of business. [. . .] The government should possess the means of ascertaining, whenever it thinks fit, that so delicate a trust is executed with fidelity and care. A right of this nature is not only desirable, as it respects the government, but it ought to be equally so to all those concerned in the institution, as an additional title to public and private confidence, and as a thing which can only be formidable to practices that imply mismanagement. The presumption must always be, that the characters who would be intrusted with the exercise of this right on behalf of the government, will not be deficient in the discretion which it may require; at least the admitting of this presumption cannot be deemed too great a return of confidence for that very large portion of it which the government is required to place in the bank.

Abandoning, therefore, ideas which, however agreeable, or desirable, are neither practicable nor safe, the following plan, for the constitution of a national bank, is respectfully submitted to the consideration of the House.

1. The capital stock of the bank shall not exceed ten millions of dollars, divided into twenty five thousand shares, each share being four hundred dollars; to raise which sum subscriptions shall be opened on the first Monday of April next, and shall continue open until the whole shall be subscribed. Bodies politic as well as individuals may subscribe.

2. The amount of each share shall be payable, one-fourth in gold and silver coin, and three-fourths in that part of the public debt which, according to the loan proposed by the act making provision for the debt of the United States, shall bear an accruing interest at the time of payment of six per centum per annum. [. . .]

6. The totality of the debts of the company, whether by bond, bill, note, or other contract, (credits for deposites excepted,) shall never exceed the amount of its capital stock. [. . .]

7. The company may sell or demise its lands and tenements, or may sell the whole or any part of the public debt, whereof its stock shall consist; but shall trade in nothing, except bills of exchange, gold and silver bullion, or in the sale of goods pledged for money lent; nor shall take more than at the rate of six per centum per annum, upon its loans or discounts. [. . .]

10. The affairs of the bank shall be under the management of twenty-five directors, one of whom shall be the President; and there shall be, on the first Monday of January, in each year, a choice of directors, by a plurality of suffrages of the stockholders, to serve for a year. The directors, at their first meeting after each election, shall choose one of their number as President.

11. The number of votes to which each stockholder shall be entitled shall be according to the number of shares he shall hold [. . .] but no person, co-partnership, or body politic, shall be entitled to a greater number than thirty votes. [. . .]

13. None but a stockholder, being a citizen of the United States, shall be eligible as a director. [...]

20. The bills and notes of the bank originally made payable, or which shall have become payable on demand in gold and silver coin, shall be receivable in all payments to the United States. [...]

22. No similar institution shall be established by any future act of the United States, during the continuance of the one hereby proposed to be established. [...]

24. And lastly, the President of the United States shall be authorized to cause a subscription to be made to the stock of the said company, on behalf of the United States, to an amount not exceeding two millions of dollars, to be paid out of the moneys which shall be borrowed by virtue of either of the acts, the one entitled "An act making provision for the debt of the United States," and the other, entitled "An act making provision for the reduction of the public debt;" borrowing of the bank an equal sum, to be applied to the purposes for which the said moneys shall have been procured, reimburseable in ten years by equal annual instalments; or at any time sooner, or in any greater proportions, that the government may think fit. [...]

The limitation of the rate of interest. [...] The natural effect of low interest is to increase trade and industry; because undertakings of every kind can be prosecuted with greater advantage. [...] The difference of one per cent, in the rate at which money may be had, is often capable of making an essential change for the better in the situation of any country or place. [...] Every thing, therefore, which tends to lower the rate of interest, is peculiarly worthy of the cares of legislators. And though laws which violently sink the legal rate of interest greatly below the market level, are not to be commended, because they are not calculated to answer their aim; yet whatever has a tendency to effect a reduction, without violence to the natural course of things, ought to be attended to and pursued. Banks are among the means most proper to accomplish this end; and the moderation of the rate at which their discounts are made, is a material ingredient towards it; with which their own interest, viewed on an enlarged and permanent scale, does not appear to clash.

All which is humbly submitted.
Alexander Hamilton,
Secretary of the Treasury

Questions

1. How would the National Bank enhance the development of the national economy, in Hamilton's view?
2. What answer would he give to those who complained that the Bank could print paper money and "debase" the currency, creating inflation and instability?
3. What elements of the Bank plan did Hamilton include in order to gain the support of the new nation's wealthiest citizens?
4. Why did Hamilton explain that while lowering the prevailing interest rate was desirable, one could not simply decree that the Bank would loan at a low interest rate?

Report on Manufactures (1791)

ALEXANDER HAMILTON

Even as the United States achieved its independence in the 1780s, Britain was building unprecedented new economic capacities that would enable it to more than compensate for its loss of much of its North American empire. Britain was becoming the world's first full-scale capitalist economy, in a process that historians often call the "Industrial Revolution." The emergence of machine-centered textile production in the cotton spinning and weaving mills of the West Midlands (i.e., the area around the city of Manchester) was leading to a new working class who lived on factory wages, ate food sold by commercial farmers, and made exportable products at ever-increasing levels of productivity. This was one of the core processes that broke the old Malthusian trap of agricultural economies. Over the next fifty to seventy years, the emerging British textile industry provided market incentives and technological models that would transform all sectors of the British economy. Eventually this process would do the same for much of the rest of the world, as well.

One aspect of the new textile production at the core of the British transformation was the way the new factories could make cloth which, even accounting for the cost of transportation, could be sold cheaper than traditionally made fabrics anywhere around the world. The history of capitalist transformation often includes the destruction of old business sectors along with the creation of new models. Whether those changes are good or bad often depend on how equitably the gains and losses are distributed, and often people disagree—based on their perspectives—about said equitability. But surely, what is especially inequitable is when a more technologically advanced economy sells its goods in a foreign market at below the cost of production with the specific purpose of destroying that other country's capacity to produce that good, thus hoping to create dependent markets. And that is exactly what British manufacturers were allegedly doing in the new United States of the 1780s. Taking advantage of the fact that under the Articles of Confederation there were thirteen separate trade policies, British merchants were "dumping" the goods of their emerging factory economy on the U.S. market—even as the angry empire kept most markets in Britain's remaining colonies, like the crucial food and timber markets of the Caribbean sugar islands, closed to American producers and middlemen.

British trade activities were one crucial target of Hamilton's pro-manufacturing agenda, which he laid out in the following document. Yet his policy, which argues for carefully targeted protective tariffs and other policies that would protect and stimulate manufacturing, seems to go against some core ideas of both his own and, more broadly, the revolution's leaders. The revolution certainly built on ideas about natural rights, as in the Declaration of Independence. American resistance to the British Crown also relied on deeply held ideas about representative government. And, as some argue, the fact that many of the revolution's leaders were slaveholders is also relevant, since they above all abhorred the idea that they would be thought of as unequal, subject, or in any way the dependents in a slavelike relationship. But the revolution was also deeply antimercantilist—deeply opposed to the rules imposed by European empires on their colonies with the specific purpose of creating trade barriers that would keep the colonies in the dependent relationship of being producers of low-value-added primary goods, while also being closed markets that could only buy from the mother country's manufacturers. The revolutionaries were, in a word, free traders.

Free trade seemed a key component of being a free citizen. Buy from whom you want, sell to whom you want, at whatever price you want. And in this the anti-merchant revolutionaries agreed with one of Hamilton's probable inspirations, the Scottish political economist Adam Smith. That kind of market freedom, Smith argued, was a key component of a broader "Society of Perfect Liberty." Even here Hamilton draws, it seems, on Smith—when, for instance, he discusses the way that the division of labor leads to greater productivity and national wealth.

And yet Hamilton argues for a nationalist policy of creating protected markets for certain kinds of manufacturing. So the question arises: Was Hamilton a prophet of a new U.S. capitalism that would emerge in the nineteenth century and beyond, or just another old-fashioned eighteenth-century mercantilist?

Thomas Jefferson certainly thought Hamilton was a mercantilist. Jefferson believed in free trade. And like many recent proponents of free trade, he thought that a country should produce what it was best suited to produce. In his *Notes on the State of Virginia*, he argued that the United States was particularly well-placed to produce agricultural commodities. Unlike British workers, American farmers were used to property ownership, and they had a whole continent laid out before them to occupy (provided they uprooted the original occupants, of course). Unlike British workers, they were also used to freedom, and Jefferson thought manufacturing towns and cities undermined the habits of self-reliant citizenship necessary to maintain such free institutions of self-government. He and his allies would oppose Hamilton's trade policies for decades to come.

So the question to think about as you read Hamilton's Report is this: is a certain kind of nationalist economic policy necessary to develop a nation's capitalism from a standing start? This debate was part of the arguments over development ideology in the 1950s. Some emergent economies, particularly in East Asia, would use a similar policy to vault into international economic power. In other cases, as in Africa, India, Latin America, and the Caribbean, such policies would by the 1970s come in for massive criticism. Developmentalist policies very similar to the ones that Hamilton here advocates for the United States would be blamed for the failure of development. International institutions like the IMF (International Monetary Fund) and the World Bank, backed by the United States and other industrialized nations, eventually imposed "structural adjustment" policies designed to open those developing economies fully to the world market. The debate still goes on today in controversies over globalization.

December 5th, 1791.

The Secretary of the Treasury, in obedience to the order of the House of Representatives, of the 15th day of January, 1790, has applied his attention, at as early a period as his other duties would permit, to the subject of Manufactures; and particularly to the means of promoting—such as will tend to render the United States independent on foreign nations, for military and other essential supplies:

And he thereupon respectfully submits the following REPORT:

It ought readily to be conceded, that the cultivation of the earth, as the primary and most certain source of national supply; as the immediate and chief source of subsistence to man; as the principal source of those materials which constitute the nutriment of other kinds of labor; as including a state most favorable to the freedom and independence of the human mind; one, perhaps, most conducive to the multiplication of the human species, has intrinsically a strong claim to pre-eminence over every other kind of industry.

But that it has a title to any thing like an exclusive predilection, in any country, ought to be admitted with great caution; that it is even more productive than every other branch of industry, requires more evidence than has yet been given in support of the position. That its real interests, precious and important as, without the help of exaggeration, they truly are, will be advanced rather than injured, by the due encouragement of manufactures, may, it is believed, be satisfactorily demonstrated. And it is also believed, that the expediency of such encouragement, in a general view, may be shown to be recommended by the most cogent and persuasive motives of national policy.

It is now proper to proceed a step further, and to enumerate the principal circumstances, from which it may be inferred, that manufacturing establishments not only occasion a positive augmentation of the produce and revenue of the society, but that they contribute essentially to rendering them greater than they could possibly be without such establishments. These circumstances are,

1. The division of labor.

2. An extension of the use of machinery.

3. Additional employment to classes of the community not ordinarily engaged in the business.

4. The promoting of emigration from foreign countries.

5. The furnishing greater scope for the diversity of talents and dispositions, which discriminate men from each other.

6. The affording a more ample and various field for enterprise.

7. The creating, in some instances, a new, and securing, in all, a more certain and steady demand for the surplus produce of the soil.

Each of these circumstances has a considerable influence upon the total mass of industrious effort in a community; together, they add to it a degree of energy and effect, which are not easily conceived. Some comments upon each of them, in the order in which they have been stated, may serve to explain their importance.

I. As to the division of labor.

It has justly been observed, that there is scarcely any thing of greater moment in the economy of a nation, than the proper division of labor. The separation of occupations causes each to be carried to a much greater perfection than it could possibly acquire if they were blended. This arises principally from three circumstances:

1st. The greater skill and dexterity naturally resulting from a constant and undivided application to a single object. It is evident that these properties must increase in proportion to the separation and simplification of objects, and the steadiness of the attention devoted to each; and must be less in proportion to the complication of objects, and the number among which the attention is distracted.

The employment of machinery forms an item of great importance in the general mass of national industry. It is an artificial force brought in aid of the natural force of man; and, to all the purposes of labor, is an increase of hands, an accession of strength, unencumbered too by the expense of maintaining the laborer. May it not, therefore, be fairly inferred, that those occupations which give greatest scope to the use of this auxiliary, contribute most to the general stock of industrious effort, and, in consequence, to the general product of industry?

It shall be taken for granted, and the truth of the position referred to observation, that manufacturing pursuits are susceptible, in a greater degree, of the application of machinery, than those of agriculture. If so, all the difference is lost to a community, which, instead of manufacturing for itself, procures the fabrics requisite to its supply from other countries. The substitution of foreign for domestic manufactures, is a transfer to foreign nations of the advantages accruing from the employment of machinery, in the modes in which it is capable of being employed, with most utility and to the greatest extent.

The cotton-mill, invented in England within the last twenty years, is a signal illustration of the general proposition which has been just advanced. In consequence of it, all the different processes for spinning cotton are performed by means of machines, which are put in motion by water, and attended chiefly by women and children; and by a smaller number of persons, in the whole, than are requisite in the ordinary mode of spinning. And it is an advantage of great moment, that the operations of this mill continue with convenience, during the night as well as through the day. The prodigious effect of such a machine is easily conceived. To this invention is to be attributed, essentially, the immense progress which has been so suddenly made in Great Britain in the various fabrics of cotton.

It is evident that the exertions of the husbandman will be steady or fluctuating, vigorous or feeble, in proportion to the steadiness or fluctuation, adequateness or inadequateness of the markets on which he must depend, for the vent of the surplus which may be produced by his labor; and that such surplus, in the ordinary course of things, will be greater or less in the same proportion.

For the purpose of this vent, a domestic market is greatly to be preferred to a foreign one; because it is, in the nature of things, far more to be relied upon.

Considering how fast, and how much the progress of new settlements in the United States, must increase the surplus produce of the soil,

This idea of an extensive domestic market for the surplus produce of the soil, is of the first consequence. It is, of all things, that which most effectually conduces to a flourishing state of agriculture. If the effect of manufactories should be to detach a portion of the hands which would otherwise be engaged in tillage, it might possibly cause a smaller quantity of lands to be under cultivation; but by their tendency to procure a more certain demand for the surplus produce of the soil, they would, at the same time, cause the lands which were in cultivation to be better improved and more productive. [...]

It merits particular observation, that the multiplication of manufactories not only furnishes a market for those articles which have been accustomed to be produced in abundance in a country; but it likewise creates a demand for such as were either unknown, or produced in inconsiderable quantities. The bowels, as well as the surface of the earth, are ransacked for articles which were before neglected. Animals, plants, and minerals, acquire an utility and value which were before unexplored.

The foregoing considerations seem sufficient to establish, as general propositions, that it is the interest of nations to diversify the industrious pursuits of the individuals who compose them. [. . .]

1st. If the system of perfect liberty to industry and commerce, were the prevailing system of nations, the arguments which dissuade a country in the predicament of the United States, from the zealous pursuit of manufactures would doubtless have great force. . . .

But the system which has been mentioned, is far from characterizing the general policy of nations. The prevalent one has been regulated by an opposite spirit. The consequence of it is, that the United States are, to a certain extent, in the situation of a country, precluded from foreign commerce. [. . .] The regulations of several countries, with which we have the most extensive intercourse, throw serious obstructions in the way of the principal staples of the United States.

In such a position of things, the United States cannot exchange with Europe on equal terms; and the want of reciprocity would render them the victim of a system which should induce them to confine their views to agriculture, and refrain from manufactures. A constant and increasing necessity, on their part, for the commodities of Europe, and only a partial and occasional demand for their own, in return, could not but expose them to a state of impoverishment, compared with the opulence to which their political and natural advantages authorize them to aspire. [. . .]

The remaining objections to a particular encouragement of manufactures in the United States, now require to be examined.

One of these turns on the proposition, that industry, if left to itself, will naturally find its way to the most useful and profitable employment. Whence it is inferred, that manufactures, without the aid of government, will grow up as soon and as fast as the natural state of things and the interest of the community may require. [...] Experience teaches, that men are often so much governed by what they are accustomed to see and practice. [...] The apprehension of failing in new attempts, is, perhaps, a more serious impediment. [...]

The superiority antecedently enjoyed by nations who have preoccupied and perfected a branch of industry, constitutes a more formidable obstacle than either of those which have been mentioned, to the introduction of the same branch into a country in which it did not before exist. To maintain, between the recent establishments of one country, and the long matured establishments of another country, a competition upon equal terms, both as to quality and price, is, in most cases, impracticable. The disparity, in the one, or in the other, or in both, must necessarily be so considerable, as to forbid a successful rivalship, without the extraordinary aid and protection of government. [...] The undertakers of a new manufacture have to contend, not only with the natural disadvantages of a new undertaking, but with the gratuities and remunerations which other governments bestow. To be enabled to contend with success, it is evident, that the interference and aid of their own governments are indispensable.

[...] One more point of view only remains, in which to consider the expediency of encouraging manufactures in the United States.

It is not uncommon to meet with an opinion, that, though the promoting of manufactures may be the interest of a part of the Union, it is contrary to that of another part. The northern and southern regions are sometimes represented as having adverse interests in this respect. Those are called manufacturing, these agricultural States; and a species of opposition is imagined to subsist between the manufacturing and agricultural interests. [...] It is nevertheless a maxim, well established by experience, and generally acknowledged, where there has been sufficient experience, that the aggregate prosperity of manufactures, and the aggregate prosperity of agriculture, are intimately connected. In the course of the discussion which has had place, various weighty considerations have been adduced, operating in support of that maxim. Perhaps the superior steadiness of the demand of a domestic market, for the surplus produce of the soil, is, alone, a convincing argument of its truth.

Ideas of a contrariety of interests between the Northern and Southern regions of the Union, are, in the main, as unfounded as they are mischievous. The diversity of circumstances on which such contrariety is usually predicated, authorizes a directly contrary conclusion. Mutual wants constitute one of the strongest links of political connexion; and the extent of these bears a natural proportion to the diversity in the means of mutual supply. [. . .]

If the northern and middle States should be the principal scenes of such establishments, they would immediately benefit the more southern, by creating a demand for productions, some of which they have in common with the other States, and others of which are either peculiar to them, or more abundant, or of better quality, than elsewhere. These productions, principally, are timber, flax, hemp, cotton, wool, raw silk, indigo, iron, lead, furs, hides, skins and coals: of these articles cotton and indigo are peculiar to the Southern States. . . .The extensive cultivation of cotton can, perhaps, hardly be expected, but from the previous establishment of domestic manufactories of the article; and the surest encouragement and vent for the others, would result from similar establishments in respect to them.

In order to a better judgment of the means proper to be resorted to by the United States, it will be of use to advert to those which have been employed with success in other countries—The principal of these are:

I. Protecting duties—or duties on those foreign
articles which are the rivals of the domestic
ones intended to be encouraged.

Duties of this nature evidently amount to a virtual bounty on the domestic fabrics; since, by enhancing the charges on foreign articles, they enable the national manufacturers to undersell all their foreign competitors. The propriety of this species of encouragement need not be dwelt upon; as it is not only a clear result from the numerous topics which have been suggested, but is sanctioned by the laws of the United States, in a variety of instances; it has the additional recommendation of being a resource of revenue. Indeed all the duties imposed on imported articles, though with an exclusive view to revenue, have the effect in contemplation, and, except where they fall on raw materials, wear a beneficent aspect towards the manufacturers of the country. [. . .]

VIII. The encouragement of new inventions and discoveries at home, and of the introduction into the United States of such as may have been made in other countries; particularly those which relate to machinery.

This is among the most useful and unexceptionable of the aids which can be given to manufactures. The usual means of that encouragement are pecuniary rewards, and, for a time, exclusive privileges. [. . .] For the last, so far as respects "authors and inventors," provision has been made by law. But it is desirable, in regard to improvements, and secrets of extraordinary value, to be able to extend the same benefit to introducers, as well as authors and inventors; a policy which has been practised with advantage in other countries. [. . .]

X. The facilitating of pecuniary remittances from place to place—

[. . .] A general circulation of bank paper, which is to be expected from the institution lately established, will be a most valuable mean to this end. But much good would also accrue from some additional provisions respecting inland bills of exchange. If those drawn in one State payable in another, were made negotiable every where, and interest and damages allowed in case of protest, it would greatly promote negotiations between the citizens of different States, by rendering them more secure; and with it the convenience and advantage of the merchants and manufacturers of each. [. . .]

XI. The facilitating of the transportation of commodities.

Improvements favoring this object intimately concern all the domestic interests of a community; but they may, without impropriety, be mentioned as having an important relation to manufactures. There is, perhaps, scarcely any thing, which has been better calculated to assist the manufactures of Great Britain, than the meliorations of the public roads of that kingdom and the great progress which has been of late made in opening canals. Of the former the United States stand much in need; for the latter they present uncommon facilities. [. . .] This is one of those improvements which could be prosecuted with more efficacy by the whole, than by any part or parts of the Union. There are cases in which the general interest will be in danger to be sacrificed to the collision of some supposed local interests. [. . .]

There are certain species of taxes, which are apt to be oppressive to different parts of the community, and among other ill effects, have a very unfriendly aspect towards manufactures. All poll or capitation taxes, are of this nature. They either proceed according to a fixed rate, which operates unequally and injuriously to the industrious poor, or they vest a discretion in certain officers, to make estimates and assessments which are necessarily vague, conjectural, and liable to abuse. They ought, therefore, to be abstained from in all but cases of distressing emergency.

All which is humbly submitted.
Alexander Hamilton,
Secretary of the Treasury.

Questions

1. Return to the question asked at the end of the introduction to this reading: was Hamilton a forward-looking capitalist prophet, or was he advising Americans to re-run the mercantilist playbook that had made Britain a great but (in many American revolutionaries' view) tyrannical empire?
2. Why, in Hamilton's view, should the U.S. *not* focus on agriculture as its main source of economic growth?
3. Which policy did the U.S. choose over the next seventy years? What about over the next two hundred and twenty-five years?
4. Are trade barriers bad for developing countries, or good? What should their economic development goals be, and how should they best achieve them?
5. As the first postcolonial country to develop into an industrial, capitalist society, does the United States have any special responsibility to assist countries that are trying to follow a similar path? What if helping actually hurts U.S. citizens in some economic sense?

PART II

MAKING CAPITALISM
AMERICAN

MODULE 6

THE HAITIAN REVOLUTION AND THE WAR OF 1812

Letters from the South: Paper Money (1835)

JAMES KIRKE PAULDING

James Kirke Paulding was a New Yorker who visited the South in the middle of the first great post–War of 1812 boom, sometime around 1816. At that time, he was a nationalist republican, anxious about the effect of slavery on the future development of the country. He wrote this account of his observations and reflections during his journey as a series of "letters," a common convention, and published it anonymously. The text includes criticism of the emerging domestic slave trade. But it also includes a parable on the evils of debt in general and, in particular, of banks' ability to issue paper banknotes as money to their borrowers.

Trained to be suspicious of banks by the Jeffersonians' long opposition to Hamilton, Paulding plays here on fears that many shared. Many Americans feared that the use of paper notes as money enabled charlatans and confidence men, some of whom sat on banks' boards of directors, to swindle hardworking farmers and others out of actual goods—in return for which producers would be holding promises to pay that could turn out to be empty. Gold and silver, they believed, were much more reliable sources of value, forms in which to contain, store, and transfer wealth. Debt in general was seen as a bad thing—as it often still is—and those who used it are still depicted as wasteful people who fritter away their earnings in the interest payments or "discounts" that they have to pay to lenders.

Sometimes those who were suspicious of the new, emerging paper-and-credit economy were right. Some banks were scams.

Some notes were fraudulent. Confidence men abounded in the nineteenth-century capitalist economy, and the revolution in credit brought the bad along with the good. But at the same time, this backward-looking sense of anxiety about innovative credit and financial practices could also hold back economic growth. At times, "specie fetishism"—the belief that only gold and silver were legitimate forms of currency—could also be used to hold back social transformation, or to transfer wealth from debtors and farmers to creditors in general and banks in particular. Even today, many Americans remain susceptible to gold and silver fixations, and knowledge about how credit can help drive economic growth is depressingly rare.

LETTER XXXV.

DEAR FRANK,

[. . .] The present paper-system is the most pernicious to the real prosperity, morals, and independence of this country, of any ever devised by the cupidity of man. It has already worked the most dangerous inroads on the virtuous independence, which was not long since the lot of all; and if suffered to continue, will place the whole community in a state of abject dependence on banks.

Power, which used to follow land, has now gone over to paper-money. The landholder does not feel this as yet, so extensively as he will by and by, when he will find his stinted independence fade away, in comparison with the short-lived splendours of the bank-dependent, and he obliged to enlist in the honourable band of bank-paupers. [. . .] Wherever a false capital is created, it will in time swallow up the real one, as a vacuum abstracts and absorbs the surrounding air.

The other evening I went to sleep, with these and such like thoughts in my head; and as people are apt to dream of what they think of when awake, I was possessed with the following curious vision.

Methought I was poring over a bank-note, which I think was issued from a place called "Owl-Creek," and happening to say to myself, "Where the deuce did this come from?" I was answered in a small squeaking voice as follows—at first I could not tell where it came from, but on closer examination, I discovered a motion in the bill of the figure of an owl, with which the note was decorated.

"I am the offspring of a bandana handkerchief, that was once worn about the neck of a learned East-Indian, acquainted with all the arts of Eastern magic, and a piece of Irish linen, whilom part of the night-cap of an old Irish witch. This accounts for my being gifted with speech. I was born in a paper-mill, and the first thing I recollect, was being nearly squeezed to death under a piece of copper, which bruised me black and blue all over. Then I was taken to the bank, and underwent a sort of transubstantiation, under the magic hands of the President and Cashier; for from a rag, I became converted into solid gold, or at least something nearly as valuable.

"I had not been here long, before I was counted out to [. . .] a merchant, who lived in a fine house drove a splendid equipage, and fared sumptuously every day. I felicitated myself mightily that I had got into such comfortable quarters; but soon discovered all was not right with my new master. As he carried me in his pocket, I had an opportunity of watching him closely, and hearing all that he said, or others said to him. I learned, that he had set out in business with a reasonable capital, which under prudent management would have led him to a comfortable independency; but was seduced by the example of those around him, and by the facility of getting discounts, into borrowing money of the banks, and trading on credit to a great amount. But he learned too late that the man who is always borrowing and paying interest for his money, is working for his creditor, and not for himself. [. . .] To add to his distresses, his wife and children, fancying him a man of immense riches, indulged in every species of extravagance, and he had not the courage to tell them a few months would probably make them beggars. In fact, I had not been with him long, before the banks, either from necessity or caprice, drew in their discounts; my master failed—the banks got all his property—the rest of his creditors got nothing; and his wife and children found themselves in beggary, with a thousand artificial wants to pamper. [. . .] This I learned afterward, for I did not accompany them, having been passed away to a shopkeeper, by my master's lady, the day before he failed, in part payment for a cashmere shawl for which she gave a hundred and fifty dollars.

[. . .]

[Later, the bill was sent to a village which had two different banks.] "These two banks made the village flourish to the eye; but this prosperity was only the bloom on the cheek of consumption. Great houses rose up in various parts, but they were all mortgaged to the banks, who lent the money, thus getting real property for rags of their own making. No man lived in his own house,—all belonged to the banks, who could at any time turn the village out of doors. Everything was done on credit, for the village having few natural advantages, depended for its summer of apparent prosperity on the discounts of the banks. The shopkeeper traded, the tavernkeeper carried on his business, the brickmaker made bricks, and the shingle-splitter, split his shingles,—with bank notes which he borrowed. The one endorsed the notes of the other; and if one failed, they all ran away together; for this is one of the great advantages of having nothing of one's own—a man can run away at a moment's warning.

[. . .]

"Nobody ever thought of working in this happy village, because it was so much easier to borrow of the banks, than to earn money by honest industry. [. . .] Every one, of course, became a speculator in something,—for the profits of a regular trade not being sufficient to pay the creditor his interest, and support the debtor at the same time, he must resort to some extraordinary means to make money, and these means are generally wild speculations that end in ruin. But for all this, everybody insisted on it that the village was flourishing beyond all example, and that banks were great blessings.

[. . .]

"It behooves the landed interest to be on the watch against these tempters, who persuade men to exchange their property for rags, or, ere long, they will be in the situation of the landholders of England, who are swallowed up by the paper system. The holders of land generally, are pursuaded that they are great gainers by the enormous plenty of paper-money, which raises the nominal price of their produce; and the merchants are fully assured that these banks are essential to their existence. But they are assuredly mistaken. [. . .] A paper aristocracy has sprung up among the people, oppressive in the highest degree, and equally dangerous to their freedom as their morals. Not only in the cities, but in the country south of Connecticut River, are people losing their habits of industry, to become dependents on banks, and speculators in something or other; but what is perhaps still worse, men are daily more and more acquiring a habit of extravagance, supported by borrowing of the banks, and not by the regular profits of their estates, or their business. That this will end in a system of bankruptcy, more extensive than any ever yet known, is sufficiently apparent. It will not be long ere the paper system will fall in Great Britain, never to rise again; and we who gained our confidence in it by witnessing her rise, will lose it in beholding her fall. The time is not far distant when the landholder, and the possessor of real estate, will resume their proper station and influence in society, and no longer shrink into comparative insignificance before the momentary magnificence of some upstart, unreal pageant."

How long the sage and learned owl would have gone on with his reflections I know not; for in rummaging my pocket for a pencil to note down some of his remarks, which I thought rather apt, I happened to bring out a half-eagle, which I had preserved as a last refuge against poverty. Sir Owl was nearly frightened out of his wits at this unexpected apparition, and began to whoop and flap his wings at such a rate, that I awoke with the terrible screeching he made, as he flew up the chimney. Adieu.

Questions

1. How is the bank-bill created—out of what materials? Where do the materials come from? What do those origins mean?
2. What changes to traditional, stable rural society does the author think are caused by the ready availability of credit that occurs at Owl Creek, and elsewhere?
3. Why is paper money so much more dangerous (says the author) than gold and silver?
4. What role do women, and women's wants, play in this little fable? Why? What does this symbolize?

Vincent Nolte Describes the
Cotton Market (1854)

VINCENT NOLTE

Vincent Nolte was born in northern Italy in the late eighteenth century. As a young man, he was apprenticed to a merchant in Germany, where he learned the skills of accounting. He also learned the games of the entrepreneurial merchant: speculating on supply and demand, arbitraging prices and currencies, and wielding the benefits that could come from leveraging credit and taking big risks. He eventually became connected with Hope and Company, international merchant bankers of Amsterdam, for whom he traveled to New Orleans before 1812 and helped link the new cotton supply in the Mississippi Valley to European demand. While Nolte was in New Orleans, the War of 1812 broke out, which interrupted the regular trade between Louisiana and Britain.

After the war, Nolte became the chief agent for Baring Brothers in New Orleans. Baring was the biggest merchant bank in the world. They bought cotton for their own speculative purposes, but their most profitable operations came from lending other merchants money, selling government and corporate bonds on European financial markets, and trading currencies. Nolte eventually launched his own cotton-trading venture, trying to buy cheap from planters who sent cotton bales to New Orleans, and sell high in Liverpool, where the Manchester textile mills bought their cotton. Along the way, Nolte helped to create the modern commodities market as a capitalist institution. He published a "Price Current" for New Orleans, a weekly document that listed the latest information on commodity prices not only in New Orleans but in other parts of the world as well. This increased the efficiency of trading by eliminating a lot of the information disparities that allowed a few players to dominate the market. He also introduced new levels of excitement and desire to the cotton market. At least twice he came close to "cornering" the New Orleans cotton market by secretly buying cotton bales before they reached the market. And he wrote eloquently about the nonrational attractions of capitalism, talking about the thrill, or "charm," of controlling a "vast extended commerce." He was a capitalist, but he was quite different form the sober, self-controlled self-improver that Benjamin Franklin (for instance) made himself out to be.

The selection below picks up after the end of the War of 1812, showing some of an entrepreneurial merchant's life in the years before instantaneous communication and rapid travel, but after the beginning of the Industrial Revolution and the rise of integrated Atlantic markets in both cotton and the credit that financed its production, purchase, and shipment. Pay attention to his language, his metaphors, and the picture of a social world and entrepreneurial work that he is painting.

I had left England but a few months previously, and having foreseen an inevitable rise in the price of cotton, wrote from New York, as I soon afterwards repeated from Louisiana, that it would be advisable to lay out some money for cotton on our account, in anticipation of this rise. [. . .] The first squad of cotton brokers called upon me on the morning after my arrival [in New Orleans]. Already acquainted with the nominal prices, I asked what was in the market. "We can offer you," said the brokers Dubuys & Longer, "two boat-loads of the best planters' marks, from the Opelousas district, at sixteen cents, each load consisting of about 400 bales." I examined the samples they had brought, the quality was good, and said that I would take both loads. At that time such a purchase was sufficient to excite remark, and the so-called English, but, properly speaking, Scotch houses, were full of curiosity to know the man who could venture, against their notions, to make so heavy a stride into the market. Two days afterwards these gentlemen began, quietly, to make certain bargains of their own, notwithstanding the discouraging news they had received from "our folks," as they called the leading houses at home, and regularly continued their purchases from time to time. The ice was broken, and my Scottish neighbors were speedily convinced that every attempt to make me dance to their music would signally fail. My position in the cotton market now became, step by step, more influential; whether I would buy, and when, or how, was, for many years afterwards, a matter of calculation which my competitors could not leave out of sight, and which often led them into false conclusions.

In the year 1818, my house was the first that sent out printed advices in relation to the eventualities of the cotton market and the crops. The meteorological weather tables had given me the idea of getting up one similar to them, which should exhibit the course and fluctuations of prices, from week to week, during the shipping period of three successive years, and designate the difference of exchange, each time, by black, red, and blue lines. These new tables were very successful, particularly among the French speculators in cotton, and led to many commissions from Havre, Rouen, and Switzerland.

In the summer of 1819, I again visited Europe. It was for both the commercial and political relations of that continent, an epoch of the greatest interest, when business had just begun to recover from the consequences of the crisis that had arisen during the preceding year. [. . .] The rapid and progressive extension of trade, upon the re-opening of its channels after the year 1815, had given rise to a certain disproportion between the general consumption and the requisite supplies: the origin of this disproportion lay chiefly in the want of accurate knowledge respecting the nature and extent of these two elements of commerce. The rapidly returning and daily increasing prosperity of trade had manifested a continually upward tendency for two years and a half—and thus the turning point had been nearly approached, where that inevitable reaction must begin, which human affairs cannot always escape; but people had not yet discovered the method of establishing a balance between consumption and the eventualities of production and supply.

[...] The business of my house had very importantly increased. In opposition to the six, seven, or eight thousand bales of cotton, which most of the houses in that city, styling themselves first class, used to purchase, my quota was seldom less than sixteen or; eighteen thousand bales. [...] [For instance, in 1821,] I had already concluded my purchases, which ran up to no less a quantity than 40,000 bales, as early as the first days in April, when, at length, a serious competition broke forth, which called for sixteen and a half cents. The shipments of my house were by this time completed, had nearly all arrived, and been advantageously sold, while my neighbors were still operating in New Orleans. The result of this anticipation of the market was very beneficial, and established our influence with planters, as well as with our neighbors and competitors. From this I was enabled to deduce a wholesome lesson, to the effect that neither combinations nor coalitions, to violently raise or lower the price of any imported article, such as cotton, can possibly succeed, since it is not given to human foresight to anticipate and count up every circumstance which may unexpectedly overthrow all such combinations. How much I would buy, and how much I was to pay for it, were matters that must escape all the foresight of my competitors; and it was precisely because they had tried to form their own conclusions in this respect, and had cast their conjectures in so wrong a direction, that it was so easy for me " to take the wind out of their sails," as nautical Englishmen would say. [...]

Just at this very time the present head of the Barings' house, Mr. Francis Baring, second son of the deceased Lord Ashburton, had arrived in New Orleans from Havana, and taken his quarters with me in my newly-built residence. We had nine large vessels receiving cargo at that moment, and he was evidently gratified when he took his first walk along the so-called Levee—the quay on the left bank of the Mississippi, in front of the town, where vessels load and unload their freight—and saw it strown, from the upper to the lower suburb, with cotton bales, on which were stamped the marks of my firm. Nothing could have given him a better idea of our activity, and he seemed to be pleased that he could take back with him to Europe a proof of it, like this one, from his own experience.

[. . .] One word about the morality of a merchant. He who does not positively despair of the possibility of an exact and strict observation of the laws of trade and commerce, must at least confess that he has fallen upon the exceptions far oftener than upon common instances. It is often said and believed of politics, that that science cannot be bound by the customary laws of morality, or in other words, that the common acceptation of the words Right and Wrong, must undergo a considerable modification when those words are politically employed—then judiciousness decides,—and whatever is judicious must be right. One may say about the same of commerce; if we allow that all that is "on the books," as merchants say, is right, because it is judicious, which means no more than that it brings the money in. According to the ideas of the day, wealth has taken the place of worth, which was the object once of the merchant's ambition. [. . .]

To this extended and ready vigilance, over all possible results connected with, or growing out of his projects and undertakings, belong the most important exigencies of the speculative merchant, by which term, I do not understand the ordinary speculator, but the man who feels himself obliged to stand out in the broad day-light, and amid his fellow-citizens, and in the sight of the whole world, to win for himself the rank that insures to him the reward of his struggles. [. . .] It is the speculative spirit alone which marks the real merchant. And the use of this spirit, when kept subordinate to his actual clearly known means, and requires from him a prevision and observation of all possible results that may occur, is what procures for him a character for prudence. And yet how often does accident, by an unusual, hidden and suddenly self-created train of circumstances change the results of the wisest combination.

[. . .] The same errors never have such powerful and stirring influence as in attempts to monopolize a branch of commerce. Thus in the whole course of my mercantile struggles, no single example of a successful speculation of this kind, that is, where a great permanent revolution of the market was aimed at, exists. A wholesale monopolizing purchase of an article is often destroyed by an attempt to sell it at paying prices. The difference between the supply and the actual regular consumption, can in these peaceful times, be easily discovered; and therefore, one ordinarily resists, until forced by necessity, to pay a compulsory speculation price.

Questions

1. Nolte seems to contradict himself when he says, on the one hand, that plans to corner the market usually fail because no one can have complete foresight, and yet on the other, he says that the entrepreneur who is truly intelligent, diligent in his planning, and so on can win a fortune. Why does he contradict himself in this way?

2. In the last paragraph, Nolte seems to suggest that normal times, as long as information is equally available, make it almost impossible for giant speculative schemes to succeed—because all of the potential buyers of a "cornered" commodity will understand that they are paying an artificially inflated price. Do you agree?

3. Does Nolte think that anything that makes a profit is therefore morally justifiable? Why or why not? If he is unclear or contradictory, why?

4. What is the difference between an "ordinary speculator" and a "real merchant"? Is "speculation" bad? And wasn't speculation exactly what Nolte did?

MODULE 7

SLAVERY AND INDUSTRIAL DEMAND

In Defense of the American System (1832)

HENRY CLAY

In the years after 1815, Alexander Hamilton's pro-banking, pro-development policies were adopted by a group of politicians who had initially come to public notice as young supporters of Thomas Jefferson and James Madison. These politicians, who included Henry Clay of Kentucky, John C. Calhoun of South Carolina, and Daniel Webster of New Hampshire and Massachusetts, came to be called "National Republicans." In the years after 1815, they helped to create the Second Bank of the United States. They spent federal money on clearing harbors and rivers for steamboats and merchant ships. They promoted canals as infrastructure investments that would open tremendous opportunities for commercial farmers, manufacturers, and others. They also supported tariffs to protect manufacturing.

Henry Clay, the most charismatic of all the National Republicans, put all the policies together in a synthesis of government-supported nationalist-capitalist development that he called "The American System." His critics charged that the American System helped well-connected citizens while hurting ordinary farmers, and worried that the Bank of the United States would corrupt the American economy as a whole. But here, in the 1832 speech, Clay argues that the tariff—one part of the system—had already provided great benefits to all actors in the American economy, not just the textile or iron manufacturers that it specifically protected from competition. Opponents wanted to reduce the tariff dramatically, and one of their claims was that the process of paying off the national debt, begun in the 1790s by Hamilton, was now almost complete—thus meaning that high surcharges on imports were no longer necessary for raising revenue. South Carolina, led by Calhoun—who had experienced a change of heart and now opposed the American System—charged that tariffs did not protect cotton growers, but only raised the prices that they paid for manufactured goods. Here Clay credits the new tariffs imposed in 1824 and 1828 not only with protecting American markets from unfair British "dumping" of goods but also allowing manufacturing to employ more workers, thus creating markets for the farmers who feed them—and markets for Southern plantation owners, as well.

This transformation of the condition of the country from gloom and distress to brightness and prosperity, has been mainly the work of American legislation, fostering American industry, instead of allowing it to be controlled by foreign legislation, cherishing foreign industry. The foes of the American System, in 1824, with great boldness and confidence, predicted [. . .] The augmentation of the price of objects of consumption, and further decline in that of the articles of our exports. Every prediction which they made has failed—utterly failed.

[. . .] It is now proposed to abolish the system to which we owe so much of the public prosperity, and it is urged that the arrival of the period of the redemption of the public debt has been confidently looked to as presenting a suitable occasion to rid the country of the evils with which the system is alleged to be fraught. [. . .] We shall see that its foes will have accomplished comparatively nothing, after having achieved their present aim of breaking down our iron founderies, our woollen, cotton, and hemp manufactories, and our sugar plantations. The destruction of these would undoubtedly lead to the sacrifice of immense capital, the ruin of many thousands of our fellow citizens, and incalculable loss to the whole community. [. . .]

[...] Its duration is worthy, also, of serious consideration. Not to go behind the Constitution, its date is coeval with that instrument. It began on the ever memorable 4th day of July—the 4th day of July, 1789. The second act which stands recorded in the statute book, bearing the illustrious signature of George Washington, laid the cornerstone of the whole system. That there might be no mistake about the matter, it was then solemnly proclaimed to the American people and to the world, that it was necessary for "the encouragement and protection of manufactures," that duties should be laid. [...] Mr. Jefferson argued that foreign restrictions, foreign prohibitions, and foreign high duties, ought to be met, at home, by American restrictions, American prohibitions, and American high duties. Mr. Hamilton, surveying the entire ground, and looking at the inherent nature of the subject, treated it with an ability which, if ever equalled, has not been surpassed, and earnestly recommended protection. [...]

The question, therefore, which we are now called upon to determine, is not whether we shall establish a new and doubtful system of policy, just proposed, and for the first time presented to our consideration; but whether we shall break down and destroy a long established system, patiently and carefully built up, and sanctioned, during a series of years, again and again, by the nation and its highest and most revered authorities. [...] The people of the United States have justly supposed that the policy of protecting their industry, against foreign legislation and foreign industry, was fully settled, not by a single act, but by repeated and deliberate acts of government, performed at distant and frequent intervals. [...]

Its beneficial effects [...] have been felt in all parts of the Union. To none, I verily believe, has it been prejudicial. To the North, everywhere testimonies are borne to the high prosperity which it has diffused. There, all branches of industry are animated and flourishing. Commerce, foreign and domestic, active; cities and towns springing up, enlarging and beautifying; navigation fully and profitably employed, and the whole face of the country smiling with improvement, cheerfulness, and abundance. The gentleman from South Carolina has supposed that we, in the West, derive no advantages from this system. He is mistaken. Let him visit us, and he will find, from the head of La Belle Riviere, at Pittsburg, to America, at its mouth, the most rapid and gratifying advances. He will behold Pittsburg itself, Wheeling, Portsmouth, Maysville, Cincinnati, Louisville, and numerous other towns, lining and ornamenting the banks of that noble river, daily extending their limits, and prosecuting, with the greatest spirit and profit, numerous branches of the manufacturing and mechanic arts. [. . .]

Nor has the system [. . .] proved injurious to the cotton-growing country. I cannot speak of South Carolina itself, where I have never been, with so much certainty; but of other portions of the Union in which cotton is grown, especially those bordering on the Mississippi, I can confidently speak. If cotton planting is less profitable than it was, that is the result of increased production; but I believe it to be still the most profitable investment of capital of any branch of business in the United States. [. . .] When gentlemen have succeeded in their design of an immediate or gradual destruction of the American System, what is their substitute? Free trade! Free trade! The call for free trade, is as unavailing as the cry of a spoiled child, in its nurse's arms, for the moon or the stars that glitter in the firmament of heaven. It never has existed; it never will exist. Trade implies at least two parties. To be free, it should be fair, equal, and reciprocal. [. . .] We may break down all barriers to free trade on our part, but the work will not be complete until foreign powers shall have removed theirs. There would be freedom on one side, and restrictions, prohibitions, and exclusions, on the other. [. . .]

Gentlemen deceive themselves. It is not free trade that they are recommending to our acceptance. It is, in effect, the British colonial system that we are invited to adopt; and, if their policy prevail, it will lead substantially to the recolonization of these states, under the commercial dominion of Great Britain. [. . .] The South Carolina policy now, is identical with the long-cherished policy of Great Britain, which remains the same as it was when the thirteen colonies were part of the British empire. [. . .] Then it was the object of this British economist to adapt the means or wealth of the colonists to the supply required by their necessities, and to make the mother country the only source of that supply. Now it seems the policy is only so far to be reversed, that we must continue to import necessaries from Great Britain, in order to enable her to purchase raw cotton from us. [. . .]

The establishment of manufactures among us excites the creation of wealth, and this gives new powers of consumption, which are gratified by the purchase of foreign objects. A poor nation can never be a great consuming nation. Its poverty will limit its consumption to bare subsistence. [. . .] If the establishment of American manufactures, therefore, had the sole effect of creating a new, and an American, demand for cotton, exactly to the same extent in which it lessened the British demand, there would be no just cause of complaint against the tariff. The gain in one place would precisely equal the loss in the other. But the true state of the matter is much more favorable to the cotton grower. It is calculated that the cotton manufactories of the United States absorb at least 200 thousand bales of cotton annually. I believe it to be more. The two ports of Boston and Providence alone received, during the last year, near 110 thousand bales. The amount is annually increasing. [. . .] Break down the home market, and you are without resource. Destroy all other interests in the country, for the imaginary purpose of advancing the cotton-planting interest, and you inflict a positive injury, without the smallest practical benefit to the cotton planter [. . .]

[O]ne topic has, I think unnecessarily, been introduced into this debate. I allude to the charge brought against the manufacturing system, as favoring the growth of aristocracy. [. . .] [W]ould gentlemen prefer supporting foreign accumulations of wealth, by that description of industry, rather than their own country? But is it correct? The joint stock companies of the North [. . .] are nothing more than associations, sometimes of hundreds, by means of which the small earnings of many are brought into a common stock. [. . .] Nothing can be more essentially democratic, or better devised to counterpoise the influence of individual wealth. [. . .] Is there more tendency to aristocracy in a manufactory, supporting hundreds of freemen, or in a cotton plantation, with its not less numerous slaves, sustaining, perhaps, only two white families—that of the master and the overseer? [. . .]

The United States, at this time, manufacture one half the quantity of cotton which Great Britain did in 1816! We possess three great advantages: First. The raw material. Second. Water power instead of that of steam, generally used in England. And third. The cheaper labor of females. [. . .] And can there be any employment more appropriate? Who has not been delighted with contemplating the clock-work regularity of a large cotton manufactory? [. . .] This brings me to consider what I apprehend to have been the most efficient of all the causes in the reduction of the prices of manufactured articles; and that is, COMPETITION. By competition, the total amount of the supply is increased, and by increase of the supply a competition in the sale ensues, and this enables the consumer to buy at lower rates. Of all human powers operating on the affairs of mankind, none is greater than that of competition. [. . .] By the American System this vast power has been excited in America, and brought into being to act in cooperation or collision with European industry. [. . .] The consequence is the reduction of prices in both hemispheres. [. . .]

Under the operation of the American system, the products of our agriculture command a higher price than they would do without it, by the creation of a home market; and, by the augmentation of wealth produced by manufacturing industry, which enlarges our powers of consumption, both of domestic and foreign articles. [. . .] It cannot be doubted that the existence of American manufactures has tended to increase the demand, and extend the consumption of the raw material. [. . .]

[. . .] I conclude this part of the argument with the hope that my humble exertions have not been altogether unsuccessful in showing—

1. That the policy which we have been considering ought to continue to be regarded as the genuine American System.

2. That the free trade system, which is proposed as its substitute, ought really to be considered as the British colonial system.

3. That the American System is beneficial to all parts of the Union, and absolutely necessary to much the larger portion.

4. That the price of the great staple of cotton, and of all our chief productions of agriculture, has been sustained and upheld, and a decline averted by the protective system.

5. That, if the foreign demand for cotton has been at all diminished by the operation of that system, the diminution has been more than compensated in the additional demand created at home.

6. That the constant tendency of the system, by creating competition among ourselves, and between American and European industry, reciprocally acting upon each other, is to reduce prices of manufactured objects.

7. That, in point of fact, objects within the scope of the policy of protection have greatly fallen in price.

8. That if, in a season of peace, these benefits are experienced in a season of war, when the foreign supply might be cut off, they would be much more extensively felt.

9. And, finally, that the substitution of the British colonial system for the American System, without benefiting any section of the Union, by subjecting us to a foreign

legislation, regulated by foreign interests, would
lead to the prostration of our manufactures, general
impoverishment, and ultimate ruin. [...]

It is for the great body of the people, and especially for the poor, that
I have ever supported the American System. It affords them profitable employment, and supplies the means of comfortable subsistence.
It secures to them, certainly, necessaries of life manufactured at home,
and places within their reach, and enables them to acquire, a reasonable share of foreign luxuries; whilst the system of gentlemen promises
them necessaries made in foreign countries, and which are beyond their
power, and denies to them luxuries which they would possess no means
to purchase. [...] Let us then adopt the measure before us, which
will benefit all classes: the farmer, the professional man, the merchant,
the manufacturer, the mechanic, and the cotton planter more than all.
[...] Our southern brethren believe that it is injurious to them, and
ask its repeal. We believe that its abandonment will be prejudicial to
them, and ruinous to every other section of the Union. [...]

Questions

1. Clay seems to be arguing for heavy regulation of trade and
   government direction of overall economic policy. Is this
   incompatible with true capitalism?
2. Who was right about the effects of the growth of northern
   industry—Clay, or his South Carolina critics?
3. Contemporary economists are nearly unanimous in their belief that
   free trade is better for consumers than tariffs. Clay seems to argue
   otherwise. What is his case for tariffs in the U.S. of 1832? Do you
   find that persuasive? Would it be persuasive at other times or places?
4. "Policymakers ought to privilege the development of a domestic
   market and a manufacturing sector over other initiatives in order
   to promote economic growth." Discuss.

Slavery in the United States (1837)

CHARLES BALL

Charles Ball grew up in slavery in Maryland, during the period in which tobacco slavery was becoming less profitable. Born about 1780, he was separated from his mother at an early age when her enslaver sold her to buyers from the growing slave region of the South Carolina and Georgia backcountry. By the time Ball grew up, and was married and the father of two young children, he might have hoped to become one of the many Maryland slaves who was able to buy his freedom from an enslaver who wasn't making much money from slavery. Instead, as we see here, in 1805 he became one of the many who was sold to the new cotton region developing down where his mother had already been sent—that was the other way that Chesapeake enslavers had to deal with the lack of profit in the decaying tobacco economy.

Ball describes his travel in the slave trader's gang (or "coffle") in greater detail than we excerpt here, but the reader should know that slave trading was also in the process of becoming a big and efficient business that used a lot of capital and incorporated many modern business practices. When the coffle he was in reached South Carolina, Ball was sold to a wealthy planter named Wade Hampton, and taken to Congaree, Hampton's labor camp, to grow and pick cotton. There Ball learned how cotton was made, and he details techniques of labor management and extraction that helped ensure that the productivity of slave labor would rise about 2 percent a year in the period from 1800 to the start of the Civil War in 1861.

Ball suffered tremendously, as he reports. He watched people tortured because they didn't meet production targets—didn't pick cotton quickly enough, in short—he didn't have enough food to eat, and he watched people all around him suffering from malaria, nutritional deficiencies, intense depression, and other diseases. But unlike most enslaved people, he was able to escape. His secret journey from the Georgia-Carolina border all the way to Maryland to reunite with his family culminated in them moving to the free state of Pennsylvania, where he told his story to an editor; it was written up and published in 1837. This was one of the first reports from someone who had truly been inside the powerful engine of much of American economic growth before 1850—the ever-more-efficient system of cotton production on slavery's expanding frontier.

My grandfather was brought from Africa, and sold as a slave in Calvert county, in Maryland, about the year 1730. [. . .] My mother was the slave of a tobacco planter, an old man, who died, according to the best of my recollection, when I was about four years old, leaving his property in such a situation that it became necessary, as I suppose, to sell a part of it to pay his debts. Soon after his death, several of his slaves, and with others myself, were sold at public venue. [This was 1785] My mother had several children, my brothers and sisters, and we were all sold on the same day to different purchasers. Our new master took us away, and I never saw my mother, nor any of my brothers and sisters afterwards. [. . .] My mother was sold to a Georgia trader, who soon after that carried her away from Maryland. [. . .] At the time I was sold I was quite naked, having never had any clothes in my life; but my new master had brought with him a child's frock or wrapper, belonging to one of his own children; and after he had purchased me, he dressed me in this garment, took me before him on his horse, and started home; but my poor mother, when she saw me leaving her for the last time, ran after me, took me down from the horse, clasped me in her arms, and wept loudly and bitterly over me. [. . .] [She] besought my master to buy her and the rest of her children, and not permit them to be carried away by the negro buyers; but whilst thus entreating him to save her and her family, the slave-driver, who had first bought her, came running in pursuit of her with a raw hide in his hand. [. . .] He gave her two or three heavy blows on the shoulders with his raw hide, snatched me from her arms, handed me to my master, and seizing her by one arm, dragged her back towards the place of sale. My master then quickened the pace of his horse; and as we advanced, the cries of my poor parent became more and more indistinct. [. . .] I never again heard the voice of my poor mother.

[. . .] [We now jump forward to 1805.] My master kept a store at a small village on the bank of the Patuxent river [. . .] although he resided at some distance on a farm. One morning he rose early, and ordered me to take a yoke of oxen and go to the village, to bring home a cart which was there, saying he would follow me. He arrived at the village soon after I did, and took his breakfast with his store-keeper. He then told me to come into the house and get my breakfast. Whilst I was eating in the kitchen, I observed him talking earnestly, but lowly, to a stranger near the kitchen door. I soon after went out, and hitched my oxen to the cart, and was about to drive off, when several men came round about me, and amongst them the stranger whom I had seen speaking with my master. This man came up to me, and, seizing me by the collar, shook me violently, saying I was his property, and must go with him to Georgia. At the sound of these words, the thoughts of my wife and children rushed across my mind, and my heart died away within me. I saw and knew that my case was hopeless, and that resistance was vain, as there were near twenty persons present, all of whom were ready to assist the man by whom I was kidnapped. I felt incapable of weeping or speaking, and in my despair I laughed loudly. My purchaser ordered me to cross my hands behind, which were quickly bound with a strong cord; and he then told me that we must set out that very day for the south. I asked if I could not be allowed to go to see my wife and children, or if this could not be permitted, if they might not have leave to come to see me; but was told that I would be able to get another wife in Georgia.

My new master [. . .] took me that same day across the Patuxent, where I joined fifty-one other slaves, whom he had bought in Maryland. Thirty-two of these were men, and nineteen were women. The women were merely tied together with a rope, about the size of a bed cord, which was tied like a halter round the neck of each; but the men, of whom I was the stoutest and strongest [. . .] A strong iron collar was closely fitted by means of a padlock round each of our necks. A chain of iron, about a hundred feet in length, was passed through the hasp of each padlock, except at the two ends, where the hasps of the padlocks passed through a link of the chain. In addition to this, we were handcuffed in pairs, with iron staples and bolts, with a short chain, about a foot long, uniting the handcuffs and their wearers in pairs. In this manner we were chained alternately by the right and left hand. [. . .] Taking up our line of march, we travelled about five miles that evening, and stopped for the night at one of those miserable public houses, so frequent in the lower parts of Maryland and Virginia, called "ordinaries."

We all lay down on the naked floor to sleep in our handcuffs and chains. The women, my fellow-slaves, lay on one side of the room; and the men who were chained with me, occupied the other. I slept but little this night, which I passed in thinking of my wife and little children, whom I could not hope ever to see again. I also thought of my grandfather, and of the long nights I had passed with him, listening to his narratives of the scenes through which he had passed in Africa. I at length fell asleep, but was distressed by painful dreams. My wife and children appeared to be weeping and lamenting my calamity; and beseeching and imploring my master on their knees, not to carry me away from them. My little boy came and begged me not to go and leave him, and endeavoured, as I thought, with his little hands to break the fetters that bound me. I awoke in agony and cursed my existence. I could not pray, for the measure of my woes seemed to be full, and I felt as if there was no mercy in heaven, nor compassion on earth, for a man who was born a slave. Day at length came, and with the dawn, we resumed our journey towards the Potomac. As we passed along the road, I saw the slaves at work in the corn and tobacco-fields. I knew they toiled hard and lacked food but they were not, like me, dragged in chains from their wives, children, and friends. Compared with me, they were the happiest of mortals. I almost envied them their blessed lot.

[Ball next recounts his month-long march to South Carolina and his sale to Wade Hampton. After the sale he was marched to Hampton's labor camp "Congaree," where the morning after his arrival he was awakened by the blowing of a loud plantation horn that summoned all of the enslaved people to their daily labor.]

The overseer then led off to the field, with his horn in one hand and his whip in the other; we following—men, women, and children, promiscuously—and a wretched looking troop we were. There was not an entire garment amongst us. More than half of the gang were entirely naked. Several young girls, who had arrived at puberty, wearing only the livery with which nature had ornamented them, and a great number of lads, of an equal or superior age, appeared in the same costume. [. . .] Not one of the others had on even the remains of two pieces of apparel. Some of the men had old shirts, and some ragged trousers, but no one wore both. Amongst the women, several wore petticoats, and many had shifts. Not one of the whole number wore both of these vestments.

We walked nearly a mile through one vast cotton field, before we arrived at the place of our intended day's labour. At last the overseer stopped at the side of the field, and calling to several of the men by name, ordered them to call their companies and turn into their rows. The work we had to do today was to hoe and weed cotton, [. . .] the men whose names had been called [. . .] were designated as captains, each of whom had under his command a certain number of the other bands. The captain was the foreman of his company, and those under his command had to keep up with him. Each of the men and women had to take one row. [. . .]The first captain, whose name was Simon, took the first row,—and the other captains were compelled to keep up with him. By this means the overseer had nothing to do but to keep Simon hard at work, and he was certain that all the others must work equally hard.

Simon was a stout, strong man, apparently about thirty-five years of age; and for some reason unknown to me, I was ordered to take the row next to his. The overseer with his whip in his hand walked about the field after us, to see that our work was well done. As we worked with hoes, I had no difficulty in learning how the work was to be performed. [. . .] The overseer had bread, butter, cold ham, and coffee for his breakfast. Ours was composed of a corn cake, weighing about three quarters of a pound to each person, with as much water as was desired. I at first supposed that this bread was dealt out to the people as their allowance; but on further inquiry I found this not to be the case. Simon, by whose side I was now at work, and who seemed much pleased with my agility and diligence in my duty, told me that here, as well as every where in this country, each person received a peck of corn at the crib door, every Sunday evening, and that in ordinary times, every one had to grind this corn and bake it, for him or herself, making such use of it as the owner thought proper; but that for some time past, the overseer, for the purpose of saving the time which had been lost in baking the bread, had made it the duty of an old woman, who was not capable of doing much work in the field, to stay at the quarter, and bake the bread of the whole gang. When baked, it was brought to the field in a cart, as I saw, and dealt out in loaves.

They still had to grind their own corn, after night. [. . .] We worked in this field all day; and at the end of every hour, or hour and a quarter, we had permission to go to the cart, which was moved about the field, so as to be near us, and get water.

Our dinner was the same, in all respects, as our breakfast, except that, in addition to the bread, we had a little salt, and a radish for each person. We were not allowed to rest at either breakfast or dinner, longer than while we were eating; and we worked in the evening as long as we could distinguish the weeds from the cotton plants. [. . .] When we could no longer see to work, the horn was again sounded, and we returned home. I had now lived through one of the days—a succession of which make up the life of a slave—on a cotton plantation.

[In August, they turned from cultivating cotton to picking it, which was—after the invention on the cotton gin in 1791—the part of the production process which slowed down everything else, the bottleneck. So enslavers pushed people to pick as much cotton as they could, and Ball tells us part of how they did that.]

This business of picking cotton, constitutes about half the labour of the year, on a large plantation. In Carolina, it is generally commenced about the first of September; though in some years, much cotton is picked in August. The manner of doing the work is this. The cotton being planted in hills, in straight rows, from four to five feet apart, each hand or picker, provided with a bag, made of cotton bagging, holding a bushel or more, hung round the neck, with cords, proceeds from one side of the field to the other between two of these rows, picking all the cotton from the open burs, on the right and left, as he goes. It is the business of the picker to take all the cotton from each of the rows, as far as the lines of the rows or hills. In this way he picks half the cotton from each of the rows, and the pickers who come on his right and left, take the remainder from the opposite sides of the rows.

The cotton is gathered into the bag, and when it becomes burdensome by its weight, it is deposited in some convenient place, until night, when it is taken home, either in a large bag or basket, and weighed under the inspection of the overseer. A day's work is not estimated by the number of hills, or rows, that are picked in the day, but by the number of pounds of cotton in the seed, that the picker brings into the cotton house, at night.

[. . .] The picking of cotton, continues from August until December, or January; and in some fields, they pick from the old plants, until they are ploughed up in February or March, to make room for the planting of the seeds of another crop. [. . .] When his or her cotton is weighed at the cotton-house, in the evening, it is found that the standard quantity has not been picked, the delinquent picker is sure to receive a whipping.

On some estates, settlements are made every evening, and the whipping follows immediately; on others, the whipping does not occur until the next morning, whilst on a few plantations, the accounts are closed twice, or three times a week. [. . .] A short day's work was always punished.

I now entered upon a new scene of life. My true value had not yet been ascertained by my present owner. [. . .] It requires some time to enable a stranger, or new hand, to acquire the sleight of picking cotton.

I had ascertained, that at the hoe, the spade, [or] the axe, [. . .] I was a full match for the best hands on the plantation; but soon discovered, when we came to the picking of cotton, that I was not equal to a boy of twelve or fifteen years of age. I worked hard the first day, and made every effort to sustain the character that I had acquired, amongst my companions, but when evening came, and our cotton was weighed, I had only thirty-eight pounds, and was vexed to see that two younger men, about my own age, had, one fifty-eight, and the other fifty-nine pounds. This was our first day's work; and the overseer had not yet settled the amount of a day's picking. It was necessary for him to ascertain, by the experience of a few days, how much the best hands could pick in a day, before he established the standard of the season. I hung down my head, and felt very much ashamed of myself, when I found that my cotton was so far behind that of many, even of the women, who had heretofore regarded me as the strongest and most powerful man of the whole gang.

I had exerted myself to-day, to the utmost of my power; and as the picking of cotton seemed to be so very simple a business, I felt apprehensive that I should never be able to improve myself, so far as to become even a second rate hand. [. . .] I knew that the lash of the overseer would soon become familiar with my back, if I did not perform as much work as any of the other young men.

[. . .] When it was all weighed, the overseer came to me where I stood, and told me to show him my hands. When I had done this, and he had looked at them, he observed—"You have a pair of good hands—you will make a good picker." This faint praise of the overseer revived my spirits greatly, and I went home with a lighter heart than I had expected to possess, before the termination of cotton-picking.

When I came to get my cotton weighed, on the evening of the second day, I was rejoiced to find that I had forty-six pounds, although I had not worked harder than I did the first day. On the third evening I had fifty-two pounds; and before the end of the week, there were only three hands in the field—two men and a young woman—who could pick more cotton in a day, than I could.

[. . .] Picking of cotton may almost be reckoned among the arts. A man who has arrived at the age of twenty-five, before he sees a cotton field, will never, in the language of the overseer, become a crack picker.

By great industry and vigilance, I was able, at the end of a month, to return every evening a few pounds over the daily rate [. . .] but the business of picking cotton was an irksome, and fatiguing labour to me, and one to which I could never become thoroughly reconciled; for the reason, I believe, that in every other kind of work in which I was engaged in the south, I was able to acquire the character of a first rate hand; whilst in picking cotton, I was hardly regarded as a prime hand.

[Most enslavers kept a cotton-picking ledger, in which they recorded the number of pounds that each slave picked. Those who failed to meet the quota were whipped, as Ball details. Those who did, as other former slaves report, often found their quotas raised.]

Questions

1. Can you name three innovations described by Ball that made the production of cotton more efficient over time?
2. Adam Smith argues that labor can become more efficient with the addition of machines or through the division of labor. Are either of these methods happening in the cotton-production process that Ball learned about first-hand?
3. Would the use of wage labor have made cotton-picking more or less efficient?

The Great Divergence: China, Europe, and the Making of the World Economy (2000)

KENNETH POMERANZ

Kenneth Pomeranz's *The Great Divergence* set the historiography of capitalism on its head when it was published in 2001. Instead of simply asking why western Europe industrialized, he also asked why East Asia did not do so, despite having a similar set of market institutions as Europe. *The Great Divergence* details both the economies of Asia and Europe, demonstrating why Europe, with access to New World resources and African labor, was able to overcome the Malthusian trap and begin the world's first industrial revolution.

Much of modern social science originated in efforts by late nineteenth- and twentieth-century Europeans to understand what made the economic development path of western Europe unique; yet those efforts have yielded no consensus. Most of the literature has focused on Europe, seeking to explain its early development of large-scale mechanized industry. Comparisons with other parts of the world have been used to show that "Europe"—or in some formulations, western Europe, Protestant Europe, or even just England—had within its borders some unique homegrown ingredient of industrial success or was uniquely free of some impediment.

Other explanations have highlighted relations between Europe and other parts of the world—particularly various forms of colonial extraction—but they have found less favor with the majority of

Western scholars. It has not helped matters that these arguments have emphasized what Marx called the "primitive accumulation" of capital through the forcible dispossession of Amerindians and enslaved Africans (and many members of Europe's own lower classes). While that phrase accurately highlights the brutality of these processes, it also implies that this accumulation was "primitive" in the sense of being the beginning step in large-scale capital accumulation. This position has become untenable as scholarship has shown the slow but definite growth of an investible surplus above subsistence through the retained earnings of Europe's own farms, workshops, and countinghouses.

This book will also emphasize the exploitation of non-Europeans—and access to overseas resources more generally—but not as the sole motor of European development. Instead it acknowledges the vital role of internally driven European growth but emphasizes how similar those processes were to processes at work elsewhere, especially in east Asia, until almost 1800. Some differences that mattered did exist, but I will argue that they could only create the great transformation of the nineteenth century in a context also shaped by Europe's privileged access to overseas resources. For instance, western Europe may well have had more effective institutions for mobilizing large sums of capital willing to wait a relatively long time for returns—but until the nineteenth century, the corporate form found few uses other than for armed long-distance trade and colonization, and long-term syndicated debt was primarily used within Europe to finance wars. More important, western Europe had by the eighteenth century moved ahead of the rest of the world in the use of various labor-saving technologies. However, because it continued to lag behind in various land-saving technologies, rapid population growth and resource demands might, in the absence of overseas resources, have forced it back onto a path of much more labor-intensive growth. In that case it would have diverged far less from China and Japan. The book thus calls upon the fruits of overseas coercion to help explain the difference between European development and what we see in certain other parts of Eurasia (primarily China and Japan)—not the whole of that development or the differences between Europe and all other parts of the Old World. A few other factors that do not fit firmly into either category, such as the location of coal supplies, also play a role. Thus the book combines comparative analysis, some purely local contingency, and an integrative or global approach.

Moreover, the comparative and integrative approaches modify each other. If the same factors that differentiate western Europe from, say, India or eastern Europe (e.g., certain kinds of labor markets) are shared with China, then comparisons cannot simply be the search for a European difference; nor can patterns shared at both ends of Eurasia be explained as unique products of European culture or history. (Nor, of course, can they be explained as outgrowths of universal tendencies, since they distinguish some societies from others.) The resemblances between western Europe and other areas that force us to turn from a purely comparative approach—one that assumes essentially separate worlds as units of comparison—to one that also looks at global conjunctures have another significance as well. They imply that we cannot understand pre-1800 global conjunctures in terms of a Europe-centered world system; we have, instead, a polycentric world with no dominant center. Global conjunctures often worked to western Europe's advantage, but not necessarily because Europeans created or imposed them. Only after nineteenth-century industrialization was well advanced does it make sense to see a single, hegemonic European "core."

There is little evidence to suggest a quantitative advantage in western Europe's capital stock before 1800 or a set of durable circumstances—demographic or otherwise—that gave Europe a significant edge in capital accumulation. Nor is it likely that Europeans were significantly healthier (i.e., advantaged in human capital), more productive, or otherwise heirs of many years of slowly accruing advantages over the more developed parts of Asia.

When we turn to comparisons of the technology embodied in the capital stock, we do find some important European advantages emerging during the two or three centuries before the Industrial Revolution; but we also still find areas of European backwardness. Europe's disadvantages were concentrated in areas of agriculture, land management, and the inefficient use of certain land-intensive products (especially fuel wood). As it worked out, some of the areas in which Europe had an edge turned out to be important for truly revolutionary developments, while the particular areas in which other societies had better techniques did not. But even Europe's technological leadership in various sectors would not have allowed a breakthrough to self-sustaining growth without other changes that made it much freer than other societies of its land base. This was partially a result of catching up in some of the land-saving technologies in which it lagged, a process that was greatly facilitated by knowledge gained through overseas empire, and partly a matter of serendipity, which located crucial resources (especially forest-saving coal) in particularly fortunate places. It was also partly due to global conjunctures. Those global conjunctures, in turn, were shaped by a combination of European efforts (many of them violent), epidemiological luck, and some essentially independent developments. (One example of the latter is China's switch to a silver-based economy, which helped keep New World mines profitable and sustain Europe's colonial presence during the long period before other products were developed.)

These global conjunctures allowed western Europeans access to vast amounts of additional land-intensive resources. Moreover, they could obtain these resources without needing to further strain a European ecology that was already hard-pressed before the great nineteenth-century boom in population and per capita resource use, and without having to reallocate vast amounts of their own labor to the various labor-intensive activities that would have been necessary to manage their own land for higher yield and greater ecological sustainability. Without these "external" factors, Europe's inventions alone might have been not much more revolutionary in their impact on economy and society than the marginal technological improvements that continued to occur in eighteenth-century China, India, and elsewhere.

One core, western Europe, was able to escape the proto-industrial cul de sac and transfer handicraft workers into modern industries as the technology became available. It could do this, in large part, because the exploitation of the New World made it unnecessary to mobilize the huge numbers of additional workers who would have been needed to use Europe's own land in much more intensive and ecologically sustainable ways—if even that could have provided enough primary products to keep ahead of nineteenth-century population growth. The New World yielded both "real resources" and precious metals, which require separate treatment. Let us begin with real resources; they, in turn, begin with plantation products from the Caribbean, northeastern Brazil, and later the southern United States.

The New World's farm exports were largely slave grown. The plantations were almost all either on islands or near the coast. Consequently, exports from the circum-Caribbean plantation zone did not plateau the way that exports from the Chinese interior to Jiangnan and Lingnan did when free laborers ran into diminishing returns and switched more of their efforts to handicrafts; nor were they beset by the soaring transport costs that Old World foresters faced once they moved away from the riverbanks. And because the proprietors of New World plantations (unlike those of eastern European estates or southeast Asian pepper fields) purchased most of their labor force from abroad and often curtailed their subsistence production, western Europe's trade with this area also escaped the "small-market problem" that had dogged its trade for eastern European raw materials. Exports had to be high enough to cover the costs of buying slaves and much of the cost of feeding and clothing them.

There were many reasons why African slaves became the principal workforce in so many New World colonies. First and foremost are the astonishing death rates among New World peoples after contact, mostly from disease. Few of Europe's poor, as we have seen, could pay their own passage before 1800, and they were only worth transporting if one could force them to produce exports. With outright enslavement of Europeans unacceptable, this meant indentures that would end with freedom and a grant of land. As survival rates for Europeans (and Africans) in the New World began to improve, this became too expensive for most plantation owners; they preferred to pay more money up front and get a slave who never had to be freed. The surviving New World peoples were sometimes enslaved (especially in Brazil), but Africans were preferred for several reasons. New World peoples were seen as fragile because so many died upon contact with Europeans; and at least some Europeans opposed their enslavement on humanitarian grounds (but not that of Africans). Amerindians also would have found it much easier to flee and to make common cause with unconquered native peoples nearby (though Africans sometimes did this, too). And since the conquest of native peoples slowed down considerably after the first half century (once smallpox had done its worst damage and various indigenous peoples had acquired guns and horses), acquiring indigenous slaves was not always easy. By contrast, the large internal slave trade in Africa made it relatively easy for Europeans to acquire slaves there, as long as they had goods that the slaveholders wanted. Meanwhile, the Spanish and the Portuguese crowns preferred the transatlantic slave trade to New World slave-raiding, because the former was much easier to monitor and tax than local slave-raiding. This was yet another way in which interstate competition and military fiscalism indirectly helped accelerate the repopulation of the New World from overseas and helped place the settlers in a context in which they (unlike, say, settlers on the Chinese frontier) would find it hard to switch away from a focus on export production. The slaves had no choice at all, and even their owners may have had little choice, since they (unlike a hypothetical group raiding locally for slaves) had to pay for their purchased workforce.

Thus, slavery helped make Euro-American trade unlike any between Old World cores and peripheries. A free-labor periphery like southwest China would not have served Europe as well, even if it had been just as ecologically bountiful; nor would a periphery like eastern Europe (or later Java) in which participants in a still-functioning subsistence-oriented economy were forced into part-time export production. Silver exports from Potosí, which fell as the native population recovered and a more self-sufficient regional economy reemerged, remind us that European demand alone did not ensure a continued flow of a commodity to Europe without either massive force or the reproduction of local needs for European goods. We will return to silver shortly. What needs emphasizing here is that it was not only ecology that made so much sugar, tobacco, and later cotton flow from the circum-Caribbean region: the region was also sociologically and politically set up to "need" almost everything else. Indeed, one of Britain's advantages was that unlike France, Holland, or Denmark, it did not need to ship food from Europe to its sugar colonies but could rely on continental North America to do so, which in turn bought English manufactures (employing labor and capital rather than land).

Thus, a combination of depopulation and repopulation with slaves made the circum-Caribbean region a perversely large market for imports and a source of land-intensive exports. In fact, it became the first periphery to assume a now familiar "Third World" profile: that of a large importer of both capital goods (in this case, walking, talking, kidnapped ones) and manufactured goods for daily use, with exports that kept falling in price as production became more efficient, capital intensive, and widespread. By contrast, the prices of most forms of energy produced in Europe, including food, rose throughout the eighteenth century, relative to both wages and other goods. Thus the plantation areas of the New World were a new kind of periphery: one that would import enough to keep its trade with the core fairly balanced. Moreover, its imports and exports stimulated each other:

more sugar exports consistently led to more slave imports, more food and clothing imports, and (often) more plantation debt, which led to selling more sugar next year, at whatever price.

Meanwhile, concentration on one or two exports in most plantation areas greatly facilitated a crucial improvement in trade itself. Transatlantic shipping costs fell roughly 50 percent during the eighteenth century, even without substantial technological change. Part of the decline was due to political change: the British Navy repressed most piracy, which reduced insurance rates and allowed more freight to travel on unarmed ships with smaller crews. However, the other major component (briefly discussed in chapter 4) was a sharp decline in the time spent acquiring cargo. This meant a faster turnover of working capital, more intensive use of ships, and large savings in sailors' wages (who had to be paid for every day away from home, even if they were waiting in port while a cargo was purchased). This reduction in port time was achieved by having a local agent collect the desired goods in a warehouse before the ship arrived, rather than having the ship visit many plantations and spend time haggling. Such delegation of responsibility was much easier when each area only sold one or two exports, rather than the numerous possibilities in, say, an Indian Ocean port.

Thus, while seeking more primary products from many Old World peripheries meant exhausting the most accessible sources, facing higher transport costs, and working against the logic of import substitution, an opposite dynamic was at work in much of the New World. With political and sociological factors working against import substitution, export monocultures brought down transatlantic transport and transaction costs. This in turn allowed Americans to incur higher local transport costs—i.e., expand further inland—and still sell enough in Europe to pay for manufactures and repay start-up costs. This dynamic operated whether the labor in question was slave, indentured, or free but in need of start-up money, and it played a crucial role in populating North America. It also helped the transatlantic exchange of manufactured goods (and kidnapped "capital goods") keep expanding, unlike the Baltic trade or the trade from the Chinese interior.

In other words, a demographic catastrophe, colonial legislation, and slavery combined to create a periphery that was an ever-expanding source of raw materials in an era before most production required expensive capital goods and when most people still had some connection to subsistence production. Indeed, this situation proved temporary even in much of the New World; as population levels recovered in Peru and Mexico, more self-sufficient economies reemerged and exports fell. Without the peculiar conditions created in the circum-Caribbean region, the mere existence of trade between a rich, free labor core and a poorer, bound labor periphery would not have had such epochal effects; western Europe's trade with eastern Europe, for instance, was in no way more important or dynamic than that between the Lower Yangzi and its various free labor peripheries. The form of labor control on the periphery was indeed crucial, as world-systems theorists insist, but we oversimplify greatly if we lump together all kinds of "coerced cash-crop producers." New World slavery and colonialism were different in very important ways.

Earlier arguments about the importance of slavery in European (especially British) industrial growth have often focused on export markets as a stimulus for burgeoning industries; they have thus been vulnerable to the "internalist" argument that domestic markets were growing, too, and off a much larger base. Such debates may be inherently inconclusive—if Caribbean demand accounted for 12 percent of the growth of British industrial output between 1748 and 1776, is the proverbial glass half full or half empty? By contrast, the argument here emphasizes that some markets mattered more than others. For the New World and the slave trade offered what an expanding home market could not have: ways in which manufactured goods created without much use of British land could be turned into ever-increasing amounts of land-intensive food and fiber (and later timber) at reasonable (and even falling) prices.

Questions

1. What are the key factors, for Pomeranz, that set Asia and Europe apart?
2. What made New World slavery different from older forms of European and African slavery?
3. Why was New World slavery essential for European industrial development?
4. What was the role of states in the transition to industrialization?

MODULE 8

THE BIRTH OF THE AMERICAN FACTORY

Chants Democratic: New York City and the Rise of the American Working Class (1984)

SEAN WILENTZ

The creation of a new economy in the early nineteenth century took place in the cotton fields where people like Charles Ball toiled, in the cotton mills of towns like Lowell, Massachusetts, in farms along New York's Erie Canal, in the countinghouses of merchants, and in the legislative halls where banks and corporations were chartered. But here, in a selection from his groundbreaking first book, Princeton historian Sean Wilentz shows that capitalism also emerged in the tenements and workshops of Manhattan. As the old artisan economy was replaced with wage labor and something like Adam Smith's division of labor, workers who in earlier generations would have had the opportunity to become journeyman and master artisans found that the masters had become capitalist entrepreneurs in their own rights. Now the workers were trapped in wage labor and did a more intense, deskilled kind of labor they called "sweated"— leading to the term "sweatshop." These laborers also formed the first mass urban market for commercially produced food and manufactured goods. They also began to create a distinctly working-class culture in the United States.

By 1825, [the master artisans of New York] were on the verge of making [Adam] Smithian ideas irrevocably their own. Haltingly, meanwhile, the organized journeymen tried to construct a consis-

tent justification for their actions. The union printers' declaration of
1817 on the inevitably opposing interests of masters and journeymen
suggested a temporary hardening of distinctions; by the early 1820s,
some journeymen had begun to examine the deeper social and economic matrix of their plight. [. . .] Their new understanding [. . .]
surfaced with peculiar force during the carpenters' strike of 1810. The
masters, joined by the city's architects and surveyors, adamantly refused to concede their privileges in the face of the "increasing evils
and distressing tendency" of the journeymen's militancy; least of all
would they grant a standard rate of wages, by which they could no
longer decide what to pay journeymen "according to their several
abilities and industry." The journeymen replied that they had struck
because their "haughty, overbearing" masters—including some "master builders in name only"—had misinterpreted their own interests
and those of all carpenters by hiring men below accepted wage rates
and by depressing the earnings of all, so that the journeymen could
not expect to become masters. Even those employers whose abilities
as workmen still held respect had forfeited all allegiance, by riding
about in their carriages, building themselves brick homes, and assuming a demeanor that "better fits them to give laws to slaves" than
to be master mechanics. The masters had denied both their fellow
tradesmen and the Republic and had become paragons of acquisitive
corruption; the journeymen struck as free men for republican justice.
"Among the inalienable rights of man are life, liberty, and the pursuit
of happiness," the journeymen declared:

"By the social contract every class in society ought to be entitled
to benefit in proportion to its qualifications. [. . .] Among the duties
which society owes individuals is to grant them just compensation
not only for current expenses of livelihood, but to the formation of
a fund for the support of that time when nature requires a cessation
of work."

[. . .] With a rhetoric rich in the republican language of corruption, equality, and independence, [journeyman artisans] remained

committed to a benevolent hierarchy of skill and the cooperative workshop. Artisan independence conjured up, not a vision of ceaseless, self-interested industry, but a moral order in which all craftsmen would eventually become self-governing, independent, competent masters—an order to match the stonemasons' ditty that they would "steal from no man." Men's energies would be devoted, not to personal ambition or profit alone, but to the commonwealth; in the workshop, mutual obligation and respect—"the strongest ties of the heart"—would prevail; in more public spheres, the craftsmen would insist on their equal rights and exercise their citizenship with a view to preserving the rule of virtue as well as to protecting their collective interests against an eminently corruptible mercantile and financial elite. [...]

[But over the first few decades of the nineteenth century, the masters' power continued to grow, and they reorganized trade after trade in order to make production more subject to a division of labor. Many of the new workers who took the less well-paid, more limited employment that emerged in the city were women, like] those female craft workers who had no man's income to help out—widows, young women with small children, the flood of country girls who came to New York in the 1830s and 1840s—faced an even greater crush to earn a bare subsistence. [...] In 1845, the New York Daily Tribune prepared a series of reports on the condition of labor in New York. What the Tribune reporters found shocked them, and they groped for explanations—especially to account for the outrageous underbidding and exploitation that riddled the city's largest trades. A few years later, after he had read the works of the greatest urban journalist of the age, a Tribune correspondent named George Foster had found the right term: it was "sweating," "the accursed system [...] so thoroughly exposed in the recent investigations of Mr. Mayhew in the 'Morning Chronicle,'" a system that had come to prevail "proportionally to as great an extent in this city as in London." One or another variation of sweating emerged in almost all of New York's early industrial trades. It arose in its purest forms in the consumer finishing trades, and most notoriously in the production of clothing.

It took only ten years, from 1825 to 1835, for New York's clothing revolution to conquer the local market; by 1850, it had created and captured the lion's share of a national trade in ready-made clothes for men. The original instigators were the city's cloth wholesalers, auctioneers, and jobbers, whose command of the English import market and broadening avenues to New England invited further adaptation and expansion of the contracting schemes of the early slopshop entrepreneurs. Their success, and that of the master tailors turned manufacturers whom they supplied with cloth and credit, was neither an act of Providence nor an inevitable working-out of the growth of commerce. Of all of New York's middlemen and manufacturers, the clothiers were the most astute at perfecting aggressive merchandizing methods; more important, it was the clothiers who first mastered the art of extending liberal credit to local retailers and country dealers, to expand their own contacts and squeeze their competitors in other cities (and smaller New York dealers) out of the market. By 1835, they had turned the New York trade in ready-mades into one of the nation's largest local industries, with some firms employing between three and five hundred hands each. A large portion of their output was for the "cheap" trade-in precut apparel for southern customers (as well as the "Negro cottons" for southern slaves), dungarees and hickory shirts for western farmers and miners, and shoddy clothing for the urban poor. Beginning in the early 1830s, the clothiers also entered the respectable market, introducing superior lines, fiercely promoted by the jobbers and retailers, for clerks, shopkeepers, and wealthy patrons who lacked the time or money to patronize a custom tailor. [. . .] With this democratization of product and the continued growth of the southern market, the New York clothing trade became an antebellum manufacturing giant. By 1850, the largest New York firms hired as many as five thousand tailors and seamstresses to turn out goods "with a degree of precision that would astonish the negligent observer."

[. . .] The focal point of the clothing outwork system was the New York version of the central shop. [. . .] Behind the scenes, the elite of the clothing work force, the in-shop cutters, prepared the predesigned patterns. The head cutters [. . .] numbered about fifty in all in the city. With an average annual income of between $1,000 and $1,500 each, they were probably the best-paid craft workers in New York. [. . .] Apart from their power to discipline workers, the head cutters (sometimes called "piece masters") were in charge of giving out all work to the journeymen, outworkers, and contractors. On the basis of their appraisal—or whims—a cutter or stitcher could earn a decent living or an excellent one. Impartiality in these matters was not among the head cutter's virtues. "Generally," the Tribune reported, "he has his favorites, perhaps a brother, or cousin, or a particular friend, who gets the 'cream of the shop' and is thus frequently able to make $30 or $40 per week." [. . .]

The cutters enjoyed relatively high wages (roughly $10 to $12 per week) and regular employment, but none of the foremen's powers. Rapid, regular work schedules prevailed in the cutting rooms. At the Devlin and Brothers' firm, cutters were divided into bureaus for coats, pants, vests, and trimmings, while the entire production process, one reporter observed, "was reduced to a system," in which every piece of work had its own number and a ticket with the workman's name. Emphasis fell on speed and accuracy in cutting predetermined designs; "Southern-trade cutting," a term synonymous with rapid rather than artful work, was the most common task in New York's major clothing firms at least as early as the mid-1830s. Any slip, momentary slowdown, or simple disagreement with the foreman could deprive a cutter of the best work in the shop; if he could not adjust to the pace, he was fired.

From the cutting rooms (again, out of sight of the customers), the head cutter or piece master distributed the cut cloth to the outworkers and contractors, and it was here that the worst depredations of sweating began. [. . .] In all cases, the system invited brutal competition and a successive lowering of outwork piece rates. At every level of the contracting network, profits came from the difference between the rates the contractors and manufacturers received and the money they paid out for overhead and labor. [. . .] The sufferings of the outwork and garret-shop hands—the vast majority of clothing-trade workers—taxed the imaginations of even the most sentimental American Victorians. [. . .] All pretensions to craft vanished in the outwork system; with the availability of so much cheap wage labor, formal apprenticing and a regular price book had disappeared by 1845. At any given moment in the 1830s and 1840s, the underbidding in the contracting network could depress outwork and garret-shop piece rates so low that stitchers had to work up to sixteen hours a day to maintain the meanest of living standards: in 1850, some of the largest southern-trade clothing firms in the Second Ward paid their male workers, on the average, well below subsistence wages. Housing was difficult to come by and could amount to no more than a cellar dwelling or a two-room flat, shared with two or more families; single men crammed into outwork boardinghouses. [. . .] The seamstresses and tailors' wives—consigned the most wearisome work (shirt sewing worst of all) and subjected to the bullying and occasional sexual abuse of the contractors—bore the most blatant exploitation; the men, working either as petty contractors or the paterfamilias of the family shops, enjoyed, by comparison, a measure of independence—but only that, as unionists noted in the 1850s. By themselves, such conditions were difficult; they were aggravated by the tendency for outwork and garret-shop wages to diminish further as workers tried to increase their earnings by intensifying their labor and by taking on larger lots of work, thus causing short-term gluts in the labor market and still lower piece rates.

Questions

1. What was the role of women in the system of clothes production, both before and after the early 1800s? Were they used by masters

and shop owners to drive down male wages? What kinds of social roles and practices made that possible?

2. What was the relationship of the sweatshops to the slave plantations?

3. Did these changes in capitalism affect the ideas of citizenship that had crystallized during the revolution and afterwards? In what ways?

The Lynn Shoemakers Strike (1860)

THE NEW YORK TIMES

In 1860, one-third of Massachusetts workers went on strike in sympathy with the shoemakers of Lynn, Marblehead, Salem, and many other communities where piecework prices had begun to fall because of the new sewing machines. In this piece, we accompany a *New York Times* reporter north from Boston to Marblehead and then Lynn, where he listens to the conversations about prices, work, nationhood, and race. The shoemakers articulate their grievances in political terms; they will not be slaves. The workers invoke the heritage of the American Revolution and refuse to allow a new form of tyranny to control them.

The Bay State Strike: Movement Among the Women—
Acts and Proceedings of Employers and Workmen—
The Female Strikers at Liberty Hall

LYNN, Tuesday, Feb. 28, 1860.

In company with some of the Boston correspondents, I yesterday visited the town of Marblehead, where the strikers have obtained an ascendancy equal almost to that of the Lynn malcontents. The immediate cause of our going was a desire to witness the doings of the mass meeting, composed of the combined forces of Lynn and Marblehead. [. . .]

About noon, the procession from Lynn, consisting of about 3,500 men, preceded by a brass band, entered the village green, escorted by 500 Marbleheaders. The sight from the hotel steps was a very interesting one. Four thousand men, without work, poor, depending partially upon the charities of their neighbors and partially upon the generosity of the tradesmen of their town, giving up a certainty for an uncertainty and involving in trouble with themselves many hundreds of women and children, while to a certain extent the wheels of trade are completely blocked, and no immediate prospect of relief appears. Their banners flaunted bravely. Their inscriptions of "Down with tyranny," "We are not slaves," "No sympathy with the rich," "Our bosses grind us," "We work and they ride," "No foreign police," and many others of like import, read very well and look very pretty, but they don't buy dinners or clothing, or keep the men at work or the women at home about their business. By this strike $25,000 weekly is kept from circulation in Lynn alone, and who can say what the effect will be on the storekeepers, dealers in articles of home consumption, if such a state of drainage is kept up for any great length of time?

However this may be, they made a grand show. The day was fine, the air balmy, the music good, the crowd great, and all the resolutions for sticking out were passed unanimously; so they passed a few hours on the green, making speeches of encouragement, and then, with three cheers for the Marblehead girls, and three groans for "grandizing bosses," the delegations parted, and the Lynnites returned home, with mud in the road up to their knees, but with enthusiasm waxing stronger at every step. [. . .]

The hall was filled to its utmost capacity. The ladies were such as you can imagine free, self-supporting, fearless, happy women to be. We have seen many assemblages of women, but have never beheld a more intelligent, earnest, "peart" set, than were in Liberty Hall last night.

The object of the meeting was the hearing the reports of Committees who had been deputed to make a list of reasonable prices, and to solicit the girls of Lynn and the surrounding towns to join the strike movement.

There are two classes of workers—those who work in the shops and those work at home—the former use the machines and materials of the bosses, while the latter work on their own machines, or work by hand, furnishing their own materials. It is evident that the latter should receive higher pay than the former, and the report not having considered this fact, was subjected to severe handling. The discussion which followed was rich beyond description—the jealousies, piques and cliques of the various circles being apparent as it proceeded. One opposed the adoption of the report because "the prices set were so high that the bosses wouldn't pay them." Cries of "Put her out," "Shut up," "Scabby," and "Shame!" arose on all sides; but, while the reporters were alarmed, the lady took it all in good part, and made up faces at the crowd. The Chairman stated that, hereafter, Pickleeomoonia boots were to be made for three cents a pair less, which announcement was received with expressions of dismay, whereupon he corrected himself, and said they were to be three cents higher; and this announcement drew forth shouts and screams of applause. "There! didn't I say so?" said an old lady behind me. "You shut up," was the response of her neighbor: "you think because you've got a couple of machines you're some; but you ain't no more than anybody else." At this point some men peeped in at the window— "Scat, scat, and put 'em out," soon drove them away, and the meeting went into a Committee of the Whole, and had a grand chabbering for five minutes. Two ladies, one representing the machine interest, and the other the shop girls, became very much excited, and were devoting themselves to an expose of each other's habits, when the Chairman, with the perspiration starting from every pore, said in a loud and authoritative tone of voice: "Ladies! look at me; stop this wranglin'. Do you care for your noble cause? Are you descendants of old MOLLY STARK or not? Did you ever hear of the spirit of '76? [Yes, yes, we've got it.] Wall, then, do behave yourselves. There ain't nobody nowhere who will aid you if you don't show 'em that you're regular built Moll Starks over again." [Cheers, clappings, &c.] [...]

Some of the statements were quite interesting. A Mrs. MILLER said that she hired a machine on which she was able to make $6 per week—out of that she paid—for the machine, $1; for the materials, $1 50; for her board, $2; for bastings, $1;—making $5.50 in all, which left her a clear profit of only fifty cents a week. One of the bosses says, however, that if a woman is at all smart she can make $10 per week with her machine, which would be clear $3, sure. In fact, from remarks which were dropped around I judged that Mrs. MILLER's estimate is rather low. The leading spirit of the meeting, Miss CLARA BROWN, a very bright, pretty girl, said that she called at a shop that day and found a friend of hers hard at work on a lot of linings. She asked what she was getting for them, and was told eight cents for sixty. "Girls of Lynn," said CLARA, "Girls of Lynn, do you hear that and will you stand it? Never, Never, NEVER. Strike, then—strike at once; DEMAND 8½ cents for your work when the binding isn't closed, and you'll get it. Don't let them make niggers of you; [Shame, there are colored persons here.] I meant Southern niggers:—keep still; don't work your machines; let 'em lie still till we get all we ask, and then go at it, as did our Mothers in the Revolution."

Questions

1. Is Mrs. Miller a worker or an independent businesswoman? What would that difference mean to her social status? How can we tell the difference?
2. Did the reporters think the strike would be successful? What did they think about the political activism of these women?
3. How did having a "machine" affect the kinds of choices that a shoemaker could make?
4. How did this political activity fit with middle-class male notions of how women "ought" to behave?
5. Why did Clara Brown use a derogatory racial epithet for slaves, and why did she tell mostly white workers not to be black?

MODULE 9

AMERICAN FINANCE

Jackson's Veto of the Second Bank (1832)

PRESIDENT ANDREW JACKSON

In 1811, the U.S. Congress—dominated by the "Republican" followers of Jefferson and Madison, who opposed Hamilton's idea of a central bank—allowed the charter of the First Bank of the United States to lapse. The next year, that same Congress declared war on the world's greatest financial, industrial, and naval power: Great Britain. The War of 1812 ended in what some historians call a "draw," but what was actually by definition a victory for the United States since the young nation managed to survive what some other historians call a "second war for independence." In the course of the war, however, the absence of a banking policy proved most of Hamilton's arguments for a strong national bank. The United States could not raise money, and currency fluctuations whipsawed the economy by sending different states (which had their own, usually unregulated banking systems) through different extremes of deflation and inflation. In the wake of the war, Madison and his followers changed their minds and adopted many elements of Hamiltonian policy. Seeking to strengthen the national government and support rapid economic growth, these new "National Republicans," like Henry Clay of Kentucky and John C. Calhoun of South Carolina, proposed federally funded enhancements to economic infrastructure. These included roads and canals, although the most successful of those projects was funded by a state: New York's astonishing Erie Canal, at first called "Clinton's Ditch" after the governor who proposed it, De Witt Clinton. But just as important as physical infrastructure for the development of American capitalism was a sound banking system that could smooth out or even prevent financial crises, make credit markets possible and reliable, and lend money to entrepreneurs. The result was the Second Bank of the United States, which Congress chartered in 1816.

The charter of the Second Bank was much like the first one. It was a private-public partnership. While the federal government would buy $7.5 million worth of bank stock, the rest of its working capital of $35 million was to be supplied by private individuals' purchases of stock. The bank would be the banker for the federal government, paying its bills—including payments of interest and principal due on the long-running national debt—and holding its tax receipts. It would have the privilege of using that working capital in its daily operations, such as loaning money out on a short-term basis to merchants. The bank would in return pay a $1.5 million "bonus" to the federal government. The Second Bank was also more clearly empowered to regulate the state-chartered banks whose irresponsible expansions and contractions of credit had been so disruptive to the wartime economy. Its directors would elect the bank's president, who would in theory be free from federal government control, for some of the same reasons that Hamilton had offered to justify the healthy independence of a national bank. But unlike the first bank, this one was to establish multiple branches, reducing the fear that capitalist development would be localized in Philadelphia only. The branches, in particular, would be very important in making both short- and long-term loans in their local catchment areas, enabling both the ordinary flow of commercial trade and the long-term investments that established new businesses and new markets.

Unfortunately for the advocates of banking, the administration of the bank in its first four years did little to combat the claims of its dyed-in-the-wool opponents, who believed that no private institution should have so much power over the money supply, over the price of credit, and over the government's finances. The first administrators of the bank played a major role in superheating the post–War of 1812 boom that exploded in the Panic of 1819. The revelation that bank directors and branch officers had been speculating with other people's deposits also led states to try to tax and regulate the branches out of existence. However, the Supreme Court, in *McCulloch v. Maryland* (1819) ruled that states could not tax the branches of the federally chartered institution. This decision, attributed to Chief Justice John Marshall, helped establish the federal government's authority over state decisions. Bank defenders would also argue that the *McCulloch* decision established the long-disputed constitutionality of a kind of institution that Hamilton had defended with the "necessary and proper" clause, and which his Jeffersonian opponents had just as resolutely denied. But in the meantime, the practical survival of the overextended bank fell to the hands of new bank president Langdon Cheves, a South Carolina planter who ruthlessly called in loans and contracted credit after the bursting of the speculative bubble in 1819.

Coming out of the panic, the majority of white Americans might have agreed with Missouri senator Thomas Hart Benton's claim that the tight-money policies of 1819–1821 meant that "the Bank was saved, but the People were lost." In much of rural America, times remained tight for the next five years or more. This was not, however, the case, in the cotton economy. Under its subsequent president, a dashing Philadelphia aristocrat, politician, and poet named Nicholas Biddle, the bank in the 1820s gradually increased its lending to cotton merchants and planters in Louisiana, Mississippi, and Alabama. They dramatically expanded their operations, and a thriving domestic slave trade developed to move enslaved people from older slave states to newer ones, separating hundreds of thousands of spouses, parents, children, and siblings. The production of cotton, the main U.S. export, grew. So did the banking sector in New Orleans, New York, and Philadelphia, and New England's new textile belt began to emerge as the second major industrial region in world history (after the British Midlands around Manchester.)

By the time that Andrew Jackson won the presidential election of 1828, the U.S. economy was expanding at an unprecedented rate, part of a transformation in the North Atlantic that was starting to move modernizing societies out of the Malthusian trap. Finance and investment were absolutely crucial to the emergence of this new kind of highly productive, industrializing capitalism, and the Second Bank of the United States was in many ways doing a great job supporting this transformative growth. But not everybody was happy with the bank, or with Nicholas Biddle. If one was among the thousands of enslaved people transported from Virginia to New Orleans over the late 1820s and early 1830s by slave-trading entrepreneurs Isaac Franklin and R. C. Ballard, one might have a lot of criticisms of the role of the Second Bank in making credit easily available for the traders and the planters who bought and transported people. Yet that wasn't the perspective which led newly elected President Jackson to criticize the bank. Instead, he thought it played favorites— lending to some white citizens and not to others, moving profits from one part of the country to another, and supporting his 1828 election opponent, incumbent president John Quincy Adams.

Nicholas Biddle tried to entice President Jackson into recognizing the ways in which the Second Bank of the United States enhanced American national development, but over the first three years of his time in office, Jackson refused to signal support for it. According to Biddle, in their private conversations Jackson expressed the suspicion that banks' ability to create money by lending was inherently speculative. So by summer of 1832, Biddle threw his support behind a congressional plan to push for an early renewal of the bank's charter, which wasn't actually set to expire until 1836. The plan was a trap for Jackson. If he supported recharter, they believed, he would lose the support of his most fervent antibank supporters, who were still resentful over its tight-money policies right after the panic. If he vetoed the bill, which passed easily, he would be putting himself in opposition to those who saw it as the source of the general economic prosperity that was driving the economy's growth rate to an unprecedented level.

Jackson vetoed the bill, and supported his act with the uncompromising document you see here. After Jackson's veto survived congressional attempts to overturn it, he and his 1832 electoral opponent, Henry Clay, made the Bank Veto the central issue of the Presidential contest. When Jackson won, he felt empowered to begin moving federal funds out of the bank, effectively overturning the charter in 1833 even though it still had three years to run. No longer able to exert control over the financial pipes and valves of the American credit economy, Biddle's bank was just another institution in a suddenly deregulated environment. And between 1834 and 1836, states embarked on a wild spree of bank chartering and bond issuing. Awash in easy credit, augmented by Europeans' desire to invest in the booming cotton economy and its derivative sectors, Americans were in fact living in a bubble economy. When the price of cotton fell in late 1836, the fortunes of all the banks and merchant firms and planters and others who had been borrowing huge amounts on the expectation of making even larger returns turned to dust. The Panic of 1837 was the opening round of a half-decade of economic doldrums that helped set the stage for eventual civil war in the United States. It also was an indication of what can happen when ideology leads policymakers to remove the regulatory brakes that prevent the creative forces of capitalist finance from running so quickly that individuals' rational decisions to take on risk accumulate so much debt that the entire economy risks broader failure if key commodities decline in price, or other shocks occur.

WASHINGTON, July 10, 1832

To the Senate:

[. . .] A bank of the United States is in many respects convenient for the Government and useful to the people. Entertaining this opinion, and deeply impressed with the belief that some of the powers and privileges possessed by the existing bank are unauthorized by the Constitution, subversive of the rights of the States, and dangerous to the liberties of the people, I felt it my duty at an early period of my Administration to call the attention of Congress to the practicability of organizing an institution combining all its advantages and obviating these objections. I sincerely regret that in the act before me I can perceive none of those modifications of the bank charter which are necessary, in my opinion, to make it compatible with justice, with sound policy, or with the Constitution of our country.

The present corporate body, denominated the president, directors, and company of the Bank of the United States, [. . .] enjoys an exclusive privilege of banking under the authority of the General Government, a monopoly of its favor and support. [. . .] The powers, privileges, and favors bestowed upon it in the original charter, by increasing the value of the stock far above its par value, operated as a gratuity of many millions to the stockholders.

[. . .] The act before me proposes another gratuity to the holders of the same stock, and [. . .] will increase at least so or 30 per cent more the market price of the stock, subject to the payment of the annuity of $200,000 per year secured by the act, thus adding in a moment one-fourth to its par value. It is not our own citizens only who are to receive the bounty of our Government. More than eight millions of the stock of this bank are held by foreigners. [. . .] The many millions which this act proposes to bestow on the stockholders of the existing bank must come directly or indirectly out of the earnings of the American people. [. . .] The twenty-eight millions of stock would probably [. . .] command in market at least $42,000,000, subject to the payment of the present bonus. The present value of the monopoly, therefore, is $17,000,000, [. . .]

But this act [. . .] seems to be predicated on the erroneous idea that the present stockholders have a prescriptive right not only to the favor but to the bounty of Government. It appears that more than a fourth part of the stock is held by foreigners and the residue is held by a few hundred of our own citizens, chiefly of the richest class. [. . .] I can not perceive the justice or policy of this course. [. . .] If gratuities must be made once in fifteen or twenty years let them not be bestowed on the subjects of a foreign government nor upon a designated and favored class of men in our own country. [. . .]

As little stock is held in the West, it is obvious that the debt of the people in that section to the bank is principally a debt to the Eastern and foreign stockholders; that the interest they pay upon it is carried into the Eastern States and into Europe, and that it is a burden upon their industry and a drain of their currency, which no country can bear without inconvenience and occasional distress. To meet this burden and equalize the exchange operations of the bank, the amount of specie drawn from those States through its branches within the last two years, as shown by its official reports, was about $6,000,000. More than half a million of this amount does not stop in the Eastern States, but passes on to Europe to pay the dividends of the foreign stockholders. [. . .] The Western States find no adequate compensation for this perpetual burden on their industry and drain of their currency. [. . .] This provision in its practical effect deprive the Eastern as well as the Southern and Western States of the means of raising a revenue from the extension of business and great profits of this institution. It will make the American people debtors to aliens in nearly the whole amount due to this bank, and send across the Atlantic from two to five millions of specie every year to pay the bank dividends.

In another of its bearings this provision is fraught with danger. Of the twenty-five directors of this bank five are chosen by the Government and twenty by the citizen stockholders. [. . .] The entire control of the institution would necessarily fall into the hands of a few citizen stockholders, and the ease with which the object would be accomplished would be a temptation to designing men to secure that control in their own hands by monopolizing the remaining stock.

There is danger that a president and directors would then be able to elect themselves from year to year, and without responsibility or control manage the whole concerns of the bank during the existence of its charter. It is easy to conceive that great evils to our country and its institutions might flow from such a concentration of power in the hands of a few men irresponsible to the people.

Is there no danger to our liberty and independence in a bank that in its nature has so little to bind it to our country? The president of the bank has told us that most of the State banks exist by its forbearance. Should its influence become concentered, as it may under the operation of such an act as this, in the hands of a self-elected directory whose interests are identified with those of the foreign stockholders, will there not be cause to tremble for the purity of our elections in peace and for the independence of our country in war? Their power would be great whenever they might choose to exert it; but if this monopoly were regularly renewed every fifteen or twenty years on terms proposed by themselves, they might seldom in peace put forth their strength to influence elections or control the affairs of the nation. But if any private citizen or public functionary should interpose to curtail its powers or prevent a renewal of its privileges, it can not be doubted that he would be made to feel its influence.

Should the stock of the bank principally pass into the hands of the subjects of a foreign country, and we should unfortunately become involved in a war with that country, what would be our condition? [. . .] Controlling our currency, receiving our public moneys, and holding thousands of our citizens in dependence, it would be more formidable and dangerous than the naval and military power of the enemy. [. . .]

It is to be regretted that the rich and powerful too often bend the acts of government to their selfish purposes. Distinctions in society will always exist under every just government. Equality of talents, of education, or of wealth can not be produced by human institutions. In the full enjoyment of the gifts of Heaven and the fruits of superior industry, economy, and virtue, every man is equally entitled to protection by law; but when the laws undertake to add to these natural and just advantages artificial distinctions, to grant titles, gratuities, and exclusive privileges, to make the rich richer and the potent more powerful, the humble members of society—the farmers, mechanics, and laborers—who have neither the time nor the means of securing like favors to themselves, have a right to complain of the injustice of their Government. There are no necessary evils in government. Its evils exist only in its abuses. If it would confine itself to equal protection, and, as Heaven does its rains, shower its favors alike on the high and the low, the rich and the poor, it would be an unqualified blessing. In the act before me there seems to be a wide and unnecessary departure from these just principles. [. . .] Many of our rich men have not been content with equal protection and equal benefits, but have besought us to make them richer by act of Congress. [. . .] We can at least take a stand against all new grants of monopolies and exclusive privileges, against any prostitution of our Government to the advancement of the few at the expense of the many, and in favor of compromise and gradual reform in our code of laws and system of political economy. [. . .] ANDREW JACKSON.

Questions

1. Why does Andrew Jackson see the Bank as an unfair monopoly?
2. How were Southern and Western interests allegedly hurt by the Bank, considering that by 1832 approximately half of the lending done by the Bank was in the cotton states?
3. What responsibility, if any, does Andrew Jackson think that the government has for supporting economic growth? How should the government operate in a rapidly changing capitalist economy? Which political or other voices today use some or all of the arguments he offers against the bank, and which arguments?

4. Using this document as a guide, how would you define Jackson's political and economic philosophy? Whose interests does he claim to be representing? Why does this matter?

5. Compare Jackson's Veto Message with Alexander Hamilton's Report on a National Bank. How much had the debate changed in the forty years between the two documents?

Toxic Debt, Liar Loans, and Securitized Human Beings (2011)

EDWARD E. BAPTIST

For generations, people wrote about slavery as if it had little or nothing to do with capitalism. This was odd, given the reality that enslaved African Americans produced virtually all the cotton that the innovative new factories of the Industrial Revolution spun and wove. But even though free wage labor definitely produced different internal social relations than did a labor system in which enslavers could buy and sell human beings, recent research has been uncovering the connections between slavery in the cotton-growing South and the development of world—and American—capitalism. Ed Baptist, who argues elsewhere that a system of measurement and torture that was deeply embedded in U.S. cotton slavery created massive increases in productivity—increases that were very important to the development of industrial capitalism—here shows how enslavers' financial innovations spread torture-extracted profit throughout the Western world. The securitization of slave mortgages generated huge amounts of capital for enslavers as well, but in the end, that was their downfall. Much like the 2008 collapse of the bubble in securitized residential mortgages, the consequences of unregulated financial innovation and "this-time-is-different" thinking would be far-reaching, complex, and unpredictable.

* * *

The Panic of 1837 launched America's biggest and most conse-quential economic depression before the Civil War. And it was the decisions and behavior of thousands of actors [like Louisiana planter Jacob Bieller] that created a perfect financial storm. [. . .] [In] the Panic of 1837, we find new evidence about the role of slavery and slave labor in the creation of our modern, industrialized—and post-modernly financialized—world. Look a little more closely at Jacob Bieller, who can tell us things worth the due diligence. In 1837 Bieller was 67 years old. He had grown up in South Carolina. [. . .] In 1809, little more than a year after Congress closed the legal Atlantic slave trade, Bieller moved west [. . .] drawn by the opportunities for an entrepreneurial slave owner in the new cotton lands opening to the west, Bieller took his son Joseph and 27 enslaved African Americans and settled just up the Mississippi River from Natchez, on the Loui-siana side.

The enslaved people that Bieller brought to Concordia Parish be-came the root of his fortune—as they and a million others like them would become the root of the prosperity of [. . .] the United States as a whole. [. . .] When Jacob Bieller put his two dozen slaves to work growing and picking cotton, his whip was also driving the creation of a new, more complex, more dynamic world economy. In the lifetime between the ratification of the Constitution and the secession of the Confederacy, enslavers moved more than a million enslaved African Americans to cotton-growing areas taken by the new nation from their original inhabitants. Forced migrations and stolen labor yielded an astonishing increase in cotton production: from 1.2 million pounds in 1790 to 2.1 billion in 1859, and an incredible dominance over the international market—by the 1830s, 80% of the cotton used by the British textile industry came from the southern U.S.

We live today with the results of the long days that Bieller's slaves sweated out in the field, but we also live in a world distantly shaped by the financial decisions of cotton entrepreneurs on both sides of the Atlantic—as well as by the forgetfulness of those who have not learned from their lessons of two centuries ago. Specifically: their decisions about how to obtain and use credit, as well as to manage risk. [. . .] Credit and risk were imminent to the task of moving the world's most important commodity through a chain of buyers and sellers that stretched from Louisiana cotton field to Liverpool cotton exchange. Prices suddenly dropped when rumors raced through New Orleans, New York, or Liverpool: "Optimism prevailed"—till the market learned that the U.S. crop is too big for the demand this year. Cloth isn't selling because of "overproduction." The mill workers in Manchester have been "turned out"—laid off. [. . .]

Beginning with Adam Smith, utopian economists have argued that the logical outcome of profit-maximizing behavior by all market actors is the maximum collective benefit. [. . .] [But] when the price of a pound of cotton plummeted, merchant firms were unable to pay back the short-term commercial loans they had taken, and so they demanded repayment from their fellow firms to whom they had made loans. This individually rational behavior—shoring up liquidity as pressure for payment increased—led to collectively irrational outcomes. Every firm was suddenly moving in the same direction, every firm faced the same crisis, each one responded in the same way. [. . .] [But] the Bank of the United States [under Nicholas Biddle] ensured a level of systemic stability. [. . .] The Bank not only worked to prevent financial panics but to drive steady growth. As the single biggest lender in the economy, it lent directly to individual entrepreneurs—including enslavers like Jacob Bieller, who were always eager to buy more human capital whom they could put to work in the cotton fields of the southwest. "The US Bank and the Planters Bank at this place has thrown a large amt of cash into circulation," wrote slave trader Isaac Franklin from Natchez in 1832. Franklin was the Sam Walton of the internal slave trade in the U.S., selling hundreds or even thousands of men and women in New Orleans and Natchez in a given year. In fact, by the early 1830s, the Natchez and

New Orleans branches had lent out a full third of the capital of the B.U.S., much of it used to buy thousands of enslaved people from the Chesapeake, Kentucky, and North Carolina. [...]

Ultimately the entire structure was bottomed on, founded on, funded by the bodies of enslaved people: on the ability of slaveholders to extract cotton from them, and on the ability of slaveholders (or bankruptcy courts) to sell them to someone else who wanted to extract cotton. And the fact that cotton fields were the place where the margins of growth were created meant that they presented lenders with both needs and opportunities to hedge against the risk that individual counterparties would default.

For there were many things that could cause individual counterparties, especially planters, to fail. [...] The cotton country of the Mississippi Valley was hot and wet, and the people transported there died of fevers in great number. [...] In 1832–33, cholera raged through the slave labor camps of Mississippi and Louisiana. [...] At the "Forks in the Road," the huge slave market just outside of Natchez, Isaac Franklin desperately hid the evidence of epidemic among his "fancy stock of wool and ivory," as his cousin coarsely put it. "The way we send out dead negroes at night and keep dark is a sin," wrote Isaac about secret burials in the woods. [...] Then there was simple failure. [...] Even as cotton markets soared in the 1830s, Jacob Bieller, for instance, plunged into his own personal crash. [...] Bieller's wife, Nancy [...] began divorce proceedings— claiming half of Bieller's property. According to Nancy, not only had Jacob threatened to shoot her in 1827, but for years "he kept a concubine in their common dwelling & elsewhere, publicly and openly." (The courts of Louisiana declined to rule on either charge when they eventually granted the couple a divorce. Jacob's last will gave tacit freedom "to my slaves Mary Clarkson and her son Coulson, a boy something more than five years old, both bright mulattoes.")

[...] The ultimate hedge for him [and] for Nancy [...] was the relative liquidity of enslaved people. (Bieller had recently purchased dozens of additional slaves on credit from Isaac Franklin, paying more than $1,000 each, bringing his total number of captives to over eighty). [. . .] He wanted to sell all those determined to be community rather than separate property, and divide the cash. She wanted to divide the men, women, and children up, "scattering them," [for] [. . .] enslaved people, Nancy said, were "susceptible to a division in kind without injury to us." [. . .] The families of the almost one hundred people listed in Bieller's documents would be melted like ice in his summer drink.

For everyone who drew profit in the system, enslaved human beings were the ultimate hedge. Cotton merchants, bankers, slave traders—everybody whose money the planter borrowed and could not pay until the time the cotton was sold at a high enough price to pay off his or her debts—all could expect that eventually enslaved people would either 1) make enough cotton to enable the planter to get clear or 2) be sold in order to generate the liquidity to pay off the debt. In 1824, Vincent Nolte, a freewheeling entrepreneur who almost cornered the New Orleans cotton market more than once in the 1810s, lent $48,000 to Louisiana-based enslaver Alonzo Walsh. The terms? Walsh had to pay the money back in four years at a rate of about eight percent. To secure payment he committed to consigning his entire crop each year to Nolte to be sold in Liverpool. And, just in case, he provided collateral: "from 90 to a 100 head of first rate slaves will be mortgaged." In 1824 those nearly five score people meant up to $80,000 on the New Orleans auction block—a form of property whose value fluctuated less than bales of cotton.

Yet enslavers had already—by the end of the 1820s—created a highly innovative alternative to the existing financial structure. The Consolidated Association of the Planters of Louisiana (despite its name, the "C.A.P.L." was still a bank) created more leverage for enslavers at less cost, and on longer terms. It did so by securitizing slaves, hedging even more effectively against the individual investors' losses—so long as the financial system itself did not fail. Here is how it worked: potential borrowers mortgaged slaves and cultivated land to the C.A.P.L., which entitled them to borrow up to half of the assessed value of their property from the C.A.P.L. in bank notes. To convince others to accept the notes thus disbursed at face value, the C.A.P.L. convinced the Louisiana legislature to back $2.5 million in bank bonds (due in ten to fifteen years, bearing five percent interest) with the "faith and credit" of the people of the state. The great British merchant bank Baring Brothers agreed to advance the C.A.P.L. the equivalent of $2.5 million in sterling bills, and market the bonds on European securities markets.

[. . .] The sale of the bonds created a pool of high-quality credit to be lent back to the planters at a rate significantly lower than the rate of return that they could expect that money to produce. That pool could be used for all sorts of income-generating purposes: buying more slaves (to produce more cotton and sugar and hence more income) or lending to other enslavers. [. . .] They had mortgaged their slaves—sometimes multiple times, and sometimes they even mortgaged fictitious slaves—but [. . .] this type of mortgage gave the enslaver tremendous margins, control, and flexibility. It was hard to imagine that such borrowers would be foreclosed, even if they fell behind on their payments. After all, the borrowers owned the bank.

Using the C.A.P.L. model, slaveowners were now able to monetize their slaves by securitizing them [. . .] on the international financial market. This also allowed a much wider group of people to profit from the opportunities of slavery's expansion. [. . .] For the investor who bought it from the House of Baring Brothers or some other seller, a bond was really the purchase of a completely commodified slave: not a particular individual, but a tiny percentage of each of thousands of slaves. The investor, of course, escaped the risk inherent in owning an individual slave, who might die, run away, or become rebellious.

[. . .] The Bank [of the United States] had pumped millions of dollars of loans into Mississippi and Louisiana in Jackson's first term—almost half of the Bank's total balance sheet was there by 1832—but it remained unpopular in the large sections of the south-west. Creditors are not always loved among those to whom they lend. Jackson vetoed the recharter of the B.U.S. in 1832, and won reelection that fall against a pro-Bank opponent. The next year, he ordered the transfer of the government's deposits out of the Bank. Jackson [. . .] [then] distributed the deposits to a horde of so-called "pet banks"—state-chartered institutions that, at least initially, were run by his political allies. [. . .] Now, nothing—no bank, no other institution—regulated the financial economy of the U.S.

Economists of financial crisis such as the late Hyman Minsky and Charles Kindleberger [. . .] argued that most historical bubbles contain three crucial elements: policymakers who believed markets were stable and did not need regulation; financial innovations that make it easier to create and expand the leverage of borrowers [and] [. . .] those who believe that, to quote the title of another recent work on financial panics, "This Time Is Different"—that the rules have changed and prices will continue to climb. [. . .] In this way, every boom takes on aspects of a Ponzi scheme. "Disaster myopia," meanwhile, refers to the common propensity of economic actors to underestimate both the likelihood and the likely magnitude of fi-nancial panic. The magnitude is exacerbated by the extent of indebt-edness (entered into because of overconfidence) and the degree to which individual hedging and unregulated over-leveraging make it likely that pulling one card will bring down the whole structure.

The anti-B.U.S. elements in Jackson's administration did not re-place Biddle's institution with any other check within the financial system, opening the way for all three developments. State politicians, to whom the ball was in effect handed, apparently assumed that noth-ing could go wrong. After 1832, the securitization, world-wide mar-keting, and multiple leveraging of enslaved people, pioneered by the C.A.P.L., proliferated. Across the southwest, cotton entrepreneurs created a series of banks, many of them far larger than the C.A.P.L.

In 1832, the state of Louisiana chartered the Union Bank of Louisiana, which issued $7 million in state bonds. The bank contracted with Baring Brothers to sell them, and Baring sent some to their American partners, Prime, Ward, and King in New York City. Soon Union Bank securities were circulating in all the financial centers of Europe and North America. Next, in 1833, came the mammoth Citizens' Bank of Louisiana, which was capitalized with an issue of $12 million in bonds that Hope and Company in Amsterdam agreed to market [. . .] until, by 1836, New Orleans was, per resident, the U.S. city with the greatest density of bank capital—$64 million in all. Other states and territories in the area, self-consciously copying Louisiana, began to create new banks of their own, each one exploiting the loopholes of the now-unregulated system with innovative financial devices. [. . .] By the end of the 1830s, the state-chartered banks of the cotton-growing states had issued bonds for well over $50 million dollars.

[. . .] Huge amounts of money were shifted around: to slave traders, to the sellers of goods like food and cheap clothing, to slave owners in the Chesapeake who sold people to the southwest, to the banks in Virginia and elsewhere who took their slice of profit as the financiers of the domestic slave traders. By the time the decade was out, at least 250,000 enslaved men, women, and children had been shifted from the old terrain of slavery to the new. [. . .] A quarter million people were moved by force, sold, mortgaged, collateralized, securitized, sold again 3,000 miles from where they actually toiled. Each summer they learned how to pick the fields clean faster, at the end of a whip. From 1831 to 1837, cotton production almost doubled, from 300 million pounds to over 600 million. Too much was reaching Liverpool for Manchester to spin and weave, much less to sell to consumers in the form of cloth. Prices per pound at New Orleans, which had begun the boom in 1834 at eighteen cents, slipped to less than ten by late 1836. [. . .] As the slowing prices began to pinch, the Bank of England, alarmed at the outflow of capital to the U.S. in the form of securities purchases, cut its lending in the late summer of 1836. [. . .] Three massive Liverpool and London firms, unable to meet their commercial debt because cotton prices had dropped, collapsed at the end of 1836. The tsunami rushed across the ocean to their trading partners in New Orleans. By late March each of the top ten cotton-buying firms there had collapsed.

[. . .] A second, bigger crash in 1839 finished off many of the survivors of the 1837 panic. [. . .] Most of the debt owed by planters and those who dealt with them was "toxic," to use a recent term. It was unpayable. The planters of Mississippi owed New Orleans banks alone $33 million, estimated one expert, and could not hope to net more than $10 million from their 1837 crop to pay off that debt. Nor could they sell off capital to raise cash because prices for slaves and land, the ultimate collateral in the system, had plummeted as the first wave of bankruptcy-driven sales tapped what little cash there was in the system. [. . .]

The southwestern banks [. . .] were unable to continue to make coupon payments—interest installments on the bonds they had sold on far-off securities markets. Some might have been able to collect from their debtors by foreclosing mortgages on slaves and land, but, of course, the markets for those two assets had collapsed. Many slave owners [. . .] [used] political leverage to protect them from the consequences of their financial over-leverage. The ultimate expression of this practice was the repudiation of the government-backed bonds by the legislatures of several southwestern states and territories, most notably Mississippi and Florida. [. . .] The power of the state had created the securitized slave, and now the power of the state destroyed it, in order to protect that slave's owner from his creditors.

[. . .] After repudiation, outside investors were cautious about lending money to Southern institutions. [. . .] By the early 1840s, Wall Street and New York had emerged as the definitive victor. Slave owners continued to supply virtually all of the industrial world's most important commodity, but the post-1837 inability of Southern planters to control their own financing or get the capital that would enable them to diversify led them to sacrifice massive skimmings of their profits to financial intermediaries and creditors. They sought greater revenues in the only ways that they could. [. . .] They forced enslaved people to achieve an incredible intensity of labor, developed new kinds of seed, and expanded their acreage . . . cotton production . . . rose from 600 million pounds in 1837 to two billion in 1859.

The second method of enhancing revenues was by seeking new territory, both in order to add to the land under cultivation and with the hope of provoking a new boom. Unleashing the animal spirits of speculation in new territories had almost worked before, so why not try it again by acquiring California, Cuba, Mexico, or Kansas for slavery? The result of the commitment of political capital to that end [. . .] was the Civil War, in which the consequences of the long-term financial difficulties of the cotton economy played a major role in Southern defeat.

Financial innovation in the 1820s and 1830s thus had massive, unforeseen, and often ironic consequences. [. . .] In the end the reverberations set off by the leveraging of slavery's inequities into further equity for those who exploited them were what brought the structure of real-life slavery crashing down.

Questions

1. In what ways was the market in bonds that were ultimately backed by enslaved people's work in the cotton fields of the American slave labor camps similar to the pre-2008 market in bonds backed by residential home mortgages? What differences come to mind?
2. When they buy assets whose prices have risen dramatically during a boom or bubble, are entrepreneurs and other market actors behaving rationally? Is capitalism a rational system? Does it depend on the rationality or rational behavior of market actors?
3. Was slavery capitalist? Was it in, but not of, capitalism, or was it actually capitalist in essence or spirit? Does the answer matter today?

MODULE 10

CASH CONSUMPTION

The Murder of Helen Jewett (1830)

The story of Helen Jewett brings into sharp focus the everyday meanings of the new cash economy of the 1830s. In this world of anonymous cash, clerks could buy anything and do anything that they wanted. Helen Jewett was a twenty-three-year-old prostitute originally named Dorcas Doyen. She had been orphaned at thirteen, and after being kicked out by her foster family, had made her way to New York City. Once there, she went to the theater to solicit men to bring back to a brothel run by a madam named Rosina Townsend. One of her frequent customers at the brothel was a young garment clerk named Richard Robinson. Townsend describes below how, after serving champagne to Jewett and Robinson, she came back the following morning to find Jewett murdered in a horrifying manner.

This murder was shocking, and it transformed what was considered appropriate for public discussion. Across the country there were debates over how Jewett (a native-born American) became a prostitute, who she was, and most pivotally (and strangely for us), whether Robinson should be jailed. As one writer put it, "no man ought to forfeit his life for the murder of a whore." Robinson defended himself: "I was an unprotected boy without female friends to introduce me to respectable society, sent to a boarding house where I could enter at what hour I pleased, subservient to no control after the business of the day was over." His boss was not his master and his father was absent. In his world, there was no moral center. The Jewett case was as much about this new class of clerks as the murder itself.

At the trial, young men wore white beaver hats in support of Robinson (who also went by the street name of "Frank Rivers"). These "Frank Rivers" caps became a fashion item for the young men in support of the liberated, cash-fueled life—everything that the genteel parlor was not. The case outlined the limits of what clerks could actually buy with their cash. Richard Robinson was acquitted.

Atrocious Murder of Helen Jewett

April 16, 1836

One of the most cold blooded murders ever perpetrated in this city took place on Saturday night last at a house of ill fame in Thomas street. Since the awful and mysterious tragedy of Gulielma Sands, upon which Fay's novel of "Norman Leslie" is founded, *no occurrence has* taken piece *among* us that has *excited* such a universal horror and consternation. It is not to be wondered at that such an excitement should pervade the public mind in relation to this almost unparalleled *atrocity*. The high respectability of the family and connexions of the unfortunate young man who is charged with *the* aggravated crime; his heretofore exemplary character and conduct his youth the superior accomplishments, beauty and attractions of the poor murdered girl, compared with those ordinarily possessed by the common herd of unfortunates; the deliberate, premeditated, ferocious character of the assassination; and the desperate means which were resorted to, to prevent exposure and detection; all combine to invest the catastrophe with an interest and a horror that have rarely, if ever, been connected with the occurrence of any homicide, however heart-rending and awful, in any country.

That our readers abroad may be in possession of the full details of this shocking affair, we extract from the daily papers the following facts.

From *Times* of Monday

The deceased, as appeared from the evidence adduced before the Coroner's jury, was a girl of ill fame, and the house of Townsend, of which she was an inmate, was one of the same character. Since the year 1834, she had been frequently visited by Robinson, a young man from the state of Maine, of highly respectable connexions and most excellent general character, a clerk in the store of Joseph Hoxie, Esq. and not yet twenty years of age. On Saturday evening, about 6 o'clock, as Townsend deposed, Robinson rapped at her street door, and she opening it, asked for the deceased, who was called out of the parlor by her; and he and Helen went together to her room. Nothing more was heard from either of them till about 11 o'clock, when Helen came partly down stairs in her night clothes, and calling to Townsend, desired her to bring a bottle of champagne up to her room. Townsend did so; and at that time Robinson was undressed and in bed. She left the wine, and neither Helen nor Robinson were seen again by any in the house, before it was closed for the night, which was about 12 o'clock.

Near 3 o'clock in the morning [. . .] She took the lamp up stairs and first applying it at the door adjoining Helen's, found it locked. She then opened the door of Helen's room; and when she did so, a large body of dense smoke instantly burst out, and nearly suffocated her. [. . .] [She] found Helen lying on her left side dead, and her ride side burned almost to a crisp. [. . .] One of the watchmen, on more closely inspecting her corpse, found a large and deep cut on the right side of her head, a little above the temple, about three inches in length, completely through the skull, and extending into the brain.

The Coroner, on arriving, and being informed of what is above stated, sent for officer Brink, whom he despatched in search of Robinson. The officer found the unfortunate young man in bed with his roommate, and apparently asleep, at his boarding-house, in Dey Street, and informing him of his arrest, Robinson calmly got up and dressed himself, and accompanied the officer to the scene of this horrid tragedy. He appeared no more affected by the horrid spectacle which there presented itself, than if he had neither lot nor part in the matter, and boldly declared that he was wholly innocent of the murder of the unfortunate girl, and ignorant of how or by whom it was perpetrated. He was, however, committed by the Coroner to prison, to await the investigation of the melancholy deed in which he is so unfortunately so deeply implicated.

Amongst the witnesses examined by the Coroner, was Robinson's roommate, who deposed that he went to bed about nine o'clock, and fell asleep, and that waking up in the course of the night, he found Robinson in bed. He asked Robinson how long he had been home, and was told by him that he came home about half-past eleven. The cloak found [at the scene of the crime] was not identified as belonging to Robinson, nor as the one he wore on the preceding night; but on being shown to his roommate the latter with much agitation acknowledged that he knew the cloak, and had seen Robinson wear it.

Whilst Robinson was dressing himself, Mr. Brink noticed that the seat and one side of his pantaloons were much covered with whitewash; and on examination it proved that one side of one of the fences he must have climbed before dropping his cloak, was whitewashed. It is a source of very great regret, that the proofs against young Robinson as the perpetrator of this, one of the most cold-blooded and cruel murders and arsons ever perpetrated in this city, are so fearfully and conclusively strong as to warrant the direct charge by a coroner's jury, and not even leave a loop to hang a doubt upon, that it was the work of his hand. The deceased was a woman of extraordinary beauty, intelligence, and accomplishments, for one in her sphere of life, and is represented to have been uncommonly high-minded and spirited.

Questions

1. This account is reproduced from a New York newspaper for circulation abroad. What do you think that tells us about this event?
2. Why do you think the journalist took such pains in describing Jewett as "uncommonly high-minded and spirited"?
3. Why do you think that the young clerks of America defended Robinson?

MODULE 11

AMERICAN CAPITALISMS AND REGIONAL DEVELOPMENT

The Financial Power of Slavery (1840)

JOSHUA LEAVITT

After Andrew Jackson "disestablished" the Second Bank of the United States, the suddenly deregulated banking sector of the U.S. economy produced a burst of innovation. Raising capital by selling to investors innovative new bonds backed by mortgages on slaves, banks in Louisiana, Alabama, Mississippi, and Florida during the 1830s helped finance the movement of 250,000 enslaved people into the rich cotton land of the Deep South. In just five years, from 1831 to 1836, the investments on slavery's frontier doubled the United States' production of cotton, the world's most widely traded commodity. The price of enslaved African Americans, who were the "capital" that generated the cotton, doubled and then tripled on the New Orleans market. Investors and speculators were making huge amounts by selling cotton, selling slaves, lending money, and producing supplies like the corn and hogs sold to plantations. The boom spread throughout most of the U.S.

But then, the bubble burst. All of the money lent to the South had generated a massive increase in the quantity of cotton being made, and that in turn led to a drop in price. In Britain, many of the biggest cotton brokers collapsed, their trading partners in New Orleans did the same, and banks around the country failed. The cold light of bankruptcy revealed that many slaveowners had mortgaged the same slaves multiple times to take advantage of the loose availability of credit. Banks, likewise, had also played fast and loose, counting on a future in which bond and stock prices, as well as cotton, slave, and land prices, would rise without pause. But this time was not different, after all, and many merchants and bankers and slave owners, in the South especially, were bankrupt. Many moved across the border to Texas, which was at that point an independent republic. Those who had lent money, including numerous Northern banks and merchants who had sold goods on credit, were also in serious financial trouble.

Joshua Leavitt, who had graduated from Yale intending to make a career of the ministry, had turned instead to secular social reform. Over the course of the 1830s, he grew closer to the small but increasingly active antislavery movement. He worked primarily with New York abolitionists like Lewis and Arthur Tappan, who were, ironically, millionaires because of their wholesaling "dry goods" business, which had many Southern customers. Leavitt and the Tappans, for instance, helped form a committee of abolitionists to secure legal representation for the *Amistad* rebels, a group of enslaved Africans who in 1839 seized the slave ship on which they were being transported. But Leavitt also developed a sweeping critique of slavery, which he believed systematically undermined the economic growth of the United States. The Bank of the United States, he argued, had artificially suppressed the cost of credit in the South, passing on the losses that everybody sustained when they lent money to slaveholders. The apparent profits of entrepreneurial endeavors in Southern markets were not real revenues driven by the wealth that cotton generated, but instead a set of unseen transfers from hard-working Northerners. Before 1837, it was harder to find a large audience for such claims, but after the Panic, many Northerners were deeply frustrated with Southern business partners who refused to or were unable to pay their debts.

In this piece, Leavitt argues that recent financial events did depend in part on the corrupt financial practices of slaveholders and their banks, but he also argues that this wasn't just an accident caused by recent policy decisions. Instead, he argues, slavery as an institution inevitably creates corruption and theft from all business partners who deal with enslavers. Like other critics who argued that slavery was actually economically backward, a brake on economic modernization, Leavitt presented slavery as antithetical to what we would now call free-market capitalism. Because slaves had no incentive to labor except fear, and because direct supervision of their labor was not always possible, Leavitt believed (like Adam Smith before him) that slave labor was always inefficient compared to the work done by free wage laborers. Over the twenty years following Leavitt's publication of *The Financial Power of Slavery*, similar attacks on the South's ruling class and its system of human enslavement would become more and more common. Critics like author Frederick Law Olmsted and New York senator William Seward would echo many of Leavitt's claims—as would the German radical economist Karl Marx. These were important because economic attacks on slavery as being essentially precapitalist convinced many white Northerners who weren't concerned by the arguments of other abolitionists, who were intent on proving the immorality of slavery. For nonabolitionist Northerners, the claim that slavery was bad for business and should not be allowed to expand was more telling. The final point Leavitt makes regards the necessity of political discussion of these questions. The two major parties of his day, the Democrats and the Whigs, each depended on Southern votes. The ability of the South to control the parties was part of what Leavitt and other critics called "the Slave Power." Only by convincing Northern whites to leave their existing parties and form one regional party opposed to Southern domination of politics and the credit economy, Leavitt believed, would his part of the country be "free from the exhausting operations of slavery."

The Substance of an Address Delivered in Ohio, in September 1840.

I come now to consider slavery as the chief source of the commercial and financial evils under which the country is groaning. I will not now dwell on the financial evils of a fluctuating policy, such as slavery is continually demanding. It must be evident to the slightest observation, that all the great changes of policy which have successively involved in disaster each and every northern interest, have been introduced by the dictation of the Slave Power.—And it is equally obvious that so long as slavery reigns, by fomenting the strife of party at the North, *we never shall have a settled policy.* The slaveholders are, at this moment, actually creating a new ferment at the North with regard to the tariff, that they may hold the balance of power, and keep the North in subjection, and above all, prevent our uniting by constitutional means to put down the grand evil that eats out our vitals.

Slavery absorbs the available capital of the North, and thus creates periodical revulsions, each one more severe than the last.

[...] When money is scarce, and produce brings a low price, and a man cannot borrow of his neighbor to meet a pressing emergency, and every one feels embarrassed, and crippled, and poor, then it is "hard times." Well, it is "hard times" now, and money is scarce. What has become of the money? It is well known that we have had a long career of industry, and enterprise, and peace. Our people have earned a vast amount of money in the last 15 years. [...] We were really growing rich. The apparent prosperity of the years 1829–36, was very much of it real. [...] [But] I overlooked the train, which was silently and rapidly carrying these accumulations of industry and economy where they could never be recovered. Had the free States been subject to no losses but those of their own extravagance, (great and foolish and criminal as that was,) none, nor all of the alleged causes of our present depression could have produced this deep and protracted embarrassment. [...]

The Boston Daily Advertiser, the leading commercial paper of that city, had an article on the 6th of July last, from an able writer, who furnished a series of essays on the finances and currency of the country. The writer states that there has been a hundred millions of dollars of banking capital sunk in this country since the year 1836, estimating what remains at current prices; but he considers the actual loss much greater, because the stocks are in fact worth much less than they are now quoted.* Then there is a loss to the country of fifteen or twenty millions in irredeemable bank notes. Then there are a hundred and fifty millions loaned to stockholders and directors, and spent in extravagance and speculation. Is it any wonder that we have hard times?

This vast amount of Capital is lost at the South [. . .] ask any man of business in our cities where his capital is gone, and where his hopeless irrecoverable debts are, and he will point to the South. Go among the merchants or the manufacturers, and you will find one complaining of his ten thousand, and other of his hundred thousand, and another of is two or five hundred thousand dollars of southern debts. He would get along very well now, if it were not for that southern debt.—And behind every one of these stands another class, who have sold goods, or lent money, or given their endorsement to others that have trusted their all to the South, and now cannot pay. And behind these another class, and another, and another, until there is hardly a remote hamlet in the free States that has not been directly or indirectly drained of its available capital by the southern debt. [. . .] Nearly every dollar of this is, directly or indirectly, southern debt. Look at Newark. I was told, three years ago, that the people of Newark had three millions of dollars at one time, of protested southern paper. [. . .]

What carried the Capital to be lost at the South?

[. . .] Eighty years ago, a great statesman, in the British Parliament, laid it down as an axiom in political economy, that planters are always in debt. The system of society in a slave-holding community is such as to lead to the contraction of debt, which the system itself does not furnish any means of paying, and which must, therefore, be wiped off by periodical bankruptcies. The ill economy of slave labor

---

* The immense depreciation of stocks since July, 1840, must have added many millions to the aggregate loss.—June, 1841.

is seen in a thousand particulars, the wastefulness of the slaves is exceeded only by the extravagance of the masters, while the social *rank* (!) which is generally conceded to him who exercises power of his fellow-men, is a passport to credit. So long as credit lasts and times are prosperous, the slaveholder is a very good paymaster, but the *general* indebtedness is all the while increasing until a commercial crisis comes, to disclose the true state of things. There is, then, this difference between a slaveholding and a free community. When a pressure comes upon a free people, they immediately begin to curtail their expenses and increase their products, they work harder and save more, wear the old coat, sell all they can, and buy nothing they can do without,—because they intend to pay their debts. The slaveholders, on the contrary, always drive their producers, (the slaves,) to the utmost, and the time of high prices is especially the time of high pressures, and this makes the poor slave pray that cotton may be cheap. Consequently, when hard times come, the slaveholder has no way to increase his products, and there is no way he can curtail the weekly peck of corn, and the yearly shirt and overalls which he expends upon his slaves. And as to his own expenses, it is of more importance to him to maintain his standing as a gentleman planter, that is to pay the rascally shopkeepers, and, therefore, when a pressure comes, we do not see in the slaveholding States any such calculations and efforts to pay the old debt, as are found in the free States. The sense of obligation to pay debts is essentially different between people who always live on the earnings of the poor, and those who have nothing but what they have earned by their own industry. [. . .] The free expect to pay their debts, if it takes years of toil and self-denial; the slaveholder likes to pay debts if it is convenient, but to work and save to pay an old debt enters not into his thoughts. [. . .]

2. Now, look at the next commercial period. The industry and economy produced by hard times among a free and moral people, naturally leads to an accumulation of capital, and, then, to an extension of credit. The productive power of free industry, aided by or-

derly habits and light taxes, has never yet been properly appreciated. [. . .] Were such a community left to its own resources, its prosperity would be constant, and without any assignable limits. But, here we again find ourselves subject to the exhausting operations of slavery— "Our glorious union" makes the slaveholder a fellow-countryman with us, and slavery one of the "institutions of the country." [. . .] The late United States Bank had a capital of 35 millions of dollars, a very small proportion being the property of slaveholders. It also enjoyed the use of the national revenues as deposits, and received and disbursed all moneys of the United States. [. . .] With all these facilities, and a credit greatly enhanced by the financial reputation of its president, Mr. Biddle undertook to equalize the exchanges between the different sections of the country. Exchange is the price paid for the transfer of money from one place to another. It is a service rendered, and has a proper measure of price, as much as carrying wheat to market has.—The principal elements which enter into the calculation of the proper price of exchanges, are the distance and difficulty of transportation, the relation of supply and demand, and the risk arising among the parties drawing and drawn upon. Exchange, if left to itself, would ordinarily make some special allowance for this last consideration in the case of a slaveholding community, because all experience shows that there is a much greater risk in doing business with slaveholders. But the Bank, in equalizing exchanges, entirely disregarded this consideration, which is a part of the real expenses of the business. [. . .] The effect of the credit system in producing the level between the two pools more speedily than could be done through the natural channels, is one of the most instructive subjects of study for our financiers and political economists. One pool is fed by the perennial spring of free labor; the other is trying to fill by the slow and reluctant percolation, through its sands, of slave labor enforced by the lash, but the waste by evaporation and the daily consumption is greater than the flow at the fountain. Our Union as one country leads to a transfer of waters to produce a level, through the natural channels of trade, but the credit system cuts a wider and deeper sluice, and hastens the result; and then slavery knocks the bottom out, and the whole is lost.

It is the Southern Debt which hangs like a mill-stone upon our banks and our individual merchants and manufacturers, and no man can as yet forsee the end. [...] The equalizing of exchanges is doubtless one of the principal causes of the delusion under which our men of business have labored in regard to the stability and real value of Southern trade. Men of business found that they could get their paper cashed, or collect, receive and transmit funds, at the South, in Alabama or Mississippi, at as low a rate as Maine or Ohio; and as such men are little accustomed to look deeply into the causes of things, it is not strange that they should conclude that a southern trade should be relied on, for the long run, as being as stable and secure as trade with northern customers. The great "regulator" assumed it to be so, and why should they not follow? [...] But the day of reckoning came [and] [...] the southern debt hangs between the bank and the merchants, a dead-weight that will probably sink them both.

[And] the great drain of northern capital to the South, to supply the ordinary defalcations of slavery, has been enhanced by the demands of the Domestic Slave Trade. The extent of this trade in human souls cannot be fully ascertained until Congress shall prepare to exercise its constitutional powers by instituting a legal inquiry and requiring a return. Some idea of the whole may be formed, however, from a statement made by a man of business purposes; in the United States Gazette, a leading commercial paper of Philadelphia, Feb. 1, 1840. The writer declares that upwards of forty thousand slaves were imported from the North into the single State of Mississippi, during the year 1836 alone; that in three years the slaves in that State increased 100,000 and that the debt incurred by the planters in those three years for slaves alone was ninety millions of dollars, the greater part secured by mortgage on the plantations and negroes. This trade was carried on by the aid of northern capital. Northern banks and brokers were involved, the United States Bank was involved, numerous banks were started in the South-west on northern capital, the States themselves contracted loans to a vast amount to aids these banks; (of course, borrowing the money at the North,) the dividends were astonishingly large, every body wanted stocks in the Vicksburgh, Grand Gulf, Brandon and other South-west Banks, never was trade so vast and so profitable, until the bubble burst, and all that capital is gone, sunk, irrecoverable. The South has nothing to show for it. Whether the State stocks will ever be paid, will be known in a few years. The bank stock is gone.

Look now at Mississippi. Her hundred thousand laborers were brought from the slave-breeding states, at a cost of a *thousand dollars* a piece, or a total of one hundred millions of dollars. Now, observe, that for this expenditure, the state of Mississippi has nothing to show but a laboring population of a hundred thousand persons. The individuals who sold these persons as property may call themselves the richer. That question I will not now argue. [...] But Mississippi was a new State, and had no available capital, no roads, no canals, no cities filled with surplus wealth, she raised no provision for all this swelling population, she manufactured no clothes, or tools, or carriages—all was to be bought and paid for, at the dearest rate, and all to be done with capital from abroad. And when it was all done, she had nothing to show for it, that was available in the world's market to raise the money from. The "union," the "compromisers of the constitution," the delusive dreams of "southern trade," and the maddening war cry of "amalgamation," blinded the men of the North to furnish first all their own surplus capital, and then, all they could borrow on either side of the ocean; but, all would not suffice to meet such a drain—to fill such a bottomless gulf, and *all broke together!* [...] [And] as long as slavery governs the public policy, the slaveholders will again and again find means to transfer these accumulations of free labor to supply the constant deficiencies of their own miserable system.

[...] There are, therefore, two things essential to the deliverance of the free industry of the North from this intolerable burthen, of supporting slavery and enduring these perilous revulsions and bankruptcies. One is, to develop the true nature of slavery, as an element of our domestic fiscal economy, so that our merchants and manufacturers will understand the danger of carrying on a southern trade. What the abolitionists have been doing for five years, and yet no one has heeded it. Notwithstanding the calamities of the last three years, the merchants and manufacturers of Philadelphia, of New York, of Newark, of Connecticut, of Rhode Island and Boston, are as blind and deaf on the subject of slavery, and as decidedly opposed to anti-slavery meetings and agitations, as they were in the palmy days of 1835. [. . .]

We shall never get the commercial community to read or to think on the subject, until the question can be made to present itself at the ballot box, and the opposers of slavery become the arbiters of destiny to political aspirants. This is one reason why we must have—In the second place, a direct resistance to the political domination of the Slave Power. [. . .] The resistance must come to the ballot box. There is where we have to meet slavery, face to face. [. . .] [Then] the whole nation will see that the great question is, and long has been, whether the Federal Government shall be administered for the good of the whole and the preservation of liberty, or for the good of a handful of slaveholders and the strengthening of slavery.

FREEMEN OF THE NORTH—WHAT IS YOUR DECREE.

Questions

1. What makes Southern slavery so dependent on credit, according to Leavitt? And why can't they borrow from lenders in their own communities?

2. Is the difference between the South and the North primarily economic or cultural, according to Leavitt? Whether or not you agree with his argument, do you think such differences persist?

What is their cause, and how do they shape American capitalism and American politics today?

3. What drove the development of capitalism, in Leavitt's view? What was the essential difference between an Alabama slave labor camp that made cotton, and a Massachusetts cotton mill that turned that cotton into cloth? How did that essential difference shape society as a whole?

4. How did the Slave Power, in Leavitt's view, shape the United States?

Address before the Wisconsin State Agricultural Society (1859)

ABRAHAM LINCOLN

Abraham Lincoln, as one of his most perceptive biographers points out, may have grown up splitting rails and plowing fields on his father's backcountry farms, but he never liked farm labor. Once he left his father's house, he never did that kind of work again, always tried to find jobs that would put him at a desk or standing before a jury, and he always thereafter lived in a town or city. When the Wisconsin State Fair, which was largely a gathering of farmers, asked him to give a keynote address in the fall of 1859, Lincoln delivered a speech that meandered for a long time about the glories of farming and the possibility of inventing a steam-powered plow. But eventually, "the rough man from Illinois" got down to brass tacks.

His main subject, it turned out, was the superiority of a society and economy based on free labor. It was this, he believed, which was creating the great change in human economic life that had become so visible in his lifetime. This provided the inducements both for more diligent labor and for inventing technological enhancements (like, perhaps, a steam plow) that would enable men and women who got to enjoy the fruits of their labor to enjoy still more of those fruits. The South's defenders, during the 1850s, had elaborated what Lincoln calls the "mudsill" theory—that those who labor the hardest are not capable of advanced thought or responsible citizenship. Better, they claimed, to assign that kind of work to a group of people who were supposedly genetically distinct and inferior anyway—that is, African Americans—and better to keep them in slavery so that they could be forced to work.

Lincoln, however, would have none of that. He believed that the community in which he had grown up—and his own climb from penniless laborer to soon-to-be presidential candidate—showed that in a society based on free labor, any man could rise. Each one who did provided more incentive for those who would follow. Those who did not rise had bad luck, or their own lack of ambition, to blame. That was the true relationship between capital and labor. The laborer could become the possessor of capital in capitalist America—at least in the free-labor part of capitalist America. This is the same ideal of America as a place where everyone had an opportunity for greatness that some (like Apollo Creed, even) would call "the American Dream."

Milwaukee, Wisconsin

Members of the Agricultural Society and Citizens of Wisconsin:

[. . .] The world is agreed that *labor* is the source from which human wants are mainly supplied. There is no dispute upon this point. From this point, however, men immediately diverge. Much disputation is maintained as to the best way of applying and controlling the labor element. By some it is assumed that labor is available only in connection with capital—that nobody labors, unless somebody else, owning capital, somehow, by the use of that capital, induces him to do it. Having assumed this, they proceed to consider whether it is best that capital shall *hire* laborers, and thus induce them to work by their own consent; or *buy* them, and drive them to it without their consent. Having proceeded so far they naturally conclude that all laborers are necessarily either *hired* laborers, or *slaves*. They further assume that whoever is once a *hired* laborer, is fatally fixed in that condition for life; and thence again that his condition is as bad as, or worse than that of a slave. This is the *"mud-sill"* theory.

But another class of reasoners hold the opinion that there is no *such* relation between capital and labor, as assumed; and that there is no such thing as a freeman being fatally fixed for life, in the condition of a hired laborer, that both these assumptions are false, and all inferences from them groundless. They hold that labor is prior to, and independent of, capital; that, in fact, capital is the fruit of labor, and could never have existed if labor had not *first* existed—that labor can exist without capital, but that capital could never have existed without labor. Hence they hold that labor is the superior—greatly the superior—of capital.

They do not deny that there is, and probably always will be, *a* relation between labor and capital. The error, as they hold, is in assuming that the *whole* labor of the world exists within that relation. [. . .] Again, as has already been said, the opponents of the *"mud-sill"* theory insist that there is not, of necessity, any such thing as the free hired laborer being fixed to that condition for life. There is demonstration for saying this. Many independent men, in this assembly, doubtless a few years ago were hired laborers. And their case is almost if not quite the general rule.

The prudent, penniless beginner in the world, labors for wages awhile, saves a surplus with which to buy tools or land, for himself; then labors on his own account another while, and at length hires another new beginner to help him. This, say its advocates, is *free* labor—the just and generous, and prosperous system, which opens the way for all—gives hope to all, and energy, and progress, and improvement of condition to all. If any continue through life in the condition of the hired laborer, it is not the fault of the system, but because of either a dependent nature which prefers it, or improvidence, folly, or singular misfortune. [. . .]

[And, Lincoln goes on to argue, an *educated* population of free laborers, especially farmers, will enable the kinds of technological discoveries that have enhanced human life and broken down the walls of the Malthusian cul-de-sac to continue on and on, pushing living standards and opportunities for both labor and capital continually forward.]

[. . .] No other human occupation opens so wide a field for the profitable and agreeable combination of labor with cultivated thought, as agriculture. I know of nothing so pleasant to the mind, as the discovery of anything which is at once *new* and *valuable*—nothing which so lightens and sweetens toil, as the hopeful pursuit of such discovery. And how vast, and how varied a field is agriculture, for such discovery. Every blade of grass is a study; and to produce two, where there was but one, is both a profit and a pleasure. And not grass alone; but soils, seeds, and seasons—hedges, ditches, and fences, draining, droughts, and irrigation—plowing, hoeing, and harrowing—reaping, mowing, and threshing—saving crops, pests of crops, diseases of crops, and what will prevent or cure them—implements, utensils, and machines, their relative merits, and [how] to improve them—hogs, horses, and cattle—sheep, goats, and poultry—trees, shrubs, fruits, plants, and flowers—the thousand things of which these are specimens—each a world of study within itself.

In all this, book-learning is available. A capacity, and taste, for reading, gives access to whatever has already been discovered by others. It is the key, or one of the keys, to the already solved problems. And not only so. It gives a relish, and facility, for successfully pursuing the [yet] unsolved ones. The rudiments of science, are available, and highly valuable. Some knowledge of Botany assists in dealing with the vegetable world—with all growing crops. Chemistry assists in the analysis of soils, selection, and application of manures, and in numerous other ways. The mechanical branches of Natural Philosophy, are ready help in almost everything; but especially in reference to implements and machinery.

The thought recurs that education—cultivated thought—can best be combined with agricultural labor, or any labor, on the principle of *thorough* work—that careless, half performed, slovenly work, makes no place for such combination. And thorough work, again, renders sufficient, the smallest quantity of ground to each man. And this again, conforms to what must occur in a world less inclined to wars, and more devoted to the arts of peace, than heretofore. Population must increase rapidly—more rapidly than in former times—and ere long the most valuable of all arts, will be the art of deriving a comfortable subsistence from the smallest area of soil. No community whose every member possesses this art, can ever be the victim of oppression of any of its forms. Such community will be alike independent of crowned-kings, money-kings, and land-kings.

Questions

1. Does Lincoln see capitalists and workers as inevitably in conflict? Why or why not? How does this differ from the view of his contemporary Karl Marx?

2. Lincoln's own experience was essential to his development of the idea that every laborer who works for wages paid by someone else can rise to greater independence over time. How typical was his experience? Is his own life history applicable to today's iteration of capitalism?

3. Why do you think Lincoln doesn't spend any time here talking about the injustice of slavery, the moral wrong of racism, or his own plans (if he had them) for a United States in which slavery would not only no longer exist, but in which all Americans would enjoy equal access to opportunity? Does he avoid the question of racial equality or slavery's morality/immorality because he is a racist?

Nature's Metropolis: Chicago and the Great West (1991)

WILLIAM CRONON

William Cronon, as University of Wisconsin historian, describes many aspects of the massive impact of the city of Chicago on the development of American capitalism. Some of the most revealing insights, however, come from his discussion of the repeated transformations in the transportation, storage, and sale of wheat. The story here starts after the invention of the grain elevator, which replaced wheat sacks by storing in bulk the wheat grown by Midwestern farmers and sent to Chicago by rail. But the innovation here was not the elevator but the process that surrounded it instead. Before the wheat ever reached the elevators, someone had graded the wheat, issued the farmer a receipt for X pounds of wheat of grade Y, and directed the wheat to a specific elevator for wheat of grade Y. And that is the beginning of how wheat was turned not only into a commodity, but into an object of financial speculation.

European demand for grain expanded during the Crimean War [. . .] American wheat exports doubled in volume and tripled in value during 1853 and 1854, while domestic prices rose by more than 50 percent. The surge of foreign buying had impressive effects in Chicago. Between 1853 and 1856, the total amount of grain shipped from Chicago more than tripled, with 21 million bushels leaving the city in 1856 alone. As volume increased and traders found it more convenient to do their business centrally, attendance at daily [Chicago Board of Trade, where wheat was often traded] meetings rose. Rather than argue over prices amid heaps of grain in streets and warehouses, traders—usually working on commission for real owners and purchasers—brought samples to the Board's meeting rooms, dickered over prices, and arranged contracts among buyers and sellers. The greater the number of traders who gathered in a single market, the more efficient and attractive that market became. By 1856, Board leaders felt confident enough of their organization's importance that they stopped serving cheese, crackers, and ale to encourage attendance. The advantages of the centralized market were soon so great that no serious grain merchant could afford not to belong, and so the Board began to issue membership cards that traders had to show to a doorkeeper before entering the meeting rooms. Daily meetings on the floor of what was beginning to be called 'Change (short for "Exchange") soon became so crowded that the Board moved to newer quarters on the corner of LaSalle and South Water streets.

[. . .] By promulgating rules which all traders using its market agreed to follow, the Board in effect set uniform standards for the city as a whole, and for its grain-raising hinterland as well. Its system of regulations, proposed for the first time in 1856, restructured Chicago's market in a way that would forever transform the grain trade of the world. In that year, the Board made the momentous decision to designate three categories of wheat in the city—white winter wheat, red winter wheat, and spring wheat—and to set standards of quality for each. . . [if] a shipment represented a particular "grade" of grain, then there was no harm in mixing it with other grain of the same grade. Farmers and shippers delivered grain to a warehouse and got in return a receipt that they or anyone else could redeem at will. Anyone who gave the receipt back to the elevator got in return not the original lot of grain but an equal quantity of equally graded grain. A person who owned grain could conveniently sell it to a buyer simply by selling the elevator receipt, and as long as both agreed that they were exchanging equivalent quantities of like grain. [. . .] The grading system allowed elevators to sever the link between ownership rights and physical grain, with a host of unanticipated consequences.

To make sure that the city's elevators applied these grades consistently in filling their bins, Board members in 1857 for the first time resolved to appoint an official "grain inspector of the city at large" who would be "competent and a good judge of the qualities of the different kinds of grain." [. . .] To enable inspectors to do their work, the Board got the city's elevator operators to agree [. . .] [to] allow inspectors to enter warehouses to make sure that the grain in individual bins was actually of the grade that the elevator claimed it to be. [. . .] Inspection underpinned the integrity of the grading system, which underpinned the integrity of the elevators, which underpinned the integrity of the Board's own markets. The Board's right to impose standardized grades and inspection rules on [. . .] the Chicago market as a whole—was written into Illinois law in 1859, when the state legislature granted the organization a special charter as "a body politic and corporate." [. . .] The effect of the charter was that the Chicago Board of Trade—a private membership organization of grain merchants—became a quasi-judicial entity with substantial legal powers to regulate the city's trade.

By 1859, then, Chicago had acquired the three key institutions that defined the future of its grain trade: the elevator warehouse, the grading system, and, linking them, the privately regulated central market governed by the Board of Trade. Together, they constituted a revolution. [. . .] The changes in Chicago's markets suddenly made it possible for people to buy and sell grain not as the physical product of human labor on a particular tract of prairie earth but as an abstract claim on the golden stream flowing through the city's elevators.

Chicagoans began to discover that a grain elevator had much in common with a bank—albeit a bank that paid no interest to its depositors. Farmers or shippers took their wheat or corn to an elevator operator as if they were taking gold or silver to a banker.

After depositing the grain in a bin, the original owner accepted a receipt that could be redeemed for grain in much the same way that a check or banknote could be redeemed for precious metal. Again as with a bank, as long as people were confident that the elevator contained plenty of grain, they did not need to cash the receipt to make it useful. [. . .] Instead of completing a sale by redeeming the receipt and turning over the physical grain to a purchaser, the original owner could simply turn over the receipt itself. The entire transaction could be completed—and repeated dozens of times—without a single kernel of wheat or corn moving so much as an inch. The elevators effectively created a new form of money, secured not by gold but by grain. Elevator receipts, as traded on the floor of 'Change, accomplished the transmutation of one of humanity's oldest foods, obscuring its physical identity and displacing it into the symbolic world of capital.

The elevator helped turn grain into capital by obscuring and distancing its link with physical nature, while another new technology extended that process by weakening its link with geography. In 1848, the same year that Chicago merchants founded the Board of Trade, the first telegraph lines reached the city. [. . .] By the Civil War, there were 56,000 miles of telegraph wire throughout the country, annually carrying some five million messages with lightning speed.

Because commodity prices were among the most important bits of information that traveled the wires, the coming of the telegraph meant that eastern and western markets began to move in tandem much more than before. As a result, those with the best access to telegraph news were often in the best position to gauge future movements of prices. [. . .] [But] although telegraphic information created speculative opportunities [. . .] it also increased the efficiency of regional markets by giving traders throughout the country speedier access to the same news. [. . .] The telegraph brought prices in distant places closer together by reducing the chance that people would act on bad information. In the wake of the telegraph, news of western harvests brought instant shifts in New York markets, while news of European wars or grain shortages just as rapidly changed prices in Chicago. Local events—a drought, say, or an early frost—ceased to be so important in setting prices for grain or other crops. If local circumstances forced up prices at one place, the telegraph allowed knowledgeable buyers to go elsewhere, driving local prices back down. As markets became more efficient, their prices discounted local conditions and converged with regional, national, and even international price levels. The wider the telegraph's net became, the more it unified previously isolated economies. The result was a new market geography that had less to do with the soils or climate of a given locality than with the prices and information flows of the economy as a whole.

[. . .] "To arrive" contracts in combination with standardized elevator receipts made possible Chicago's greatest innovation in the grain trade: the futures market. "To arrive" contracts solved a problem for grain shippers by ending their uncertainty about future price changes; at the same time, they opened up new opportunities for speculators who were willing to absorb the risk of price uncertainty themselves. If one was willing to gamble on the direction of future price movements, one could make a "to arrive" contract for grain one did not yet own, since one could always buy grain from an elevator to meet the contract just before it fell due. This is exactly what speculators did. Contracting to sell grain one didn't yet own—"selling short"—enabled one to gamble that the price of grain when the contract fell due would be lower than the contract's purchaser was legally bound to pay. By promising to deliver ten thousand bushels of wheat at seventy cents a bushel by the end of June, for instance, one could make $500 if the price of wheat was actually only sixty-five cents at that time, since the buyer had contracted to pay seventy cents whatever the market price. When June came to an end, one had only to buy the necessary number of elevator receipts at their current price on the Chicago Board of

Trade, and use them to fulfill the terms of the contract. [. . .] It is impossible to fix the earliest date at which a full-fledged futures market existed in Chicago. The city's newspapers commented on the frequency of sales for future delivery as early as the Crimean War (1853–56). [. . .] During the Civil War, the Union army's demand for oats and pork generated a huge speculative market in those commodities, which finally helped institutionalize futures trading as a standard feature of the Chicago Board of Trade. It was no accident that the Board adopted its first formal rules governing futures contracts in 1865.

[. . .] By the second half of the 1860s[,] alongside the older, more familiar market, in which traders bought and sold elevator receipts for grain actually present in the city, there was a growing market in contracts for the future delivery of grain that perhaps did not even exist yet. These new contracts [. . .] referred not to actual physical grain but to fixed quantities of standardized grades of grain. They called for delivery not at the moment the contract was struck but at a future date and time that was also standardized by the Board's rules. The contract, in other words, followed a rigidly predefined form, so that, as Henry Emery noted, "only the determination of the total amount and the price is left open to the contracting parties." This meant that futures contracts—like the elevator receipts on which they depended—were essentially interchangeable, and could be bought and sold quite independently of the physical grain that might or might not be moving through the city.

Moreover, the seller of such a contract did not necessarily even have to deliver grain on the day it fell due. As long as the buyer was willing, the two could settle their transaction by simply exchanging the difference between the grain's contracted price and its market price when the contract expired. Imagine, for instance, that Jones sold Smith a futures contract for 10,000 bushels of No. 2 spring wheat at 70 cents a bushel, to be delivered at the end of June. If that grade was in fact selling for 68 cents a bushel on June 30, Jones could either purchase 10,000 bushels at the lower price and deliver the receipts to Smith or—more conveniently still—accept a cash payment of $200 from Smith to make up the difference between the contract price and the market price. Had the wheat cost 72 cents on June 30, on the other hand, Jones would have paid Smith the $200.

In either case, Jones and Smith could complete their transaction without any grain ever changing hands. Although those who sold futures contracts were legally bound to deliver grain if requested to do so, in practice they rarely had to. As the historian Morton Rothstein has aptly put it, the futures market, when viewed in the most cynical terms, was a place where "men who don't own something are selling that something to men who don't really want it." Resolving this apparent paradox reveals the extent to which the Chicago grain market had distanced itself from the agricultural world around it. The futures market was a market not in grain but in the price of grain. By entering into futures contracts, one bought and sold not wheat or corn or oats but the prices of those goods as they would exist at a future time. Speculators made and lost money by selling each other legally binding forecasts of how much grain prices would rise or fall.

Questions

1. What kind of effects might you think that the increased volume of grain coming through Chicago, plus the increased efficiency and production and trade, would have had on the overall real price of wheat? Could that have influenced life outside of the U.S.? If so, how? What about the lives of traditional wheat farmers in Europe?
2. How did the telegraph help make futures contracts not only possible but also potentially *necessary*—if, that is, entrepreneurs were going to be interested in putting money into wheat?

3. Did the government (of the U.S., or Illinois, or Chicago) shape the emergence of this wheat market at all, or was it a creation of the free market?
4. Think about the possible economic, social, environmental, or cultural effects of futures contracts. Were futures contracts a good thing or a bad thing, or is that distinction irrelevant?

The Monied Metropolis: New York City and the Consolidation of the American Bourgeoisie, 1850-1896 (2001)

SVEN BECKERT

In the late nineteenth century, technological changes like the emergence of massive railroad networks, world markets linked by steam travel, the mass production of steel and other basic goods, and the emergent American corporation began to produce rapid economic transformations in the United States. The economy was becoming thoroughly industrial, and that, in turn—along with the victory of the North over the South in the Civil War—led to profound social changes. One of the most important was the development of a new economic elite, one that thought of itself as fundamentally different from the people whom it employed and who bought the products of its factories. Nor did this new elite directly manage the factories, or design their production processes. The new rich didn't pretend to be equal citizens of a republic, or try to hide their incredible wealth; instead, they displayed it in the showiest ways possible.

In all of these ways, the late-nineteenth-century American elite was very different from the people who had reaped the gains of the first, pre–Civil War era of industrial transformation. In the following passages from the introduction of his important book about the emergence of America's new superwealthy class, Harvard historian Sven Beckert explains how these millionaires, multimillionaires, and hangers-on increasingly defined the new industrial working classes as a dangerous and unworthy group, not to be trusted with the reins of democracy. In short, the "American bourgeoisie," as he calls them, were also defining themselves as a separate and distinct class.

On February 10, 1897, at the tail end of the most severe economic depression the United States had experienced in the nineteenth century, 700 merchants, industrialists, bankers, and professionals assembled at New York's Waldorf-Astoria Hotel for a costume ball. Invited by lawyer Bradley Martin and his wife Cornelia, the guests arrived in fancy historic costumes. Fifty celebrants impersonated Marie Antoinette, while others, according to the *New York Times*, came dressed as "Kings and Queens, nobles, knights, and courtiers whose names and personalities take up pages of history." Real estate mogul John Jacob Astor, wearing a Henry of Navarre costume, brandished a sword decorated with jewels; Ruth Hoe, daughter of printing press manufacturer Robert Hoe, "appeared in a dainty Louis XIV"; banker J. P. Morgan donned a Moliere costume; and Caroline Astor had gems worth $250,000 sewn into her dress. Cornelia Martin, not to be outdone, wore a necklace once owned by none other than Marie Antoinette herself. To receive her guests, Cornelia Martin sat on a raised platform resembling a throne, her husband, Bradley Martin, standing next to her, wearing a "Court dress of Louis XV., white and pink brocaded satin, knee breeches, white silk hose, diamond buckles on low, red-heeled shoes; powdered wig." Furthering such aristocratic pretensions, the rooms themselves were decorated to resemble the great hall of Versailles, and the guests dined on such delicacies as "Terrapene decossee a la Baltimore" and "Sorbet fin de Siecle." [...]

The ball was so lavish and ostentatious that it galvanized all of New York, making it the "universal and engrossing subject of interest and discussion." Cornelia Martin had justified the extravaganza as helping the country overcome the depression, arguing that it would "give an impetus to trade." Many New Yorkers, if we are to believe the *New York Times*, objected to such rationalizations in the midst of economic crisis, and threats of bombs kept not only New York's police but also a hired army of Pinkerton detectives on alert, watching "for thieves or for men of socialistic tendencies." As a further precaution, the first-floor windows of the Waldorf Hotel were nailed shut.

This "most elaborate entertainment that has ever taken place in the history of the metropolis" pointed to a dramatic departure from the past." The event and the frame of mind that inspired it were part of a series of transformations that had remade the city's economic elite between 1840 and 1890, economically, socially, ideologically, and politically. Forty years earlier, New York's wealthy citizenry, steeped in the country's republican heritage and the moral imperatives of frugality and thrift, would have looked with disdain upon the ostentatious displays of wealth and conspicuous consumption that flourished at century's end. Championing northern society as the land of liberty and equal opportunity in opposition to Europe and the American South, they could not have imagined a world of such deep class hostilities evident in bomb threats, boarded windows, and Pinkertons. And in contrast to the armed-camp setting in which bourgeois New Yorkers of the 1890s displayed their social position to the world, New York's "respectable classes" forty years earlier had proudly paraded up and down Broadway each afternoon exhibiting their status to one another and to the city, a ritual in which they shared public space with other social groups. Indeed, the Martins' ball was far removed from a time when Alexis de Tocqueville observed that "in the United States the more opulent citizens take great care not to stand aloof from the people; on the contrary, they constantly keep on easy terms with the lower classes: they listen to them, they speak to them every day." The ball symbolized other changes as well: Forty years earlier, manufacturers and merchants would hardly ever have assembled at the same social occasions. And while forty years earlier "society" events usually brought only upper-class New Yorkers together, now the Martins' ball was national in scope, with "people [coming] from distant cities to attend." The ostentatious display of riches, the depth of class conflict, the national reach of social networks, and the unification of New York's upper class across economic sectors evident at the ball symbolized a significant departure from antebellum times. [. . .]

This book [. . .] is about the making of a social class: New York City's bourgeoisie [. . .] [and] about the tremendous power upper-class New Yorkers amassed during the second half of the nineteenth century and how they employed this power. [. . .] From the factory floor to the opera house, from the family parlor to Congress [. . .] bourgeois New Yorkers dominated the drama of production, culture, ideas, and politics. [. . .] Their capital helped to revolutionize the way most Americans worked and lived, effectively forging their firms into the most powerful institutions of nineteenth-century America. [. . .] [They played an] active role in making the trajectory of American labor "exceptional."

It is striking, indeed, that nowhere else in the world did an economic elite emerge as powerful as that of New York City. [. . .] Upper-class power was such that more than a hundred years later, it is not presidents but prominent bourgeois New Yorkers, such as John D. Rockefeller and J. P. Morgan, who still symbolize the age to most Americans. Consequently, understanding the history of this economic elite in the nation's greatest metropolis is critical to understanding the history of the United States in the last half of the nineteenth century. [. . .]

It was in New York that these developments unfolded most dramatically and from there had the greatest impact on the rest of the nation. Capital and capitalists gather in cities, and nowhere did economic, social, and political power coalesce more than in New York City. New York's bourgeoisie dominated the nation's trade, production, and finance and served as the gatekeeper of America's most important outpost in the Atlantic economy. The city's merchants, bankers, and industrialists staged the most elaborate social events anywhere, setting the bourgeois standard for the nation. And their economic, social, and political power reverberated from California to South Carolina, from the factory to the farm, from City Hall to the White House. [. . .] Throughout the Western world, the nineteenth century saw the rise of the bourgeoisie and bourgeois society. As a result of the unfolding of capitalist economies and the emancipation of society from the state, owners of capital decisively shaped economic change and the newly emerging societies. As the first elite not to derive its status from the accidents of birth and heritage, the rising bourgeoisie worked hard, lived in modest comfort, and celebrated individual accomplishment. Accumulating ever more capital and power, this new social class gained the upper hand over an older, feudal, social elite and eventually shaped the economy, ideology, and politics of all Western nations.

In the United States, the history of this social class was exceptional. In the absence of an aristocracy or a feudal state, bourgeois society and the bourgeoisie burst more powerfully onto the scene than anywhere else. By the end of the American Revolution, a socially distinct group of merchants had gained ever more prominence in the cities of the eastern seaboard. During the second quarter of the nineteenth century, these traders were joined by a group of artisans who had recently turned into manufacturers, and who were accumulating capital in production, not commerce. Unlike in Europe, where conflicts with an entrenched aristocracy at times drove bourgeois citizens to articulate shared identities as early as midcentury, the economic elite of the United States did not forge such bonds. While both merchants and industrialists developed social networks, cultural orientations, and institutions, as well as ideas and politics that diverged from those of farmers on the one side and workers on the other, even by as late as the 1850s they remained divided, articulating sharply different identities, creating competing social networks, and envisioning very different kinds of political economies.

By the 1870s and 1880s, however, bourgeois New Yorkers articu-
lated a consciousness of separate class identity. In a process that ac-
celerated during the depression of the 1870s, upper-class social life
and politics increasingly manifested a new and greater distance from
other groups—especially from workers, whom the economic elite
perceived as a double threat to their economic and political power.
As a result of these fears, many elite New Yorkers abandoned their
belief in a socially cohesive society without deep class divisions and
their reluctant wartime support for a state-sponsored social revolution in the South. Instead, they advocated the unquestioned primacy
of unregulated markets and, most dramatically, restriction of suffrage
rights in municipal elections. [. . .]

The overthrow of slavery and the destruction of the political
power of slaveholders sped the economic development of the North,
benefiting industrialists and bankers while increasing the political
power of the northern bourgeoisie over the federal government. It
also provided the basis upon which different capitalists could find
common ground. Before the war, the city's industrialists, in particular,
had embraced the emancipatory promises of republicanism, seeing
in the eradication of slavery, or at least its limitation, the possibility
for preventing the emergence of a permanent proletariat. Merchants,
in contrast, aimed at building a paternalist relationship to the city's
workers, supported by the profits derived from a slave-based plantation economy. When the war destroyed slavery, it also destroyed the
grounds for these arrangements.

The destruction of slavery, in effect, moved the process of pro-
letarianization to center stage. During the war and its aftermath,
those segments of New York's economic elite who based their
economic activities on wage labor—namely, industrialists and
financiers—became the dominant segment within the bourgeoisie itself. A coincidental challenge from the increasingly militant
workers in the North compelled merchants, financiers, and industrialists to unify in defense of property rights, and to become more

ambivalent about democracy, in fact, challenging some of their older assumptions about the nature of society. Many of them also increased the amount of capital they controlled, thus sharpening social inequality. As a result, the emancipatory vision of many antebellum bourgeois New Yorkers, with its universalist preoccupations, gave way to an articulation of class identities. Their political ideas focused ever more narrowly on the guarding of their own elevated social position. A new industrial liberalism replaced the producerist liberalism of antebellum manufacturers and the communitarian liberalism of merchants. New York's bourgeoisie was made and had made itself.

Questions

1. What role did the destruction of slavery play in transforming the upper class in the late nineteenth-century United States? Those who tore down the system of slavery often said that they were destroying "aristocracy," so the outcome Beckert describes was an ironic one. Are there similar causes and effects in more recent U.S. history, perhaps leading to the emergence of new elites based on finance or technology?

2. What did the display put on by the New York elite indicate? With labor unrest and complaints about plutocrats on the rise, plus the tensions engendered by a national depression, why would they go to such lengths to impersonate a French aristocracy that died under the guillotine?

3. Why did this new elite group concentrate above all in New York, rather than in Chicago? What developments in corporate, financial, political, or transportation networks would have led them to focus on New York as their center of social gravity?

PART III

MAKING CORPORATE
CAPITALISM

MODULE 12

SECOND INDUSTRIAL
REVOLUTION

Railroaded: The Transcontinentals and the Making of Modern America (2011)

RICHARD WHITE

The work of historian Richard White has long been considered among the most innovative around, whether he is writing about the environment or Native Americans, or using the resources and possibilities of digital history to get students and scholars alike to think about the importance of geography, distance, and the space in between things. But his book on the expansion of U.S. railroad networks across the continent to the Pacific touched a number of nerves, proving highly controversial. Instead of seeing the men whose companies built and operated the transcontinental railroads as heroes who linked a continent together, he seemed to depict them as scam artists who convinced investors, the tax-paying public, and government officials to hand over the equivalent of billions of dollars in financing for railroads that could never be profitable. Is he being unfair? Or do these railroad tycoons sound all too familiar?

This selection begins with the 1884 arrival of Charles Francis Adams, Jr., the grandson of former president John Quincy Adams, as the president of the Union Pacific Railroad. The Union Pacific had completed the first intercontinental railroad in 1869. Not long afterward, it was revealed that the Union Pacific had bribed numerous congressmen, who in return helped the railroad issue bonds underwritten by the federal government. Many other financial shenanigans followed, and by 1880 the Wall

Street tycoon Jay Gould had emerged as the company's dominant shareholder.

In June of 1884 Charles Francis Adams became president of the Union Pacific Railroad. [. . .] In 1878 he had been named a government director on the board of the Union Pacific and then had rejoined the board as a regular member in 1882. Adams had often been critical of railroad practice, particularly Union Pacific practice. Western railroads issued too many securities, received too little money from them, and, as a result, carried large loads of debt. They were too often corrupt and run for the profit of insiders. Poorly constructed and poorly managed, these railroads expanded too quickly into regions without the traffic to sustain them and duplicated their rivals' tracks where there was traffic. Adams came to the Union Pacific to rescue it. [. . .] Adams knew that he was taking on a "concern [. . .] in bad repute, heavily loaded with obligations, odious in the territory it served." He became president in the midst of the Panic of 1883–84, after workers on the railroad had just forced the management to rescind wage cuts. Congress was demanding the immediate payment of money due. [. . .]

Many of the Union Pacific's problems could be traced back to Jay Gould. [. . .] The Adams family was as illustrious and well-connected as any in the United States; Gould rose from poor beginnings. [. . .] Adams wanted the railroad out of politics; Gould knew that the railroad depended on politics. In some ways, however, Gould and Adams were not so different. [. . .] Both Gould and Adams had the same grim view of western railroads as hopelessly overbuilt, badly managed, and in need of reordering. [. . .] [Adams concluded that] "on any honest basis of capitalization the road would, even at the lowest rate which has ever been proposed, return not only a fair, but a large profit." Jay Gould did not differ on the essentials. In 1887 he rather disingenuously told the Pacific Railway Commission [. . .] that the Union Pacific "would be all right if it were capitalized on a moderate basis" but that it could not compete with new roads costing $12,000 per mile.

In calling the Union Pacific overcapitalized, Adams and Gould meant that its outstanding securities had a greater par value than its actual assets. Late nineteenth- and early twentieth-century economists made a distinction between actual capital and capitalization. Capital was "tangible assets, such as real estate, rails, locomotives and cars, [. . .] good will [. . .] contracts, alliances, and reputation." In short, all the assets of a corporation "intended for continuing productive use." Capitalization, on the other hand, represented the firm's outstanding securities: "the aggregate of this paper certification of value, taken at par."

In a well-run corporation funded debt and other securities—money obtained from stocks and bonds—translated rather easily into capital assets, and overcapitalization signified the acquisition of debt without the parallel acquisition of equivalent assets. The commonplaces of transcontinental financing—the giving away of stock, the selling of bonds at deep discounts, and the insider contracts for construction—virtually ensured that these roads' capitalization was far in excess of their assets. A company with low capitalization could charge lower rates and required less income to pay interest and reasonable dividends than a company with high capitalization. This was the problem that Adams was describing in the case of the Union Pacific, but the real question was how the Union Pacific came to be overcapitalized.

The concept of overcapitalization is now largely unfashionable and a little archaic. The idea of leverage has largely replaced it. Even in the nineteenth century Jay Gould argued that the value of securities, like the value of assets, was simply what people were willing to pay for them. Sometimes it was wise to accrue large debts to acquire assets; sometimes it wasn't. Time and the markets would make it

clear whether accruing debt was wise. The issue was one of risk. If you
could borrow at high rates and still make a profit with the borrowed
money, then you were simply being an entrepreneur, a risk taker, and
a person to be admired, not condemned. [...]

Jay Gould, widely suspected of looting the Union Pacific, wanted
to shift attention elsewhere [...] so he told a story that made overcapitalization the story of risk, the monetary cost of a heroic past.
When the Union Pacific was built, he told the members of the Pacific
Railway Commission in 1887, it paid "as high as $5 or $10 a piece for
ties, and the iron rails, I think, cost $300 a ton, and men had to take
their lives in their hands to go out there. You know the Indians were
after them." With a minimum of 2,640 ties to a mile, Gould conjured
up a road whose ties alone cost from $13,200 to $26,400 for each
mile built. With iron at $300 a ton, an additional $26,400 would be
necessary to build a mile of road. The unassembled, ungraded road—
without spikes, wooden trestles, fishbars, bolts, buildings, ballast, and
the labor to assemble them—already supposedly cost from $39,000
to $52,800 a mile. Listen to Gould's story, and overcapitalization was
simple. [...] The reason the railroad cost so much was that such a
risky enterprise forced promoters to promise great rewards and pay
high prices. Economists in more mundane ways still tell Gould's
story. The high cost of capital in the Pacific Railway—the difference
between the face value of securities and what people actually paid for
them—can be taken as investors' rational calculation of risk.

Gould knew all about risk, but he was also a magician. Like any
magician, he sought to create an illusion by attracting spectators' eyes
to one thing and away from the action that actually achieved the
desired result. Gould told simple stories of a heroic past, not complicated stories about exchanges of paper. Slight, perhaps smiling,
speaking softly as he always did, the small, dapper man sitting at
number 10 Wall Street testifying before the Pacific Railway Commission told stories and performed railroad finance. . . .Gould drew
attention to risk in order to attract it away from fraud. [...] That was

the magician's trick. It concealed the secret that both he and Adams, in a rare moment of agreement, wanted kept quiet: overcapitalization was more the result of fraud, deception, and insider dealing than of entrepreneurial risk taking. [. . .] Every Union Pacific train carried its consequences, and every Union Pacific customer paid its freight. [. . .] The Associates [financiers and railroad entrepreneurs like Leland Stanford and Collis P. Huntington, who had organized most of the transcontinental corporations and secured various land grants and support for bond issues from federal and state governments], were chimeras able to change form at will, and by changing form, they created value. . . the Central Pacific, the Southern Pacific, the WDC, and others "were but convertible terms with these four or five movers in them, and they were fused constantly one into the other, and there was no distinction. The corporations were the individuals, and the individuals were the corporations. The Associates proffered a deal, went to the other side of the table, put on another set of hats, and accepted the deal. In the books and ledgers of these companies, trades that appeared to be between a wide variety of entities were not what they seemed. [. . .]

If a western Rip Van Winkle had fallen asleep in 1869 and awakened in 1896, he would not have recognized the lands that the railroads had touched. Bison had yielded to cattle; mountains had been blasted and bored. Great swaths of land that had once whispered grass now screamed corn and wheat. Nation-states had conquered Indian peoples, slaughtering some of them and confining and controlling most of them. Population had increased across much of this vast region, and there were growing cities along its edges. A land that had once run largely north-south now ran mainly east-west. Each change could have been traced back to the railroads.

The railroads' initial contribution to conquest and development was their transport of troops and their supplies. Native resistance to Mexican, Canadian, and American state control persisted longest at a distance from the railroads. The world of isolated posts adrift in a native sea gave way to a world where troops concentrated by rail to the places nearest an outbreak to crush resistance. [. . .] But conquering and dispossessing Indians did little for the railroads in and of itself; to generate traffic, western railroads had to induce both producers and consumers to move west. Henry George, Terence Powderly, and other antimonopolists were wrong in thinking that the railroad corporations sought to hold land for speculative profit. The men who managed the railroads recognized that the most profitable traffic came from a thickly settled country of small freeholders. [. . .] Railroads dealt with speculators, but they preferred selling land to small farmers. [. . .] Like so many carnival barkers, railroad publicity bureaus promoted the virtues of the West and cajoled potential settlers to seize the opportunity that the railroads offered. [. . .] Virtually all the big land grant roads invested in publicity bureaus and immigration agencies to attract settlers. [. . .]

That railroads produced settlement is one of two great truths about agricultural settlement in the American West, and it is modified by a second one: somewhere between the 98th meridian and the 100th meridian the possibilities for agricultural settlement narrowed. Here were the semiarid lands of the American steppe. And farther west lay even less promising lands: the most arid sections of the Great Plains, the Rocky Mountains, and then, running south to north, the Sonoran Desert, the high deserts of the Great Basin, the semiarid Columbian Plateau, and, finally, more mountains to the west. Even on the West Coast, only Oregon's Willamette Valley, sections of the Central Valley in California, and parts of the Santa Clara Valley provided the kind of arable agricultural land for which eastern and European farmers yearned. Everywhere else heavily timbered, infertile, or arid lands promised little for small farmers without large investments of labor and capital. Much of the agricultural history of the late nineteenth and early twentieth centuries was simply the attempt of railroad men, boosters, and farmers to extend settlement deeper into the arid regions. [. . .] West of the 98th meridian settlers came relatively slowly and in disappointingly small numbers. [. . .] Between 1880 and 1890 the Sacramento Valley had lost twenty thousand of its natural increase in population. Nevada actually shrank in population after the railroad arrived. Yet over the course of the generation between 1870 and 1900 the cumulative impact of western railroads on the entire region was tremendous. There were 2 million non-Indians in states lying all or in part west of the line of the Missouri River in 1870. The vast majority of them were in eastern Texas, eastern Kansas, and California. In 1900 there were 10.4 million.

It had taken Anglo-Americans roughly two and half centuries to secure the continent up to the Missouri River. They used the railroads to control the remainder in a generation. Canada and Mexico accomplished the equivalents.

[. . .] [But] the equation of progress with growth, wealth, religion, and "civilization" [. . .] are all part of a long line of "say what you will" justifications of what otherwise might seem unsavory episodes in the American experience. In the end there were more Americans, more American things and products, more American churches and more "civilization," and who could argue with that? In the more pedestrian terms of modern social science, the social benefits of the railroads trumped their costs. [. . .] [Yet] The railroads seemed unable to achieve a balance between too much and too little. They enabled farmers and miners to produce far more cattle, wheat, and silver than the world needed. They opened up some of the most productive farmlands in the world and some of the most unproductive. Poverty, as Henry George observed, increased in the midst of progress.

Regional lines in California and the Midwest could have handled most of the productive traffic. Rail lines connecting Chicago, Kansas City, and St. Louis with the lands east of the 98th meridian would have allowed the settlement of the prairies and other lines connecting California and western Nevada with San Francisco Bay would have created a sufficient Pacific rail network. Long before the Northern Pacific and the Great Northern arrived, the Oregon Railroad and

Navigation Company had given the Northwest a combination of river and rail transportation that allowed the settlement of the great wheat-raising region of the Palouse.

The development of the rest of the region would have been delayed without multiple transcontinentals, but what would have been lost? Mines that glutted the market for silver? The catastrophes that befell both cattle and buffalo on the Great Plains? The suffering of those who settled lands that could not sustain them all over the West? The calamities that afflicted Indians who lost their land, their way of life, and often their lives?

For Joseph Schumpeter the damage capitalism did was the source of its power. In his famous phrase, "creative destruction was its essence." Schumpeter made the entrepreneur's benefits available in the short term, while society often had to wait for its share. The classic deferred gratification of the bourgeoisie was the farthest thing from the entrepreneur's mind. He wanted great wealth, and he wanted it now. As Schumpeter saw it, entrepreneurs must reap more than they sow so that the children of those displaced by their innovations will eat more than their parents. In Schumpeter the abuses of capitalist enterprises, while real, were always transitory; their achievements, at least in the economic realm, seemingly permanent in that they set the stage for further progress as long as the process of creative destruction was allowed to continue. [. . .] [But] in assessing the social utility of the railroads, I want to include social costs harder for economists to measure. I want to be conscious of the price—not necessarily calculated in losses that markets measure—and to consider who benefited and who lost. The issue facing the transcontinental railroads was a simple one. Having built ahead of demand, they had to create traffic in places where there was precious little to sell. Given their high fixed costs, the railroads could not simply wait for profitable traffic to appear. Hauling something, even at a loss, was better than hauling nothing. In attempting to cut economic losses, the railroads helped create both what might be called dumb growth and environmental catastrophes.

Questions

1. How do you evaluate White's argument that the social cost of the transcontinentals was greater than their benefits?
2. The railroads were private corporations, but they made the argument that without special help from the government—land grants and underwriting of securities, in particular—they would have been unable to create the social good that the railroads represented. Was this plausible?
3. Take another look at White's conclusion. Should we side with Schumpeter, or with White? What if we look at our own time?

MODULE 13

LEGITIMATING CAPITALISM

How the Other Half Lives (1890)

JACOB RIIS

Jacob Riis's great documentary study of the slums of Manhattan helped inspire progressive reforms that aimed to right many of the social wrongs he depicted. The New York he studied was increasingly populated by non–English speakers, non-Protestants, and others whom the new American wealthy were defining as fundamentally different from themselves. Xenophobia was rising. In contrast to earlier reform efforts, Riis attempted to present the realities he found as factual data, eschewing the explicit appeal to religiously inspired sentiments of moral benevolence that had been so important to earlier generations of reformers.

The problem of the children becomes, in these swarms, to the last degree perplexing. Their very number makes one stand aghast. I have already given instances of the packing of the child population in East Side tenements. They might be continued indefinitely until the array would be enough to startle any community. For, be it remembered, these children with the training they receive—or do not receive—with the instincts they inherit and absorb in their growing up, are to be our future rulers, if our theory of government is worth anything. More than a working majority of our voters now register from the tenements. I counted the other day the little ones, up to ten years or so, in a Bayard Street tenement that for a yard has a triangular space in the centre with sides fourteen or fifteen feet long, just room enough for a row of ill-smelling closets at the base of the triangle and a hydrant at the apex. There was about as much light in this "yard" as in the average cellar. [. . .] The house contained one hundred and seventy children. [. . .] Sometimes I have doubted that anybody knows just how many there are about. Bodies of drowned children turn up in the rivers right along in summer whom no one seems to know anything about. When last spring some workmen, while moving a pile of lumber on a North River pier, found under the last plank the body of a little lad crushed to death, no one had missed a boy, though his parents afterward turned up. The truant officer assuredly does not know, though he spends his life trying to find out, somewhat illogically, perhaps, since the department that employs him admits that thousands of poor children are crowded out of the schools year by year for want of room. There was a big tenement in the Sixth Ward, now happily appropriated by the beneficent spirit of business that blots out so many foul spots in New York—it figured not long ago in the official reports as an out-and-out hogpen—that had a record of one hundred and two arrests in four years among its four hundred and seventy-eight tenants, fifty-seven of them for drunken and disorderly conduct. I do not know how many children there were in it, but the inspector reported that he found only seven in the whole house who owned that they went to school. The rest gathered all the instruction they received running for beer for their elders. Some of them claimed the "flat" as their home as a mere matter of form. They slept in the streets at night. The official came upon a little party of four drinking beer out of the cover of a milk-can in the hallway. They were of the seven good boys and proved their claim to the title by offering him some.

The old question, what to do with the boy, assumes a new and serious phase in the tenements. [. . .] Caught in the street by the truant officer, or by the agents of the Children's Societies, peddling, perhaps, or begging, to help out the family resources, he runs the risk of being sent to a reformatory, where contact with vicious boys older than himself soon develop the latent possibilities for evil that lie hidden in him. [. . .] [But] I have not forgotten the deputation of raga-muffins from a Mulberry Street alley that knocked at my office door one morning on a mysterious expedition for flowers, not for themselves, but for " a lady," and having obtained what they wanted, trooped off to bestow them, a ragged and dirty little band, with a solemnity that was quite unusual. It was not until an old man called the next day to thank me for the flowers that I found out they had decked the bier of a pauper, in the dark rear room where she lay waiting in her pine-board coffin for the city's hearse. [. . .] With such human instincts and cravings, forever unsatisfied, turned into a haunting curse; with appetite ground to keenest edge by a hunger that is never fed, the children of the poor grow up in joyless homes to lives of wearisome toil that claims them at an age when the play of their happier fellows has but just begun. [. . .] Out of forty-eight boys twenty had never seen the Brooklyn Bridge that was scarcely five minutes' walk away, three only had been in Central Park, fifteen had known the joy of a ride in a horse-car. The street, with its ash-barrels and its dirt, the river that runs foul with mud, are their domain. What training they receive is picked up there. And they are apt pupils. If the mud and the dirt are easily reflected in their lives, what wonder? Scarce half-grown, such lads as these confront the world with the challenge to give them their due, too long withheld, or . . . ? Our jails supply the answer to the alternative.

Questions

1. In Riis's opinion, what seems to shape the behavior of the poor most strongly: environment, or their own choices? What kind of social policy does that conclusion suggest?
2. What kinds of policies would be the most efficient? What kinds of policies with dealing with the social problem of truant youth who sometimes become criminals?

3. What kinds of beliefs about capitalism support prisons, and what kinds of beliefs support interventions like removing children from slums, giving them access to different environments, and moving them to schools where the desperately poor are not the main constituents?

The Omaha Platform (1892)

The Populist Party, also known as the National People's Party, was the most successful third party in American political history. While other democracies have many parties that come in and out of power, the United States has only had three major parties in its history (Whig, Democratic, and Republican) and only two dominant parties since the dissolution of the Whigs in the 1850s. The Populists rose to national prominence in the last decades of the nineteenth century on a rising tide of rural anger. Farmers and small businessmen felt marginalized in an era of rising financial and industrial power. The Populist era's arcane arguments about currency are less about gold than about power. Farmers had borrowed for their mortgages, but with a deflationary currency in an ever-more-global commodities market, they found their profits falling while the real value of their debts rose. The Populists were not communists or socialists. They believed in private property and free markets. What they did not believe in was an economy that, in their view, produced only "tramps and millionaires." The cause of this inequality, they thought, was the rising power of financial and industrial cartels. The problem with capitalism, then, was simply monopolistic conspiracy—a problem that could be solved by federal action.

Assembled upon the 116th anniversary of the Declaration of Independence, the People's Party of America, in their first national convention, invoking upon their action the blessing of Almighty God, put forth in the name and on behalf of the people of this country, the following preamble and declaration of principles:

PREAMBLE

The conditions which surround us best justify our co-operation; we meet in the midst of a nation brought to the verge of moral, political, and material ruin. Corruption dominates the ballot-box, the Legislatures, the Congress, and touches even the ermine of the bench. The people are demoralized; most of the States have been compelled to isolate the voters at the polling places to prevent universal intimidation and bribery. The newspapers are largely subsidized or muzzled, public opinion silenced, business prostrated, homes covered with mortgages, labor impoverished, and the land concentrating in the hands of capitalists. The urban workmen are denied the right to organize for self-protection, imported pauperized labor beats down their wages, a hireling standing army, unrecognized by our laws, is established to shoot them down, and they are rapidly degenerating into European conditions. The fruits of the toil of millions are boldly stolen to build up colossal fortunes for a few, unprecedented in the history of mankind; and the possessors of those, in turn, despise the republic and endanger liberty. From the same prolific womb of governmental injustice we breed the two great classes—tramps and millionaires.

The national power to create money is appropriated to enrich bondholders; a vast public debt payable in legal tender currency has been funded into gold-bearing bonds, thereby adding millions to the burdens of the people.

Silver, which has been accepted as coin since the dawn of history, has been demonetized to add to the purchasing power of gold by decreasing the value of all forms of property as well as human labor, and the supply of currency is purposely abridged to fatten usurers, bankrupt enterprise, and enslave industry. A vast conspiracy against mankind has been organized on two continents, and it is rapidly taking possession of the world. If not met and overthrown at once it forebodes terrible social convulsions, the destruction of civilization, or the establishment of an absolute despotism.

We have witnessed for more than a quarter of a century the struggles of the two great political parties for power and plunder, while grievous wrongs have been inflicted upon the suffering people. We charge that the controlling influences dominating both these parties have permitted the existing dreadful conditions to develop without serious effort to prevent or restrain them. Neither do they now promise us any substantial reform. They have agreed together to ignore, in the coming campaign, every issue but one. They propose to drown the outcries of a plundered people with the uproar of a sham battle over the tariff, so that capitalists, corporations, national banks, rings, trusts, watered stock, the demonetization of silver and the oppressions of the usurers may all be lost sight of. They propose to sacrifice our homes, lives, and children on the altar of mammon; to destroy the multitude in order to secure corruption funds from the millionaires.

Assembled on the anniversary of the birthday of the nation, and filled with the spirit of the grand general and chief who established our independence, we seek to restore the government of the Republic to the hands of "the plain people," with which class it originated. We assert our purposes to be identical with the purposes of the National Constitution; to form a more perfect union and establish justice, insure domestic tranquility, provide for the common defense, promote the general welfare, and secure the blessings of liberty for ourselves and our posterity.

We declare that this Republic can only endure as a free government while built upon the love of the whole people for each other and for the nation; that it cannot be pinned together by bayonets; that the civil war is over, and that every passion and resentment which grew out of it must die with it, and that we must be in fact, as we are in name, one united brotherhood of free men.

Our country finds itself confronted by conditions for which there is no precedent in the history of the world; our annual agricultural productions amount to billions of dollars in value, which must, within a few weeks or months, be exchanged for billions of dollars' worth of commodities consumed in their production; the existing currency supply is wholly inadequate to make this exchange; the results are falling prices, the formation of combines and rings, the impoverishment of the producing class. We pledge ourselves that if given power we will labor to correct these evils by wise and reasonable legislation, in accordance with the terms of our platform.

We believe that the power of government—in other words, of the people—should be expanded (as in the case of the postal service) as rapidly and as far as the good sense of an intelligent people and the teachings of experience shall justify, to the end that oppression, injustice, and poverty shall eventually cease in the land.

While our sympathies as a party of reform are naturally upon the side of every proposition which will tend to make men intelligent, virtuous, and temperate, we nevertheless regard these questions, important as they are, as secondary to the great issues now pressing for solution, and upon which not only our individual prosperity but the very existence of free institutions depend; and we ask all men to first help us to determine whether we are to have a republic to administer before we differ as to the conditions upon which it is to be administered, believing that the forces of reform this day organized will never cease to move forward until every wrong is remedied and equal rights and equal privileges securely established for all the men and women of this country.

PLATFORM

We declare, therefore—

First.—That the union of the labor forces of the United States this day consummated shall be permanent and perpetual; may its spirit enter into all hearts for the salvation of the Republic and the uplifting of mankind.

Second.—Wealth belongs to him who creates it, and every dollar taken from industry without an equivalent is robbery. "If any will not work, neither shall he eat." The interests of rural and civic labor are the same; their enemies are identical.

Third.—We believe that the time has come when the railroad corporations will either own the people or the people must own the railroads, and should the government enter upon the work of owning and managing all railroads, we should favor an amendment to the Constitution by which all persons engaged in the government service shall be placed under a civil-service regulation of the most rigid character, so as to prevent the increase of the power of the national administration by the use of such additional government employes.

FINANCE.—We demand a national currency, safe, sound, and flexible, issued by the general government only, a full legal tender for all debts, public and private, and that without the use of banking corporations, a just, equitable, and efficient means of distribution direct to the people, at a tax not to exceed 2 per cent. per annum, to be provided as set forth in the sub-treasury plan of the Farmers' Alliance, or a better system; also by payments in discharge of its obligations for public improvements.

1. We demand free and unlimited coinage of silver and gold at the present legal ratio of 16 to 1.

2. We demand that the amount of circulating medium be speedily increased to not less than $50 per capita.

3. We demand a graduated income tax.

4. We believe that the money of the country should be kept as much as possible in the hands of the people, and hence we demand that all State and national revenues shall be

limited to the necessary expenses of the government, economically and honestly administered.

5. We demand that postal savings banks be established by the government for the safe deposit of the earnings of the people and to facilitate exchange.

TRANSPORTATION—Transportation being a means of exchange and a public necessity, the government should own and operate the railroads in the interest of the people. The telegraph, telephone, like the post-office system, being a necessity for the transmission of news, should be owned and operated by the government in the interest of the people.

LAND.—The land, including all the natural sources of wealth, is the heritage of the people, and should not be monopolized for speculative purposes, and alien ownership of land should be prohibited. All land now held by railroads and other corporations in excess of their actual needs, and all lands now owned by aliens should be reclaimed by the government and held for actual settlers only.

EXPRESSION OF SENTIMENTS

Your Committee on Platform and Resolutions beg leave unanimously to report the following:

Whereas, Other questions have been presented for our consideration, we hereby submit the following, not as a part of the Platform of the People's Party, but as resolutions expressive of the sentiment of this Convention.

1. RESOLVED, That we demand a free ballot and a fair count in all elections and pledge ourselves to secure it to every legal voter without Federal Intervention, through the adoption by the States of the unperverted Australian or secret ballot system.

2. RESOLVED, That the revenue derived from a graduated income tax should be applied to the reduction of the burden of taxation now levied upon the domestic industries of this country.

3. RESOLVED, That we pledge our support to fair and liberal pensions to ex-Union soldiers and sailors.

4. RESOLVED, That we condemn the fallacy of protecting American labor under the present system, which opens our ports to the pauper and criminal classes of the world and crowds out our wage-earners; and we denounce the present ineffective laws against contract labor, and demand the further restriction of undesirable emigration.

5. RESOLVED, That we cordially sympathize with the efforts of organized workingmen to shorten the hours of labor, and demand a rigid enforcement of the existing eight-hour law on Government work, and ask that a penalty clause be added to the said law.

6. RESOLVED, That we regard the maintenance of a large standing army of mercenaries, known as the Pinkerton system, as a menace to our liberties, and we demand its abolition. [...]

7. RESOLVED, That we commend to the favorable consideration of the people and the reform press the legislative system known as the initiative and referendum.

8. RESOLVED, That we favor a constitutional provision limiting the office of President and Vice-President to one term, and providing for the election of Senators of the United States by a direct vote of the people.

9. RESOLVED, That we oppose any subsidy or national aid to any private corporation for any purpose.

10. RESOLVED, That this convention sympathizes with the Knights of Labor and their righteous contest with the tyrannical combine of clothing manufacturers of Rochester, and declare it to be a duty of all who hate tyranny and oppression to refuse to purchase the goods made by the said manufacturers, or to patronize any merchants who sell such goods.

Questions

1. "The interests of rural and civic labor are the same; their enemies are identical." Who were their mutual enemies? And were all the interests of rural farmers and urban laborers really the same? Where might they have differed?
2. Why did American farmers literally run out of money every harvest?
3. Where would Populist politics intersect with and/or contradict the politics of other groups (Communists, Knights of Labor, American Federation of Labor)?
4. What distinctions did the Populists draw between the U.S. and Europe? Why did those differences matter?

The Populist Vision (2007)

CHARLES POSTEL

The Populist Movement, and its associated People's Party, was the largest third party in American history. Its platforms demanded a complete reconsideration of an industrial "progress" that left rural farmers with unpayable mortgages while urban financiers grew wealthy. Whenever historians have written about populism, interpretations have been heavily inflected by the historians' hopes and fears. Populists have been seen as reactionary racists. Populists have been seen as visionary socialists. In Postel's take, Populists are small business people fighting back against a world based on bigness, where profits are based on economies of scale and not hard work. In his account, which takes account of all the earlier interpretations, Populists are above all a practical group seeking out a way to balance their belief in the market with their desire for individual autonomy. Instead of being "reactionaries," Populists here are activists trying to imagine an alternative capitalism in which progress meant leaving no hardworking American behind.

On Bastille Day, 1894, the *Chicago Times* ran an item on a small revolution in American business. Under the headline, "Florists Nowadays Can Fill Orders in Any Part of the World," the story reported on the telegraphic trade in flowers: "Please send immediately to Mrs.—, at such and such an address in Paris, a dozen American beauty roses, and please have them there in time for dinner." It took several years of experimentation to make such orders a practical reality. "Now it is as easy and only a little more expensive," the Times noted, "to send flowers to an address in any part of the United States or Europe as to an address across your street."

The telegraph had "annihilated time and space," to use the language of the day. The success of this new business, however, was only partly driven by technology. The decisive innovation was in the collective action of the florists, who embraced the new technology, regulated and standardized the flower market, and thereby revolutionized the flower trade. The flower sellers accomplished this through voluntary association—the International Florists' League and later the Florists' Telegraph Delivery (FTD)—reflecting the cooperative impulse coursing through American life.

Although the Times heralded flower sales by telegraph as "one of the remarkable business evolutions of the age," most Americans had far more pressing concerns during the summer of 1894. The country was suffering economic depression. The unemployed marched on Washington. Coal miners and railway workers struck to protect their livelihoods, only to be defeated by state militia and federal troops. Farmers faced another year of falling prices and despair. The great innovations in transport, industry, communications, and global trade had landed American capitalism in the proverbial ditch.

Yet the industrial and agricultural crises brought more than trauma and suffering. They also triggered innovative responses including the Populist revolt—one of the most powerful independent political movements in American history. The political, business, and intellectual elites greeted the Populists with equal shares of fear and derision. The Populists themselves—a broad coalition of farmers, wage earners, and middle-class activists—worked with self-confidence to challenge the status quo. Like the flower sellers, the participants in this movement believed that they could collectively wield new technological and organizational methods to serve their own interests. The power of the Populist movement lay in the efforts of common citizens to shape the national economy and governance. In the process millions of men and women at the lower rungs of society began, to use C. Vann Woodward's phrase, "to think as well as to throb."

Most Populists sought economic and political reform, not the overthrow of existing systems. Culturally, too, the Populists, even those of an iconoclastic bent, tended to share common assumptions with many other Americans. The ethos of modernity and progress swept across the cultural landscape of late nineteenth-century America, driven by the winds of commercial capitalism. The Populists mainly shared this ethos. They mobilized to put their own stamp on commercial development. In doing so, the farmers and other reformers of the Populist movement were as committed to the notion of progress as any social group in post-Civil War America. A firm belief in progress gave them confidence to act. Because they believed in the transforming power of science and technology, they sought to attain expertise and acknowledge for their own improvement. Because they believed in economies of scale, they strove to adapt the model of large-scale enterprise to their own needs of association and marketing. Because they believed in the logic of modernity, the Populist "clodhoppers" attempted to fashion an alternative modernity suitable to their own interests.

The Populist world was too commercially and intellectually dynamic to resemble a traditional society in any meaningful sense of the term. This tells us something important about the nature of late nineteenth-century reform: the men and women of the Populist movement were modern people. The term modern does not mean "good." Nor is it a value judgment across the political spectrum from right to left. Moreover, to say that the Populists were modern does not imply that they were more modern than, say, their Republican or Democratic opponents. Nor does it imply that all rural people shared the Populists' modern sensibility. On the contrary, the Populists understood that the transformations they sought required the uprooting of rural ignorance, inertia, and force of habit. Across much of

America's rural territory, Populism formed a unique social movement that represented a distinctly modernizing impulse.

The Populist country, however, was a commercial environment, bound to global markets. It was an environment of boom and bust, which stretched across most of a continent of commodity farming, mining, railroads, and urban centers. "It is a mixed country in its productive pursuits," as a Farmers' Alliance newspaper explained, "and commercial throughout." The men and women of the reform movement focused their attention on what they understood to be the economic underpinnings of political influence, wealth distribution, and commercial advantage. An Iowa journalist attributed the rise of Populism to this new preoccupation with economics. Prior to the Civil War, he wrote, talk of economics "would have cleared the benches of any town-hall." But the Civil War "obliterated" sentimentality, and the discussion of economics, finance, and revenue "are now heard with attention, intelligence and enthusiasm."

How then to account for the Sturm und Drang of the 1880s and 1890s? Late nineteenth-century social conflict cannot be attributed to a cultural war of resistance against the commercial ethos of progress because this ethos was widely diffused among the contesting camps. This does not signify, however, that the contest lacked substance. Much was at issue.

Farmers' efforts at market regulation collided with the efforts of wholesale agents and other middlemen to accomplish similar ends. The demands of farmers for currency inflation—whether by printing greenbacks or coining silver—threatened the dogmas and profits of bankers and creditors. Workers' struggles for the right to build industrial organizations provoked virtual warfare, as industrialists claimed such rights exclusively for themselves. The capitalist elite pursued a corporate power that left little room for the organized power of the men and women of the fields, mines, or factories. Their corporate vision clashed with the Populist vision of an alternative capitalism in which private enterprise coalesced with both cooperative and state-based economies [. . .] a conflict that all concerned understood as vital to the future of a modern America.

Questions

1. Why do you think historians have such difficulty placing Populism on a political spectrum?
2. Does Postel think that Populists would like to return to a subsistence economy outside the market?
3. Populists took pains to differentiate small business from big business. In what ways was this distinction valid, and in what ways was it not?
4. Agricultural cooperatives that emerged from the Populist movement, like FTD or Sunkist, are still strong in the U.S. agricultural sector. Why do you think cooperative organizations in manufacturing or services have not assumed such a central role in our economy?

The Gospel of Wealth (1901)

ANDREW CARNEGIE

Andrew Carnegie was one of the great industrialists of the nineteenth century. Though he arrived in America as an immigrant and went to work at thirteen, he nonetheless accumulated one of the largest fortunes in history as the founder of Carnegie Steel, which became the core of the future U.S. Steel. He came from nothing, and the meaning of his ascent to stupendous wealth weighed on his conscience as Americans began to wrestle with the meaning of the industrial revolution's success. During the 1880s, he wrote a succession of essays that were eventually gathered into a short book titled *The Gospel of Wealth*, in which he explained how the extreme inequality of industrial capitalism could be squared with a notion of justice. Despite its nod to Christianity, Carnegie dismissed charity to the poor. He believed that the best philanthropy provided education to the poor, who then would be able to better themselves. His *Gospel* was extremely influential in the Gilded Age, and we can see its echoes today in philanthropic organizations like the Gates Foundation.

The problem of our age is the proper administration of wealth, so that the ties of brotherhood may still bind together the rich and poor in harmonious relationship. The conditions of human life have not only been changed, but revolutionized, within the past few hundred years. In former days there was little difference between the dwelling, dress, food, and environment of the chief and those of his retainers.

The contrast between the palace of the millionaire and the cottage of the laborer with us to-day measures the change which has come with civilization.

The farmer has more luxuries than the landlord had, and is more richly clad and better housed. The landlord has books and pictures rarer, and appointments more artistic, than the King could then obtain.

But whether the change be for good or ill, it is upon us, beyond our power to alter, and therefore to be accepted and made the best of. It is a waste of time to criticise the inevitable.

The price we pay for this salutary change is, no doubt, great. We assemble thousands of operatives in the factory, in the mine, and in the counting-house, of whom the employer can know little or nothing, and to whom the employer is little better than a myth. All intercourse between them is at an end. Rigid Castes are formed, and, as usual, mutual ignorance breeds mutual distrust. Each Caste is without sympathy for the other, and ready to credit anything disparaging in regard to it. Under the law of competition, the employer of thousands is forced into the strictest economies, among which the rates paid to labor figure prominently, and often there is friction between the employer and the employed, between capital and labor, between rich and poor. Human society loses homogeneity.

The price which society pays for the law of competition, like the price it pays for cheap comforts and luxuries, is also great; but the advantage of this law are also greater still, for it is to this law that we owe our wonderful material development.

Objections to the foundations upon which society is based are not in order, because the condition of the race is better with these than it has been with any others which have been tried. Of the effect of any new substitutes proposed we cannot be sure. The Socialist or Anarchist who seeks to overturn present conditions is to be regarded as attacking the foundation upon which civilization itself rests, for civilization took its start from the day that the capable, industrious workman said to his incompetent and lazy fellow, "If thou dost not sow, thou shalt not reap," and thus ended primitive Communism by separating the drones from the bees. To these who propose to substitute Communism for this intense Individualism the answer, therefore, is: The race has tried that. All progress from that barbarous day to the present time has resulted from its displacement. Not evil, but good, has come to the race from the accumulation of wealth by those who have the ability and energy that produce it.

We start, then, with a condition of affairs under which the best interests of the race are promoted, but which inevitably gives wealth to the few. Thus far, accepting conditions as they exist, the situation can be surveyed and pronounced good. The question then arises,—and, if the foregoing be correct, it is the only question with which we have to deal,—What is the proper mode of administering wealth?

It will be understood that fortunes are here spoken of, not moderate sums saved by many years of effort, the returns on which are required for the comfortable maintenance and education of families. This is not wealth, but only competence which it should be the aim of all to acquire.

There are but three modes in which surplus wealth can be disposed of. It can be left to the families of the decedents; or it can be bequeathed for public purposes; or, finally, it can be administered during their lives by its possessors. Under the first and second modes most of the wealth of the world that has reached the few has hitherto been applied. Let us in turn consider each of these modes. The first is the most injudicious. In monarchical countries, the estates and the greatest portion of the wealth are left to the first son. The condition of this class in Europe to-day teaches the futility of such hopes or ambitions. The successors have become impoverished through their follies or from the fall in the value of land. Under republican institutions the division of property among the children is much fairer, but the question which forces itself upon thoughtful men in all lands is: Why should men leave great fortunes to their children? If this is done from affection, is it not misguided affection?

As to the second mode, that of leaving wealth at death for public uses, it may be said that this is only a means for the disposal of wealth, provided a man is content to wait until he is dead before it becomes of much good in the world. The cases are not few in which the real object sought by the testator is not attained, nor are they few in which his real wishes are thwarted. In many cases the bequests are so used as to become only monuments of his folly. It is well to remember that it requires the exercise of not less ability than that which acquired the wealth to use it so as to be really beneficial to the community. Men who leave vast sums in this way may fairly be thought men who would not have left it at all, had they been able to take it with them. The memories of such cannot be held in grateful remembrance, for there is no grace in their gifts.

There remains, then, only one mode of using great fortunes; but in this we have the true antidote for the temporary unequal distribution of wealth. Under its sway we shall have an ideal state, in which the surplus wealth of the few will become, in the best sense the property of the many, because administered for the common good, and this wealth, passing through the hands of the few, can be made a much more potent force for the elevation of our race than if it had been distributed in small sums to the people themselves. Even the poorest can be made to see this.

These who, would administer wisely must, indeed, be wise, for one of the serious obstacles to the improvement of our race is indiscriminate charity. It were better for mankind that the millions of the rich were thrown in to the sea than so spent as to encourage the slothful, the drunken, the unworthy. Of every thousand dollars spent in so called charity to-day, it is probable that $950 is unwisely spent; so spent, indeed as to produce the very evils which it proposes to mitigate or cure. He only gratified his own feelings, saved himself from annoyance,—and this was probably one of the most selfish and very worst actions of his life, for in all respects he is most worthy.

If we consider what results flow from the Cooper Institute, for instance, to the best portion of the race in New York not possessed of means, and compare these with those which would have arisen for the good of the masses from an equal sum distributed by Mr. Cooper in his lifetime in the form of wages, which is the highest form of distribution, being for work done and not for charity, we can form some estimate of the possibilities for the improvement of the race which lie embedded in the present law of the accumulation of wealth. Much of this sum if distributed in small quantities among the people, would have been wasted in the indulgence of appetite, some of it in excess, and it may be doubted whether even the part put to the best use, that of adding to the comforts of the home, would have yielded results for the race, as a race, at all comparable to those which are flowing and are to flow from the Cooper Institute from generation to generation. Let the advocate of violent or radical change ponder well this thought.

The rich man is thus almost restricted to following the examples of Peter Cooper, Enoch Pratt of Baltimore, Mr. Pratt of Brooklyn, Senator Stanford, and others, who know that the best means of benefiting the community is to place within its reach the ladders upon which the aspiring can rise—parks, and means of recreation, by which men are helped in body and mind; works of art, certain to give pleasure and improve the public taste, and public institutions of various kinds, which will improve the general condition of the people; in this manner returning their surplus wealth to the mass of their fellows in the forms best calculated to do them lasting good.

Individualism will continue, but the millionaire will be but a trustee for the poor. "The man who dies thus rich dies disgraced."

Questions

1. Carnegie advocates that the wealthiest dispose of their wealth while still alive to form institutions that are "ladders upon which the aspiring can rise," that is, free libraries, free schools, and

free universities. His vision of justice focuses not on present inequality but intergenerational inequality. Do you think his outlook would justify extreme inequality? Should the present-day "appetites" of underpaid workers be neglected for their children's future educated entrepreneurship?

2. Why does Carnegie oppose simple charity?

3. Why does Carnegie oppose waiting until death to dispose of wealth?

4. In the era of the internet, with all its free information, what might Carnegie advocate? Do you think this free information (like MOOCs and Wikipedia) has eliminated barriers to class mobility?

5. The libraries that Carnegie funded were closed by the time his steelworkers got off work each day. Does this undermine his argument?

Twenty Years at Hull-House: With Autobiographical Notes (1910)

JANE ADDAMS

Jane Addams was one of America's most outspoken advocates for the poor during the Progressive era. Settlement houses, like her Hull House in Chicago, were outreach organizations for the poor, especially immigrants and women. Settlement workers like Addams usually came from privileged backgrounds and have been criticized by historians for their attempts to "Americanize" immigrants and their often condescending attitudes toward the poor. While they clearly had assumptions about the causes of poverty that were rooted in a certain middle-class moralism of the period, Addams and her colleagues were exceptionally tolerant of cultural difference. Settlement house women were devoted advocates for those at the bottom of the society struggling to survive in an industrial economy. During the 1890s, they supported a pluralist vision of economic change, believing that some solution, rooted in Christian charity, to the inequities of industrialization would eventually be possible.

Chapter VI: Subjective Necessity for Social Settlements

Other motives which I believe make toward the Settlement are the result of a certain renaissance going forward in Christianity. The impulse to share the lives of the poor, the desire to make social service, irrespective of propaganda, express the spirit of Christ, is as old as Christianity itself. We have no proof from the records themselves that the early Roman Christians, who strained their simple art to the point of grotesqueness in their eagerness to record a "good news" on the walls of the catacombs, considered this good news a religion. Jesus had no set of truths labeled Religious. On the contrary, his doctrine was that all truth is one, that the appropriation of it is freedom. I believe that there is a distinct turning among many young men and women toward this simple acceptance of Christ's message. They resent the assumption that Christianity is a set of ideas which belong to the religious consciousness, whatever that may be. They insist that it cannot be proclaimed and instituted apart from the social life of the community and that it must seek a simple and natural expression in the social organism itself. The Settlement movement is only one manifestation of that wider humanitarian movement which throughout Christendom, but preeminently in England, is endeavoring to embody itself, not in a sect, but in society itself. I believe that this turning, this renaissance of the early Christian humanitarianism, is going on in America, in Chicago, if you please, without leaders who write or philosophize, without much speaking, but with a bent to express in social service and in terms of action the spirit of Christ. There must be the overmastering belief that all that is noblest in life is common to men as men, in order to accentuate the likenesses and ignore the differences which are found among the people whom the Settlement constantly brings into juxtaposition.

The Settlement then, is an experimental effort to aid in the solution of the social and industrial problems which are engendered by the modern conditions of life in a great city. It insists that these problems are not confined to any one portion of a city. It is an attempt to relieve, at the same time, the overaccumulation at one end of society and the destitution at the other; but it assumes that this overaccumulation and destitution is most sorely felt in the things that pertain to social and educational privileges. From its very nature it can stand for no political or social propaganda. It must, in a sense, give the warm welcome of an inn to all such propaganda, if perchance one of them be found an angel. The only thing to be dreaded in the Settlement is that it lose its flexibility, its power of quick adaptation, its readiness to change its methods as its environment may demand. It must be open to conviction and must have a deep and abiding sense of tolerance. It must be hospitable and ready for experiment. It should demand from its residents a scientific patience in the accumulation of facts and the steady holding of their sympathies as one of the best instruments for that accumulation. It must be grounded in a philosophy whose foundation is on the solidarity of the human race, a philosophy which will not waver when the race happens to be represented by a drunken woman or an idiot boy. . . . Their neighbors are held apart by differences of race and language which the residents can more easily overcome. They are bound to see the needs of their neighborhood as a whole, to furnish data for legislation, and to use their influence to secure it. In short, residents are pledged to devote themselves to the duties of good citizenship and to the arousing of the social energies which too largely lie dormant in every neighborhood given over to industrialism. They are bound to regard the entire life of their city as organic, to make an effort to unify it, and to protest against its over-differentiation.

Chapter VIII: Problems of Poverty

This piteous dependence of the poor upon the good will of public officials was made clear to us in an early experience with a peasant woman straight from the fields of Germany, whom we met during our first six months at Hull-House. Her four years in America had been spent in patiently carrying water up and down two flights of stairs, and in washing the heavy flannel suits of iron foundry workers. For this her pay had averaged thirty-five cents a day. Three of her daughters had fallen victims to the vice of the city.

We early found ourselves spending many hours in efforts to secure support for deserted women, insurance for bewildered widows, damages for injured operators, furniture from the clutches of the installment store. The Settlement is valuable as an information and interpretation bureau. It constantly acts between the various institutions of the city and the people for whose benefit these institutions were erected. The hospitals, the county agencies, and State asylums are often but vague rumors to the people who need them most. Another function of the Settlement to its neighborhood resembles that of the big brother whose mere presence on the playground protects the little one from bullies.

I recall a similar case of a woman who had supported her three children for five years, during which time her dissolute husband constantly demanded money for drink and kept her perpetually worried and intimidated. One Saturday, before the "blessed Easter," he came back from a long debauch, ragged and filthy, but in a state of lachrymose repentance. The poor wife received him as a returned prodigal, believed that his remorse would prove lasting, and felt sure that if she and the children went to church with him on Easter Sunday and he could be induced to take the pledge before the priest, all their troubles would be ended. After hours of vigorous effort and the expenditure of all her savings, he finally sat on the front doorstep the morning of Easter Sunday, bathed, shaved and arrayed in a fine new suit of clothes. She left him sitting there in the reluctant spring sunshine while she finished washing and dressing the children. When she finally opened the front door with the three shining children that they might all set forth together, the returned prodigal had disappeared, and was not seen again until midnight, when he came back in a glorious state of intoxication from the proceeds of his pawned clothes and clad once more in the dingiest attire. She took him in without comment, only to begin again the wretched cycle.

Chapter IX: A Decade of Economic Discussion

Fanaticism is engendered only when men, finding no contradiction to their theories, at last believe that the very universe lends itself as an exemplification of one point of view. "The Working People's Social Science Club" was organized at Hull-House in the spring of 1890 by an English workingman, and for seven years it held a weekly meeting. At eight o'clock every Wednesday night the secretary called to order from forty to one hundred people; a chairman for the evening was elected, a speaker was introduced who was allowed to talk until nine o'clock; his subject was then thrown open to discussion and a lively debate ensued until ten o'clock, at which hour the meeting was declared adjourned.

The enthusiasm of this club seldom lagged. Its zest for discussion was unceasing, and any attempt to turn it into a study or reading club always met with the strong disapprobation of the members. In these weekly discussions in the Hull-House drawing room everything was thrown back upon general principles and all discussion save that which "went to the root of things," was impatiently discarded as an unworthy, halfway measure.

I recall one evening in this club when an exasperated member had thrown out the statement that "Mr. B. believes that socialism will cure the toothache." Mr. B. promptly rose to his feet and said that it certainly would, that when every child's teeth were systematically cared for from the beginning, toothaches would disappear from the face of the earth, belonging, as it did, to the extinct competitive order, as the black plague had disappeared from the earth with the ill-regulated feudal regime of the Middle Ages. "But," he added, "why do we spend time discussing trifles like the toothache when great social changes are to be considered which will of themselves reform these minor ills?" Even the man who had been humorous fell into the solemn tone of the gathering.

It was, perhaps, here that the socialist surpassed everyone else in the fervor of economic discussion. He was usually a German or a Russian, with a turn for logical presentation, who saw in the concentration of capital and the growth of monopolies an inevitable transition to the socialist state. He pointed out that the concentration of capital in fewer hands but increased the mass of those whose interests were opposed to a maintenance of its power, and vastly simplified its final absorption by the community; that monopoly "when it is finished doth bring forth socialism." Opposite to him, springing up in every discussion was the individualist, or, as the socialist called him, the anarchist, who insisted that we shall never secure just human relations until we have equality of opportunity; that the sole function of the state is to maintain the freedom of each, guarded by the like freedom of all, in order that each man may be able to work out the problems of his own existence.

I recall a brilliant Frenchwoman who was filled with amazement because one of the shabbiest men reflected a reading of Schopenhauer. She considered the statement of another member most remarkable—that when he saw a carriage driving through the streets occupied by a capitalist who was no longer even an entrepreneur, he felt quite as sure that his days were numbered and that his very lack of function to society would speedily bring him to extinction, as he did when he saw a drunkard reeling along the same street.

It was doubtless owing largely to this club that Hull-House contracted its early reputation for radicalism. Visitors refused to distinguish between the sentiments expressed by its members in the heat of discussion and the opinions held by the residents themselves. At that moment in Chicago the radical of every shade of opinion was vigorous and dogmatic; of the sort that could not resign himself to the slow march of human improvement; of the type who knew exactly "in what part of the world Utopia standeth."

This decade of discussion between 1890 and 1900 already seems remote from the spirit of Chicago of *today*. So far as I have been able to reproduce this earlier period, it must reflect the essential provisionality of everything.

Questions

1. Jane Addams emphasizes the experimental nature of Hull House in an era of "provisionality." What were some of the political and economic contradictions evident in the programs of Hull House?

2. What do you think Addams would have said was the cause of poverty?

3. Why did Addams permit "radical" social gatherings at Hull House? What do you think she thought the relationship was between "The Working People's Social Science Club" in the evening and daytime support for deserted women?

4. What do you think Andrew Carnegie would have thought about the long-term effects of Hull House? What do you think Jane Addams would have thought about the long-term effects of Carnegie Steel?

MODULE 14

JIM CROW CAPITALISM

The Souls of Black Folk (1903)

W. E. B. DUBOIS

After the failure of Reconstruction and the success of Southern white landlords in rebuilding the cotton economy around a
new system of sharecropping and debt, opportunities for most
Southern African Americans shrank toward the vanishing point.
Already trapped in a devastated, colonial economy made more
intolerable by everyday segregation and political disfranchise-
ment, African Americans were also denied access to jobs in most
of the new industries that sprang up in the South. And yet they
could not easily leave the South, either. In the late nineteenth
century, many Northern communities reconfigured themselves
as "sundown towns," in which African Americans were not welcome. Factory jobs were often de facto segregated. Though some
left, one enduring feature of post–Civil War, pre–World War I
capitalist development in the United States was that most African Americans were stuck in the South, as impoverished and indebted producers of cotton.

In 1899, when he was living in the "New South" city of Atlanta
with his young family, Clark Atlanta University professor W. E. B.
DuBois was walking past a store when he happened to see a strange
object displayed behind the window glass. It was the knuckles of an
African-American man named Sam Hose. They were all that was
left of Hose after he had been tortured and then burned to death
by a mob of two thousand white people in a small town outside
Atlanta. DuBois, who mentions the murdered man in this selection, was an African American man, born in Massachusetts, who

was on his way to becoming one of the greatest American thinkers of the twentieth century. Although he had earned his PhD at Harvard a few years earlier, the institution had refused to award it to him because of racism. He'd had to travel to Germany to actually receive a doctorate. But he was not interested in a merely academic career. The sight of the burned trophies to which a human being's hands had been reduced galvanized DuBois, for he believed "one could not be a calm, cool, and detached scientist while Negroes were lynched, murdered, and starved." The *Souls of Black Folk* is one part of his effort to document the lives of African Americans who lived "behind the veil" (as he put it) of segregation and violence. But documentation was not enough, for DuBois wanted to act. Opposing the accomodationist program represented by the Tuskegee Institute's Booker T. Washington, DuBois helped to found the NAACP (National Association for the Advancement of Colored People). Throughout his life, he would be politically active. Unlike some African American activists, he was more than willing to work with socialist groups, for DuBois was a major critic of capitalism.

In DuBois's view, capitalism used racism as a tool to divide and conquer working classes. Without exempting white working-class murderers from guilt in the lynching of Sam Hose, he sees debt as a driving force that keeps people in "the Black Belt" trapped in a second-class economy. As you read this selection, also pay attention to the way that DuBois sees the legacy of a capital-intensive, commodity-generating, entrepreneurial brand of slavery as a force that still hovers over the southwestern Georgia that he visited at the very beginning of the twentieth century. And remember that the scenes he described, and the general sense of a one-crop economy with nowhere to go but down, persisted in many parts of the cotton South from the 1870s until the decades after World War II. That is a very long time for any part of the U.S. economy to stay frozen.

VII: Of the Black Belt

Out of the North the train thundered, and we woke to see the crimson soil of Georgia stretching away bare and monotonous right and left. Here and there lay straggling, unlovely villages, and lean men loafed leisurely at the depots; then again came the stretch of pines and clay. Yet we did not nod, nor weary of the scene; for this is historic ground. [. . .] Just this side Atlanta is the land of the Cherokees and to the southwest, not far from where Sam Hose was crucified, you may stand on a spot which is to-day the centre of the Negro problem,—the centre of those nine million men who are America's dark heritage from slavery and the slave-trade. [. . .] If you wish to ride with me you must come into the "Jim Crow Car." There will be no objection,—already four other white men, and a little white girl with her nurse, are in there. Usually the races are mixed in there; but the white coach is all white. Of course this car is not so good as the other, but [. . .] the discomfort lies chiefly in the hearts of those four black men yonder—and in mine.

We rumble south in quite a business-like way. [. . .] Below Macon the world grows darker; for now we approach the Black Belt,—that strange land of shadows, at which even slaves paled in the past, and whence come now only faint and half-intelligible murmurs to the world beyond. [. . .] The sun is setting, but we can see the great cotton country as we enter it,—the soil now dark and fertile, now thin and gray, with fruit-trees and dilapidated buildings,—all the way to Albany.

At Albany, in the heart of the Black Belt, we stop. Two hundred miles south of Atlanta, two hundred miles west of the Atlantic, and one hundred miles north of the Great Gulf lies Dougherty County, with ten thousand Negroes and two thousand whites. [. . .] Albany is to-day a wide-streeted, placid, Southern town, with a broad sweep of stores and saloons, and flanking rows of homes,—whites usually to the north, and blacks to the south. [. . .] On Saturday suddenly the whole county disgorges itself upon the place, and a perfect flood of black peasantry pours through the streets, fills the stores, blocks the sidewalks, chokes the thoroughfares, and takes full possession of the town. They are black, sturdy, uncouth country folk, good-natured and simple, talkative to a degree, and yet [...] silent and brooding [...]

It gets pretty hot in Southern Georgia in July. [...] The whole land seems forlorn and forsaken. Here are the remnants of the vast plantations of the Sheldons, the Pellots, and the Rensons; but the souls of them are passed. The houses lie in half ruin, or have wholly disappeared; the fences have flown, and the families are wandering in the world. Strange vicissitudes have met these whilom masters. Yonder stretch the wide acres of Bildad Reasor; he died in war-time, but the upstart overseer hastened to wed the widow. Then he went, and his neighbors too, and now only the black tenant remains; but the shadow-hand of the master's grand-nephew or cousin or creditor stretches out of the gray distance to collect the rack-rent remorselessly, and so the land is uncared-for and poor. Only black tenants can stand such a system, and they only because they must. [...]

A restless feeling of depression falls slowly upon us, despite the gaudy sunshine and the green cottonfields. This, then, is the Cotton Kingdom,—the shadow of a marvellous dream. And where is the King? Perhaps this is he,—the sweating ploughman, tilling his eighty acres with two lean mules, and fighting a hard battle with debt. [...] As we turn a corner on the sandy road, there comes a fairer scene suddenly in view,—a neat cottage snugly ensconced by the road, and near it a little store. A tall bronzed man rises from the porch as we hail him, and comes out to our carriage. He is six feet in height, with a sober face that smiles gravely. He walks too straight to be a tenant,—yes, he owns two hundred and forty acres. "The land is run down since the boom-days of eighteen hundred and fifty," he explains, and cotton is low. [...] Here is his gin-house with new machinery just installed. Three hundred bales of cotton went through it last year. Two children he has sent away to school. Yes, he says sadly, he is getting on, but cotton is down to four cents; I know how Debt sits staring at him. [. . .]

On we wind, through sand and pines and glimpses of old plantations, till there creeps into sight a cluster of buildings. [. . .] It seemed quite a village. As it came nearer and nearer, however, the aspect changed: the buildings were rotten, the bricks were falling out, the mills were silent, and the store was closed. [. . .] I could imagine the place under some weird spell, and was half-minded to search out the princess. An old ragged black man, honest, simple, and improvident, told us the tale. The Wizard of the North—the Capitalist—had rushed down in the seventies to woo this coy dark soil. He bought a square mile or more, and for a time the field-hands sang, the gins groaned, and the mills buzzed. Then came a change. The agent's son embezzled the funds and ran off with them. Then the agent himself disappeared. Finally the new agent stole even the books, and the company in wrath closed its business and its houses, refused to sell, and let houses and furniture and machinery rust and rot. So the Waters-Loring plantation was stilled by the spell of dishonesty, and stands like some gaunt rebuke to a scarred land. [. . .]

How curious a land is this,—how full of untold story. [. . .] Day after day the clank of chained feet marching from Virginia and Carolina to Georgia was heard in these rich swamp lands. Day after day the songs of the callous, the wail of the motherless, and the muttered curses of the wretched echoed from the Flint to the Chickasawhatchee, until by 1860 there had risen in West Dougherty perhaps the richest slave kingdom the modern world ever knew. A hundred and fifty barons commanded the labor of nearly six thousand Negroes, held sway over farms with ninety thousand acres tilled land, valued even in times of cheap soil at three millions of dollars. Twenty thousand bales of ginned cotton went yearly to England, New and Old; and men that came there bankrupt made money and grew rich. In a single decade the cotton output increased four-fold and the value of lands was tripled. [. . .] "This land was a little Hell," said a ragged, brown, and grave-faced man to me. We were seated near a roadside blacksmith shop, and behind was the bare ruin of some master's home. "I've seen niggers drop dead in the furrow, but they were kicked aside, and the plough never stopped. Down in the guard-house, there's where the blood ran." [. . .] Then came the revolution of war and Emancipation, the bewilderment of Reconstruction,— and now, what is the Egypt of the Confederacy, and what meaning has it for the nation's weal or woe?

It is a land of rapid contrasts and of curiously mingled hope and pain. Here sits a pretty blue-eyed quadroon hiding her bare feet; she was married only last week, and yonder in the field is her dark young hus-band, hoeing to support her, at thirty cents a day without board. [. . .] Five miles below here is a town owned and controlled by one white New Englander. He owns almost a Rhode Island county, with thou-sands of acres and hundreds of black laborers. Their cabins look better than most, and the farm, with machinery and fertilizers, is much more business-like than any in the county, although the manager drives hard bargains in wages. [. . .] There on the edge of town are five houses of prostitutes,—two of blacks and three of whites; and in one of the houses of the whites a worthless black boy was harbored too openly two years ago; so he was hanged for rape. And here, too, is the high whitewashed fence of the "stockade," as the county prison is called; the white folks say it is ever full of black criminals,—the black folks say that only colored boys are sent to jail, and they not because they are guilty, but because the State needs criminals to eke out its income by their forced labor.

[. . .] A pall of debt hangs over the beautiful land; the mer-chants are in debt to the wholesalers, the planters are in debt to the merchants, the tenants owe the planters, and laborers bow and bend beneath the burden of it all. Here and there a man has raised his head above these murky waters. [. . .] Here and there are black free-holders: there is the gaunt dull-black Jackson, with his hundred acres. [. . .] I turn from these well-tended acres with a comfortable feeling that the Negro is rising. Even then, however, the fields, as we proceed, begin to redden and the trees disappear. Rows of old cabins appear filled with renters and laborers,—cheerless, bare, and dirty, for the most part, although here and there the very age and decay makes the scene picturesque. A young black fellow greets us. He is twenty-two, and just married. Until last year he had good luck renting; then cotton fell, and the sheriff seized and sold all he had. So he moved here, where the rent is higher, the land poorer, and the owner inflexible; he rents a forty-dollar mule for twenty dollars a year. Poor lad!—a slave at twenty-two. [. . .] Why should he strive? Every year finds him deeper in debt. [. . .] The poor land groans with its birth-pains, and brings forth scarcely a hundred pounds of cotton to the acre, where fifty years ago it yielded eight times as much.

[. . .] They are not happy, these black men whom we meet throughout this region. [. . .] And now and then it blazes forth in veiled but hot anger. I remember one big red-eyed black whom we met by the roadside. Forty-five years he had labored on this farm, beginning with nothing, and still having nothing. [. . .] He stopped us to inquire after the black boy in Albany, whom it was said a policeman had shot and killed for loud talking on the sidewalk. And then he said slowly: "Let a white man touch me, and he dies; I don't boast this,—I don't say it around loud, or before the children,—but I mean it. I've seen them whip my father and my old mother in them cotton-rows till the blood ran; by—" and we passed on. [. . .]

Questions

1. In 1903, DuBois asked: What is the role of this part of the country, and especially the millions of African Americans in it, in the modern United States? So, what was that role, and was that an effective use of the human and physical resources of the country?
2. Why weren't more of the people of southwestern Georgia moving elsewhere to work at higher-wage jobs, or perhaps to homestead in the Midwest?

3. Was the South a "colonial economy," as some complained? Or were its continued economic deficiencies created by the insistence of Southern whites on keeping African Americans trapped in conditions that were as close to slavery as possible?
4. What role did the memory of slavery play in shaping DuBois' analysis of capitalism in the Black Belt?
5. How did some capitalists benefit from the racial barriers, inequity, and violence that DuBois noted? Would it be possible to quantify those benefits?

Selection of Jim Crow Laws (1880s–1960s)

Jim Crow was not a holdover from slavery but the modern reestablishment of a new racial order in the midst of an industrializing South. White legislators designed laws to maintain a racial hierarchy in public spaces, but also in families. It is difficult to comprehend today, but all interracial children were born of an illegal relationship. The rules molded places that we consider important (e.g., schools) and places that we probably do not (e.g., circuses). The profusion of regulations and their exhaustiveness is a stupefying reminder of how intensely racial lines needed to be policed to keep the division of the races appearing "natural."

Amateur Baseball: It shall be unlawful for any amateur white baseball team to play baseball on any vacant lot or baseball diamond within two blocks of a playground devoted to the Negro race, and it shall be unlawful for any amateur colored baseball team to play baseball in any vacant lot or baseball diamond within two blocks of any playground devoted to the white race. Georgia

Barbers: No colored barber shall serve as a barber [to] white women or girls. Georgia

Blindness: The board of trustees shall . . . maintain a separate building . . . on separate ground for the admission, care, instruction, and support of all blind persons of the colored or black race. Louisiana

Burial: The officer in charge shall not bury, or allow to be buried, any colored persons upon ground set apart or used for the burial of white persons. Georgia

Buses: All passenger stations in this state operated by any motor transportation company shall have separate waiting rooms or space and separate ticket windows for the white and colored races. Alabama

Child Custody: It shall be unlawful for any parent, relative, or other white person in this State, having the control or custody of any white child, by right of guardianship, natural or acquired, or otherwise, to dispose of, give or surrender such white child permanently into the custody, control, maintenance, or support, of a negro. South Carolina

Circus Tickets: All circuses, shows, and tent exhibitions, to which the attendance of . . . more than one race is invited or expected to attend shall provide for the convenience of its patrons not less than two ticket offices with individual ticket sellers, and not less than two entrances to the said performance, with individual ticket takers and receivers, and in the case of outside or tent performances, the said ticket offices shall not be less than twenty-five (25) feet apart. Louisiana

Cohabitation: Any negro man and white woman, or any white man and negro woman, who are not married to each other, who shall habitually live in and occupy in the nighttime the same room shall each be punished by imprisonment not exceeding twelve (12) months, or by fine not exceeding five hundred ($500.00) dollars. Florida

Education: [The County Board of Education] shall provide schools of two kinds; those for white children and those for colored children. Texas

Education: Separate free schools shall be established for the education of children of African descent; and it shall be unlawful for any colored child to attend any white school, or any white child to attend a colored school. Missouri

Education: Separate rooms [shall] be provided for the teaching of pupils of African descent, and [when] said rooms are so provided, such pupils may not be admitted to the school rooms occupied and used by pupils of Caucasian or other descent. New Mexico

Education: Separate schools shall be maintained for the children of the white and colored races. Mississippi

Education: The schools for white children and the schools for negro children shall be conducted separately. Florida

Fishing, Boating, and Bathing: The [Conservation] Commission shall have the right to make segregation of the white and colored races as to the exercise of rights of fishing, boating, and bathing. Oklahoma

Hospital Entrances: There shall be maintained by the governing authorities of every hospital maintained by the state for treatment of white and colored patients separate entrances for white and colored patients and visitors, and such entrances shall be used by the race only for which they are prepared. Mississippi

Housing: Any person . . . who shall rent any part of any such building to a negro person or a negro family when such building is already in whole or in part in occupancy by a white person or white family, or vice versa when the building is in occupancy by a negro person or negro family, shall be guilty of a misdemeanor and on conviction thereof shall be punished by a fine of not less than twenty-five ($25.00) nor more than one hundred ($100.00) dollars or be imprisoned not less than 10, or more than 60 days, or both such fine and imprisonment in the discretion of the court. Louisiana

Intermarriage: All marriages between a white person and a negro, or between a white person and a person of negro descent to the fourth generation inclusive, are hereby forever prohibited. Florida

Intermarriage: All marriages between a white person and a negro, or between a white person and a person of negro descent, to the third generation, inclusive, or between a white person and a member of the Malay race; or between the negro and a member of the Malay race; or between a person of Negro descent, to the third generation, inclusive, and a member of the Malay race, are forever prohibited, and shall be void. Maryland

Intermarriage: All marriages between . . . white persons and negroes or white persons and Mongolians . . . are prohibited and declared absolutely void . . . No person having one-eighth part or more of negro blood shall be permitted to marry any white person, nor shall any white person be permitted to marry any negro or person having one-eighth part or more of negro blood. Missouri

Intermarriage: All marriages of white persons with Negroes, Mulattos, Mongolians, or Malaya hereafter contracted in the State of Wyoming are and shall be illegal and void. Wyoming

Intermarriage: It shall be unlawful for a white person to marry anyone except a white person. Any marriage in violation of this section shall be void. Georgia

Intermarriage: The marriage of a person of Caucasian blood with a Negro, Mongolian, Malay, or Hindu shall be null and void. Arizona

Intermarriage: The marriage of a white person with a negro or mulatto or person who shall have one-eighth or more of negro blood, shall be unlawful and void. Mississippi

Juvenile Delinquents: There shall be separate buildings, not nearer than one fourth mile to each other, one for white boys and one for negro boys. White boys and negro boys shall not, in any manner, be associated together or worked together. Florida

Libraries: Any white person of such county may use the county free library under the rules and regulations prescribed by the commissioners court and may be entitled to all the privileges thereof. Said court shall make proper provision for the negroes of said county to be served through a separate branch or branches of the county free library, which shall be administered by [a] custodian of the negro race under the supervision of the county librarian. Texas

Libraries: The state librarian is directed to fit up and maintain a separate place for the use of the colored people who may come to the library for the purpose of reading books or periodicals. North Carolina

Lunch Counters: No persons, firms, or corporations, who or which furnish meals to passengers at station restaurants or station eating houses, in times limited by common carriers of said passengers, shall furnish said meals to white and colored passengers in the same room, or at the same table, or at the same counter. South Carolina

Mental Hospitals: The Board of Control shall see that proper and distinct apartments are arranged for said patients, so that in no case shall Negroes and white persons be together. Georgia

Militia: The white and colored militia shall be separately enrolled, and shall never be compelled to serve in the same organization. No organization of colored troops shall be permitted where white troops are available, and where whites are permitted to be organized, colored troops shall be under the command of white officers. North Carolina

Mining: The baths and lockers for the negroes shall be separate from the white race, but may be in the same building. Oklahoma

Nurses: No person or corporation shall require any white female nurse to nurse in wards or rooms in hospitals, either public or private, in which negro men are placed. Alabama

Parks: It shall be unlawful for colored people to frequent any park owned or maintained by the city for the benefit, use and enjoyment of white persons . . . and unlawful for any white person to frequent any park owned or maintained by the city for the use and benefit of colored persons. Georgia

Pool and Billiard Rooms: It shall be unlawful for a negro and white person to play together or in company with each other at any game of pool or billiards. Alabama

Prisons: The warden shall see that the white convicts shall have separate apartments for both eating and sleeping from the negro convicts. Mississippi

Promotion of Equality: Any person . . . who shall be guilty of printing, publishing or circulating printed, typewritten or written matter urging or presenting for public acceptance or general information, arguments or suggestions in favor of social equality or of intermarriage between whites and negroes, shall be guilty of a misdemeanor and subject to fine or not exceeding five hundred (500.00) dollars or imprisonment not exceeding six (6) months or both. Mississippi

Railroads: All railroad companies and corporations, and all persons running or operating cars or coaches by steam on any railroad line or track in the State of Maryland, for the transportation of passengers, are hereby required to provide separate cars or coaches for the travel and transportation of the white and colored passengers. Maryland

Railroads: The conductor of each passenger train is authorized and required to assign each passenger to the car or the division of the car, when it is divided by a partition, designated for the race to which such passenger belongs. Alabama

Railroads: The conductors or managers on all such railroads shall have power, and are hereby required, to assign to each white or colored passenger his or her respective car, coach or compartment. If the passenger fails to disclose his race, the conductor and managers, acting in good faith, shall be the sole judges of his race. Virginia

Reform Schools: The children of white and colored races committed to the houses of reform shall be kept entirely separate from each other. Kentucky

Restaurants: All persons licensed to conduct a restaurant, shall serve either white people exclusively or colored people exclusively and shall not sell to the two races within the same room or serve the two races anywhere under the same license. Georgia

Restaurants: It shall be unlawful to conduct a restaurant or other place for the serving of food in the city, at which white and colored people are served in the same room, unless such white and colored persons are effectually separated by a solid partition extending from the floor upward to a distance of seven feet or higher, and unless a separate entrance from the street is provided for each compartment. Alabama

Teaching: Any instructor who shall teach in any school, college or institution where members of the white and colored race are received and enrolled as pupils for instruction shall be deemed guilty of a misdemeanor, and upon conviction thereof, shall be fined in any sum not less than ten dollars ($10.00) nor more than fifty dollars ($50.00) for each offense. Oklahoma

Telephone Booths: The Corporation Commission is hereby vested with power and authority to require telephone companies . . . to maintain separate booths for white and colored patrons when there is a demand for such separate booths. That the Corporation Commission shall determine the necessity for said separate booths only upon complaint of the people in the town and vicinity to be served after due hearing as now provided by law in other complaints filed with the Corporation Commission. Oklahoma

Textbooks: Books shall not be interchangeable between the white and colored schools, but shall continue to be used by the race first using them. North Carolina

Theaters: Every person . . . operating . . . any public hall, theatre, opera house, motion picture show or any place of public entertainment or public assemblage which is attended by both white and colored persons, shall separate the white race and the colored race and shall set apart and designate . . . certain seats therein to be occupied by white persons and a portion thereof, or certain seats therein, to be occupied by colored persons. Virginia

Toilet Facilities, Male: Every employer of white or negro males shall provide for such white or negro males reasonably accessible and separate toilet facilities. Alabama

Transportation: The . . . Utilities Commission . . . is empowered and directed to require the establishment of separate waiting rooms at all stations for the white and colored races. North Carolina

Wine and Beer: All persons licensed to conduct the business of selling beer or wine . . . shall serve either white people exclusively or colored people exclusively and shall not sell to the two races within the same room at any time. Georgia

Questions

1. Why do you think so many areas of Jim Crow legislation concerned the regulation of consumer spaces (parks, theaters, circuses, saloons, restaurants, etc.)?
2. Why do you think that someone who was ⅞ "white" was considered to be "colored"? Why did railroad operators need the authority to "judge" someone's race?
3. Why do you think there were so many laws on "intermarriage"?

The Socialist Party and the Working Class
(1904)

EUGENE V. DEBS

Eugene Debs is perhaps the best-known of all American leftist leaders. He came to fame initially as the leader of the Pullman Strike of 1894, in which he attempted to parlay a railroad strike into a national general strike. Without the support of Samuel Gompers and the AFL, the Pullman Strike failed and Debs went to jail. For the next two decades, Debs remained prominent as the political voice of American socialism. Here is a speech of his from 1904, where he outlines the promise of socialism and how it could be attained in the United States through the ballot, not the bullet. Like Marx, Debs believed that the class struggle was a political struggle.

Mr. Chairman, Citizens and Comrades:

There has never been a free people, a civilized nation, a real republic on this earth. Human society has always consisted of masters and slaves, and the slaves have always been and are today, the foundation stones of the social fabric.

Wage-labor is but a name; wage-slavery is the fact. The twenty-five millions of wage-slavery in the United States are twenty-five millions of twentieth century slaves. This is the plain meaning of what is known as the Labor Market. And the labor market follows the capitalist flag. [...]

Let me say at the very threshold of this discussion that the workers have but the one issue in this campaign, the overthrow of the capitalist system and the emancipation of the working class from wage-slavery. The capitalists may have the tariff, finance, imperialism and other dust-covered and moth-eaten issues entirely to themselves. The rattle of these relics no longer deceives workingmen whose heads are on their own shoulders. They know by experience and observation that the gold standard, free silver, fiat money, protective tariff, free trade, imperialism and anti-imperialism all mean capitalist rule and wage-slavery. Their eyes are open and they can see; their brains are in operation and they can think. The very moment a workingman begins to do his own thinking he understands the paramount issue, parts company with the capitalist politician and falls in line with his own class on the political battlefield. The political solidarity of the working class means the death of despotism, the birth of freedom, the sunrise of civilization.

Having said this much by way of introduction I will now enter upon the actualities of my theme.

The Class Struggle

We are entering tonight upon a momentous campaign. The struggle for political supremacy is not between political parties merely, as appears upon the surface, but at bottom it is a life and death struggle between two hostile economic classes, the one the capitalist, and the other the working class.

The capitalist class is represented by the Republican, Democratic, Populist and Prohibition parties, all of which stand for private ownership of the means of production, and the triumph of any one of which will mean continued wage-slavery to the working class.

As the Populist and Prohibition sections of the capitalist party represent minority elements which propose to reform the capitalist system without disturbing wage-slavery, a vain and impossible task, they will be omitted from this discussion with all the credit due the rank and file for their good intentions.

The Republican and Democratic parties, or, to be more exact, the

Republican-Democratic party, represent the capitalist class in the class struggle. They are the political wings of the capitalist system and such differences as arise between them relate to spoils and not to principles. With either of those parties in power one thing is always certain and that is that the capitalist class is in the saddle and the working class under the saddle.

Under the administration of both these parties the means of production are private property, production is carried forward for capitalist profit purely, markets are glutted and industry paralyzed, workingmen become tramps and criminals while injunctions, soldiers and riot guns are brought into action to preserve "law and order" in the chaotic carnival of capitalistic anarchy.

Deny it as may the cunning capitalists who are clear-sighted enough to perceive it, or ignore it as may the torpid workers who are too blind and unthinking to see it, the struggle in which we are engaged today is a class struggle, and as the toiling millions come to see and understand it and rally to the political standard of their class, they will drive all capitalist parties of whatever name into the same party, and the class struggle will then be so clearly revealed that the hosts of labor will find their true place in the conflict and strike the united and decisive blow that will destroy slavery and achieve their full and final emancipation.

In this struggle the workingmen and women and children are represented by the Socialist party and it is my privilege to address you in the name of that revolutionary and uncompromising party of the working class. [. . .]

The Ballot

The ballot of united labor expresses the people's will and the people's will is the supreme law of a free nation. The ballot means that labor is no longer dumb, that at last it has a voice, that it may be heard and if united shall be heeded. Centuries of struggle and sacrifice were required to wrest this symbol of freedom from the mailed clutch of tyranny and place it in the hand of labor as the shield and lance of attack and defense. The abuse and not the use of it is responsible for its evils. The divided vote of labor is the abuse of the ballot and the penalty is slavery and death. The united vote of those who toil and have not will vanquish those who have and toil not, and solve forever the problems of democracy. [. . .]

The Republican Party

[. . .] For precisely the same reason that all the millionaires are opposed to the Socialist party, all workers should be opposed to the Republican party. It is a capitalist party, is loyal to capitalist interests and entitled to the support of capitalist voters on election day. All it has for workingmen is its "glorious past" and a "glad hand" when it wants their votes. The Republican party is now and has been for several years, in complete control of government. What has it done for labor? What has it not done for capital? [. . .]

The labor platforms of the Republican and Democratic parties are interchangeable and non-redeemable. They both favor "justice to capital and justice to labor." This hoary old platitude is worse than meaningless. It is false and misleading and so intended. Justice to labor means that labor shall have what it produces. This leaves nothing for capital. Justice to labor means the end of capital.

The old parties intend nothing of the kind. It is false pretense and false promise. It has served well in the past. Will it continue to catch the votes of unthinking and deluded workers? What workingmen had part in the Republican national convention or were honored by it? The grand coliseum swarmed with trust magnates, corporation barons, money lords, stock gamblers, professional politicians, lawyers, lobbyists and other plutocratic tools and mercenaries, but there was no room for the horny-handed and horny-headed sons of toil. They built it, but were not in it. [. . .]

The Democratic Party

In referring to the Democratic party in this discussion we may save time by simply saying that since it was born again at the St. Louis convention it is near enough like its Republican ally to pass for a twin brother. The former party of the "common people" is no longer under the boycott of the plutocracy since it has adopted the Wall street label and renounced its middle class heresies. The radical and progressive elements of the former Democracy have been evicted and must seek other quarters. They were an unmitigated nuisance in the conservative counsels of the old party. They were for the "common people" and the trusts have no use for such a party.

Where but to the Socialist party can these progressive people turn? They are now without a party and the only genuine Democratic party in the field is the Socialist party, and every true Democrat should thank Wall street for driving him out of a party that is democratic in name only and into one that is democratic in fact. [. . .]

The Socialist Party

[. . .] The people are as capable of achieving their industrial freedom as they were to secure their political liberty, and both are necessary to a free nation. The capitalist system is no longer adapted to the needs of modern society. It is outgrown and fetters the forces of progress. Industrial and commercial competition are largely of the past. The handwriting blazes on the wall. Centralization and combination are the modern forces in industrial and commercial life. Competition is breaking down and co-operation is supplanting it.

The hand tools of early times are used no more. Mammoth machines have taken their place. A few thousand capitalists own them and many millions of workingmen use them.

All the wealth the vast army of labor produces above its subsistence is taken by the machine owning capitalists, who also own the land and the mills, the factories, railroads and mines, the forests and fields and all other means of transportation.

Hence wealth and poverty, millionaires and beggars, castles and caves, luxury and squalor, painted parasites on the boulevard and painted poverty among the red lights. Hence strikes, boycotts, riots, murder, suicide, insanity, prostitution on a fearful and increasing scale. [...]

Closing Words

These are stirring days for living men. The day of crisis is drawing near and Socialists are exerting all their power to prepare the people for it. [...]

The overthrow of capitalism is the object of the Socialist party. It will not fuse with any other party and it would rather die than compromise. The Socialist party comprehends the magnitude of its task and has the patience of preliminary defeat and the faith of ultimate victory. The working class must be emancipated by the working class. Woman must be given her true place in society by the working class. Child labor must be abolished by the working class. Society must be reconstructed by the working class. The working class must be employed by the working class. The fruits of labor must be enjoyed by the working class. War, bloody war, must be ended by the working class.

These are the principles and objects of the Socialist party and we fearlessly proclaim them to our fellowmen. We know our cause is just and that it must prevail. With faith and hope and courage we hold our heads erect and with dauntless spirit marshal the working class for the march from Capitalism to Socialism, from Slavery to Freedom, from Barbarism to Civilization.

Questions

1. Where does Debs differ from other leftists in the progressive era, like those of the IWW?
2. Why does he lump the Populists with the Democrats and Republicans?
3. Many people, then and now, would argue that free markets underpin "political liberty." How would Debs respond?
4. Debs calls workers who are not socialists "blind and unthinking." How might those workers respond to Debs?
5. What made the wage system "wage-slavery" for Debs? How might Samuel Gompers respond? Why would even "good wages" still be "wage-slavery"?
6. Why did Debs believe that capitalism "fetters the forces of progress"? How would his vision of socialism unfetter those forces?

Preamble to the IWW Constitution (1905)

INDUSTRIAL WORKERS OF THE WORLD

The IWW, or the Wobblies, as its members were called, holds a special place in American labor history. While the AFL was practical, the Wobblies were utopian. While the AFL fought for wages, the Wobblies, in every possible sense, fought for freedom. While the AFL embraced white privilege, nativism, and gender hierarchies, the Wobblies fought racism, xenophobia, and sexism. The IWW, according to one of its pamphlets, was "not a white man's union, not a black man's union, not a red man's union, but a working man's union." From our early twenty-first century multicultural perspective, it is hard not to see them as the "good guys."

Wobblies fought capitalism not only in strikes, but in song. Their most famous songwriter, Joe Hill, penned American Left classics like "Rebel Girl" and "Give Me That Old Wooden Shoe." Their book of songs, called the Little Red Songbook, turned American folk music into a radical art form that would later shape the music of the 1960s.

Their vision of the world was not just about race and gender. It was a vision of class conflict radically at odds with mainstream visions of capitalism. William Foster's pamphlet from 1913 outlines their theory of revolution. Their vision of economy left no middle ground for accommodation. The Wobblies were not interested in wages, and work control, and job security. They were interested in total liberation from capitalism. Their philosophy, called syndicalism, harkened back to French trade unionism, which took the general strike as the foundation of worker power. A general strike, where the laborers left the factories, was a prelude to the revolution when the workers would, in committees, reopen them again—but under worker control. Foster would go on to lead the Great Steel Strike of 1919, which ended in defeat. In the aftermath, many Wobblies were deported or imprisoned during the Red Scare. Nonetheless, in an era when many workers felt broken and exploited by industrialization, the Wobblies offered a supportive, collectivist vision that enabled mass action.

The working class and the employing class have nothing in common. There can be no peace so long as hunger and want are found among millions of the working people and the few, who make up the employing class, have all the good things of life.

Between these two classes a struggle must go on until the workers of the world organize as a class, take possession of the means of production, abolish the wage system, and live in harmony with the Earth.

We find that the centering of the management of industries into fewer and fewer hands makes the trade unions unable to cope with the ever growing power of the employing class. The trade unions foster a state of affairs which allows one set of workers to be pitted against another set of workers in the same industry, thereby helping defeat one another in wage wars. Moreover, the trade unions aid the employing class to mislead the workers into the belief that the working class have interests in common with their employers.

These conditions can be changed and the interest of the working class upheld only by an organization formed in such a way that all its members in any one industry, or in all industries if necessary, cease work whenever a strike or lockout is on in any department thereof, thus making an injury to one an injury to all.

Instead of the conservative motto, "A fair day's wage for a fair day's work," we must inscribe on our banner the revolutionary watchword, "Abolition of the wage system."

It is the historic mission of the working class to do away with capitalism. The army of production must be organized, not only for everyday struggle with capitalists, but also to carry on production when capitalism shall have been overthrown. By organizing industrially we are forming the structure of the new society within the shell of the old.

Questions

1. In the preamble to its constitution, the IWW attacks "the wage system" but not low wages. What is the difference between this critique and that of the American Federation of Labor?
2. What do you think Samuel Gompers would have thought about the ideas of the IWW?

Syndicalism (1913)

WILLIAM Z. FOSTER

Syndicalism was one of many radical tracts published during the Progressive Era. Its author, William Foster, was an influential IWW member who, after World War I, led the failed Great Steel Strike of 1919. For syndicalists like the IWW, the labor union was only a means to a greater end. Capitalism, for him, was fundamentally unjust, and political action was useless since a society based on wages could not reformed. The success at Lawrence, Massachusetts, in 1912, as Foster wrote about here, emboldened the IWW in its hopes for a revolution. In *Syndicalism,* Foster outlines a theory and a practice of class war based on the idea of the general strike—where workers refuse to work, capitalism collapses, and workers' councils run the economy. Unlike later Soviet Communists, Foster believed that in the absence of capitalism, the state would no longer be necessary. Like many radical writers, he denounced the accomodationist stance of the American Federation of Labor and other craft unions. While the IWW's program never succeeded, it marked, in many ways, the high water mark of leftist radicalism in American labor history.

The Situation—Its Cause and Cure

The American workingman who arouses himself from the customary state of indifference characterizing workingmen and gazes about him in a critical mood, must-be struck by the great inequalities in the conditions of the beings surrounding him.

On the one hand, he sees vast masses of workers working long hours, often at most dangerous and unhealthy occupations, and getting in return hardly the scantiest of the necessities of life.

On the other hand, he sees a comparatively small number of idle rich revelling in all the luxuries that modern society can produce. Though they do nothing useful for society, society pours its vast treasures into their laps, and they squander this wealth in every way that their depraved and sated appetites can suggest.

The insane methods of the American aristocracy to flaunt its wealth are too well known to need recapitulation here. Our observing worker must indeed conclude that something is radically wrong in a society that produces such extremes of poverty and wealth, and toil and idleness.

The Revolution.—The wages system is the most brazen and gigantic robbery ever perpetrated since the world began. So disastrous are its consequences on the vast armies of slaves within its toils that it is threatening the very existence of society. If society is even to be perpetuated—to say nothing of being organized upon an equitable basis—the wages system must be abolished. The thieves at present in control of the industries must be stripped of their booty, and society so reorganized that every individual shall have free access to the social means of production. This social reorganization will be a revolution. Only after such a revolution will the great inequalities of modern society disappear.

The Means to the Revolution

The Class Struggle.—For years progressive workers have realized the necessity for this revolution. They have also realized that it must be brought about by the workers themselves.

The wages system has divided the immense bulk of society into two classes—the capitalist class and the working class. The interests of these two classes are radically opposed to each other.

It is the interest of the capitalist class to rob the workers of as much of their product as possible and the interest of the workers to prevent this robbery as far as they can. A guerrilla warfare—known as the class struggle and evidenced by the many strikes, working class political eruptions and the many acts of oppression committed by capitalists upon their workers—constantly goes on between these opposing classes. The capitalists, who are heartlessness and cupidity personified, being the dominant class of society and the shapers of its institutions, have organized the whole fabric of society with a view to keeping the working class in slavery. It is, therefore, evident that if the workers arc to become free it must be through their own efforts and directly against those of the capitalists.

Rejection of Political Action and Acceptance of Direct Action.—This rejection of political action and acceptance of direct action has been caused by the failure of the former and the success of the latter. Working class political parties, in spite of the great efforts spent upon them, have been distinct failures, while, on the other hand, labor unions, though often despised and considered as inter-lopers by revolutionists, have been pronounced successes.

The Syndicalist movement is a labor union movement, which, in addition to fighting the every-day battles of the working class, intends to overthrow capitalism and reorganize society in such a manner that exploitation of man by man through the wages system shall cease.

The Operation of the Industries

Anti-Statism.—At this early date, though many of the minor details of the organization plan of the new society can only be guessed at, many of its larger outlines are fairly clear. One of these is that there will be no State. The Syndicalist sees in the State only an instrument of oppression and a bungling administrator of industry, and proposes to exclude it from the future society. He sees no need for any general supervising governmental body, and intends that the workers in each industry shall manage the affairs of their particular industry; that "the fighting groups of today will be the producing and distributing groups of tomorrow."

In the future Syndicalist society the ordinarily unscientific custom of majority rule will be just about eliminated. It will be superseded by the rule of facts and figures. Not only will the industries be operated in the undemocratic manner above outlined; but, the responsible positions in them will be filled in a manner all at variance with democratic principles.

The question of the system for the division of the social product in the new society has not been the subject of much discussion by Syndicalists. However, they very generally accept the Anarchist formula: "From each according to his ability; to each according to his needs." They will abolish all ownership in the social means of livelihood and make them free for each, to take what he needs. The prevailing code of ethics will prevent would-be idlers from taking advantage of this system.

The General Strike Theory.—By the term "general strike," used in a revolutionary sense, is meant the period of more or less total cessation of labor by the workers, during which period, the workers, by disorganizing the mechanism of capitalist minority, will realize its weakness and their own strength; whereupon, perceiving themselves possessed of the power to do so, they will seize control of the social means of production and proceed to operate them in their own interest, instead of in the interest of a handful of parasites, as heretofore. The general strike is the first stage of the revolution proper.

The power of the workers to disorganize and paralyze the delicately adjusted capitalist society and the inability of the capitalists to cope with this power are shown by every large strike conducted by modern methods.

The everyday tactics of the workers strongly indicate the truth of the conclusion that they will expropriate the capitalists as soon as they learn they have the power to do so. In their daily strikes they pit their strength against that of their employers and wring from them whatever concessions they can. They don't remain long content with these concessions, and as soon as they are able, they proceed to win more. They are insatiable, and, when the general strike proves their ability to do so, they will have no scruples against expropriating the capitalists. This expropriation will seem the more natural to them then, as they will be fortified by the Syndicalist conception that the capitalists are thieves and have no "right" to their property.

The partial strike of today, in which a comparatively few workers disorganize an industry and force concessions from their employers, is but a miniature of the general strike of the future, in which the whole working class will disorganize all the industries and force the whole capitalist class to give up its ownership of them.

The Syndicalist knows that the general strike will be a success, and the timid fears of its opponents will never turn him from it, any more than will their arguments that it is an "illegal," "unfair" and "uncivilized" weapon.

Reasons for Superiority of Direct Action.—The chief cause for the greater success of the labor unions than the political party is found in the superior efficacy of direct action to political action. The former is a demonstration of real power, the latter merely an expression of public sentiment. A couple of instances, taken from late labor history, will illustrate this point:

During the recent Lawrence textile strike, 24,000 workers, in the course of a couple of months, won important concessions in wages and improved working conditions, not only for themselves, but also for some 350,000 other workers in the same industry who took no part in the strike.

For either of these groups of workers to have secured the same ends by political action would have been next to impossible. Of themselves alone they never could have done so, as minorities are negligible quantities in politics. To have accomplished even the pre-liminary steps to such victories they would have had to secure the political support of practically the whole working class. Even then they have had no guarantee that their efforts had not all been in vain, as the financial powers—who are only to be coerced by demonstrations of force—have time and again flagrantly disobeyed the political mandates of the working class.

Political Action as a Revolutionary Weapon.—In addition to being superior to the political party in accomplishments to date, the labor unions are also manifestly superior as the means to bring about the revolution.

Syndicalism and the American Labor Movement

"A Fair Day's Pay For a Fair Day's Work."—This formula expresses the vague ideal for which the majority of American labor unions are striving. Such unions grant the right to their masters to exploit them, only asking in return that they be given a "fair" standard of living. It is a slave ideal.

Harmony of Interests of Capital and Labor.—Along with the slave ideal of "a fair day's pay for a fair day's work" must go the idiotic doctrine of the harmony of interests of capital and labor, which many labor leaders are so fond of enunciating.

Craft Unionism and the Contract.—Craft Unionism—or, more properly, Sectional Unionism, as all non-revolutionary labor unions, whether organized on craft or industrial lines, are alike commonly designated "craft" unions—is a prolific source of weakness to the labor movement. By its division of the working class into various sections, each of which, knowing and caring little about the interests of the others, shortsightedly tries to defend the narrow, immediate interests of its own members, Craft Unionism cripples the fighting power of the workers. It sends the working class piecemeal to light the united capitalists, who, in addition to their own power, artfully use that of the great mass of workers at peace with them to crush the few in revolt.

Questions

1. Foster's faith in progress and science is evident by his demand for the abolition of the "unscientific custom of majority rule." In what other ways does Foster invoke notions of inevitable scientific progress in the coming of the revolution?
2. Why is he opposed to more mainstream unions?
3. What makes the general strike different from a normal strike?
4. How does Foster imagine goods will be distributed after the revolution?
5. Why does he think that wages are inherently unjust?
6. Foster criticizes capitalists as "idlers." What do you think of this critique?

IWW Songs to Fan the Flames of Discontent (1917)

JOE HILL

Wobblies fought capitalism not only in strikes but in song. Their most famous songwriter, Joe Hill, penned American left classics like "Rebel Girl" and "Give Me that Old Wooden Shoe." Their book of songs, also called the Little Red Songbook, turned American folk music into a radical art form that would later shape the music of the 1960s. While most of their songs are now little known, some like "Solidarity Forever" have become an enduring part of the labor movement.

The Rebel Girl
Words and Music by Joe Hill

There are women of many descriptions
In this queer world, as everyone knows,
Some are living in beautiful mansions,
And are wearing the finest of clothes
There are blue blooded queens and princesses
Who have charms made of diamonds and pearl;
But the only and thoroughbred lady
Is the Rebel Girl.

CHORUS
To the working class she's a precious pearl.
She brings courage, pride and joy

To the fighting Rebel Boy.
We've had girls before, but we need some more
In the Industrial Workers of the World.
For it's great to fight for freedom
With a Rebel Girl.

Yes, her hands may be hardened from labor,
And her dress may not be very fine;
But a heart in her bosom is beating
That is true to her class and her kind.
And the grafters in terror are trembling
When her spite and defiance she'll hurl;
For the only and thoroughbred lady
Is the Rebel Girl

Mr. Block
By Joe Hill
(Air: "It Looks to Me Like a Big Time Tonight")

Please give me your attention, I'll introduce to you
A man that is a credit to "Our Red, White and Blue";
His head is made of lumber, and solid as a rock;
He is a common worker and his name is Mr. Block.
And Block he thinks he may
Be President some day.

CHORUS
Oh, Mr. Block, you were born by mistake,
You take the cake,
You make me ache.
Tie on a rock to your block and then jump in the lake,
Kindly do that for Liberty's sake.

Yes, Mr. Block is lucky; he found a job, by gee!
The sharks got seven dollars, for job and fare and fee.

They shipped him to a desert and dumped him with his
    truck,
But when he tried to find his job, he sure was out of luck.
He shouted, "That's too raw, I'll fix them with the law."

Block hiked back to the city, but wasn't doing well.
He said, "I'll join the union—the great A. F. of L."
He got a job next morning, got fired in the night,
He said, "I'll see Sam Gompers and he'll fix that foreman
    right."
Sam Gompers said, "You see,
You've got our sympathy."

Election day he shouted, "A Socialist for Mayor!"
The "comrade" got elected, he happy was for fair,
But after the election he got an awful shock.
A great big socialistic Bull did rap him on the block.
And Comrade Block did sob,
"I helped him to his job."

Poor Block, he died one evening, I'm very glad to state;
He climbed the golden ladder up to the pearly gate.
He said, "Oh, Mr. Peter, one word I'd like to tell,
I'd like to meet the Astorbilts and John D. Rockefell."
Old Pete said, "Is that so?
You'll meet them down below."

Questions

1. Why did IWW leaders like Joe Hill spend so much time writing
   songs? Is it a fair question to ask if that time would have been
   better used organizing? Do you think songs are an effective way
   to sway the minds of workers like "Mr. Block"?

2. The IWW has had a lasting influence on American labor culture, from an early emphasis on feminism and civil rights to the song "Solidarity Forever," yet it is less well known than other American activist movements. Why do you think that the IWW faded after World War I?

MODULE 15

FORDISM

Principles of Scientific Management (1913)

FREDERICK TAYLOR

Taylor's *Principles of Scientific Management* systematized Progressive Era notions of efficiency in labor. His ideas weren't particularly innovative, but they were widely disseminated. Today, we still refer to the process of reducing labor time by studying and regulating workers' body movements as Taylorism. Along with Henry Ford, Taylor defined twentieth-century manufacturing. Until the rise of Toyota in the 1960s and '70s, Taylorist ideas of labor efficiency structured all production in capitalist factories.

PRESIDENT ROOSEVELT, in his address to the Governors at the White House, prophetically remarked that "The conservation of our national resources is only preliminary to the larger question of national efficiency." The whole country at once recognized the importance of conserving our material resources and a large movement has been started which will be effective in accomplishing this object. As yet, however, we have but vaguely appreciated the importance of "the larger question of increasing our national efficiency."

We can see our forests vanishing, our water-powers going to waste, our soil being carried by floods into the sea; and the end of our coal and our iron is in sight. But our larger wastes of human effort, which go on every day through such of our acts as are blundering, ill-directed, or inefficient, and which Mr. Roosevelt refers to as a lack of "national efficiency," are less visible, less tangible, and are but vaguely appreciated.

In the past the prevailing idea has been well expressed in the saying that "Captains of industry are born, not made"; and the theory has been that if one could get the right man, methods could be safely left to him. In the future it will be appreciated that our leaders must be trained right as well as born right, and that no great man can (with the old system of personal management) hope to compete with a number of ordinary men who have been properly organized so as efficiently to cooperate.

In the past the man has been first; in the future the system must be first. This in no sense, however, implies that great men are not needed. On the contrary, the first object of any good system must be that of developing first-class men; and under systematic management the best man rises to the top more certainly and more rapidly than ever before.

[. . .] The principal object of management should be to secure the maximum prosperity for the employer, coupled with the maximum prosperity for each employ.

The words "maximum prosperity" are used, in their broad sense, to mean not only large dividends for the company or owner, but the development of every branch of the business to its highest state of excellence, so that the prosperity may be permanent.

In the same way maximum prosperity for each employ means not only higher wages than are usually received by men of his class, but, of more importance still, it also means the development of each man to his state of maximum efficiency, so that he may be able to do, generally speaking, the highest grade of work for which his natural abilities fit him, and it further means giving him, when possible, this class of work to do.

No one can be found who will deny that in the case of any single individual the greatest prosperity can exist only when that individual has reached his highest state of efficiency; that is, when he is turning out his largest daily output.

In the case of a more complicated manufacturing establishment, it should also be perfectly clear that the greatest permanent prosperity for the workman, coupled with the greatest prosperity for the employer, can be brought about only when the work of the establishment is done with the smallest combined expenditure of human effort, plus nature's resources, plus the cost for the use of capital in the shape of machines, buildings, etc.

If the above reasoning is correct, it follows that the most important object of both the workmen and the management should be the training and development of each individual in the establishment, so that he can do (at his fastest pace and with the maximum of efficiency) the highest class of work for which his natural abilities fit him.

These principles appear to be so self-evident that many men may think it almost childish to state them.

[. . .] A great deal has been and is being constantly said about "sweat-shop" work and conditions. The writer has great sympathy with those who are overworked, but on the whole a greater sympathy for those who are under paid. For every individual, however, who is overworked, there are a hundred who intentionally underwork—greatly underwork—every day of their lives, and who for this reason deliberately aid in establishing those conditions which in the end inevitably result in low wages. And yet hardly a single voice is being raised in an endeavor to correct this evil. [. . .]

The body of this paper will make it clear that, to work according to scientific laws, the management must take over and perform much of the work which is now left to the men; almost every act of the workman should be preceded by one or more preparatory acts of the management which enable him to do his work better and quicker than he otherwise could. And each man should daily be taught by and receive the most friendly help from those who are over him, instead of being, at the one extreme, driven or coerced by his bosses, and at the other left to his own unaided devices.

The 30 per cent, to 100 per cent, increase in wages which the workmen are able to earn beyond what they receive under the old type of management, coupled with the daily intimate shoulder to shoulder contact with the management, entirely removes all cause for soldiering. And in a few years, under this system, the workmen have before them the object lesson of seeing that a great increase in the output per man results in giving employment to more men, instead of throwing men out of work, thus completely eradicating the fallacy that a larger output for each man will throw other men out of work. [. . .]

The Bethlehem Steel Company had five blast furnaces, the product of which had been handled by a pig-iron gang for many years. This gang, at this time, consisted of about 75 men. They were good, average pig-iron handlers, were under an excellent foreman who himself had been a pig-iron handler, and the work was done, on the whole, about as fast and as cheaply as it was anywhere else at that time.

We found that this gang were loading on the average about 12½ long tons per man per day. We were surprised to find, after studying the matter, that a first-class pig-iron handler ought to handle between 47½ and 48 long tons per day, instead of 12½ tons.

It was our duty to see that the 80,000 tons of pig iron was loaded on to the cars at the rate of 47 tons per man per day, in place of 12½ tons, at which rate the work was then being done. And it was further our duty to see that this work was done without bringing on a strike among the men, without any quarrel with the men, and to see that the men were happier and better contented when loading at the new rate of 47 tons than they were when loading at the old rate of 12½ tons.

Our first step was to find the proper workman to begin with. We therefore carefully watched and studied these 75 men for three or four days, at the end of which time we had picked out four men who appeared to be physically able to handle pig iron at the rate of 47 tons per day. A careful study was then made of each of these men. We looked up their history as far back as practicable and thorough inquiries were made as to the character, habits, and the ambition of each of them. Finally we selected one from among the four as the most likely man to start with. He was a little Pennsylvania Dutchman who had been observed to trot back home for a mile or so after his work in the evening, about as fresh as he was when he came trotting down to work in the morning. We found that upon wages of $1.15 a day he had succeeded in buying a small plot of ground, and that he was engaged in putting up the walls of a little house for himself in the morning before starting to work and at night after leaving. He also had the reputation of being exceedingly "close," that is, of placing a very high value on a dollar. As one man whom we talked to about him said, "A penny looks about the size of a cart-wheel to him." This man we will call Schmidt.

The task before us, then, narrowed itself down to getting Schmidt to handle 47 tons of pig iron per day and making him glad to do it. This was done as follows. Schmidt was called out from among the gang of pig-iron handlers and talked to somewhat in this way:

"Schmidt, are you a high-priced man?"

"Veil, I don't know vat you mean."

"Oh yes, you do. What I want to know is whether you are a high-priced man or not."

"Veil, I don't know vat you mean."

"Oh, come now, you answer my questions. What I want to find out is whether you are a high-priced man or one of these cheap fellows here. What I want to find out is whether you want to earn $1.85 a day or whether you are satisfied with $1.15, just the same as all those cheap fellows are getting."

"Did I vant $1.85 a day? Vas dot a high-priced man? Veil, yes, I vas a high-priced man."

"Oh, you're aggravating me. Of course you want $1.85 a day—every one wants it! You know perfectly well that that has very little to do with your being a high-priced man. For goodness sake answer my questions, and don't waste any more of my time. Now come over here. You see that pile of pig iron?"

"Yes."

"You see that car?"

"Yes."

"Well, if you are a high-priced man, you will load that pig iron on that car to-morrow for $1.85. Now do wake up and answer my question. Tell me whether you are a high-priced man or not."

"Veil—did I got $1.85 for loading dot pig iron on dot car tomorrow?"

"Yes, of course you do, and you get $1.85 for loading a pile like that every day right through the year. That is what a high-priced man does, and you know it just as well as I do."

"Veil, dot's all right. I could load dot pig iron on the car to-morrow for $1.85, and I get it every day, don't I?"

"Certainly you do—certainly you do."

"Veil, den, I vas a high-priced man."

"Now, hold on, hold on. You know just as well as I do that a high-priced man has to do exactly as he's told from morning till night. You have seen this man here before, haven't you?"

"No, I never saw him."

"Well, if you are a high-priced man, you will do exactly as this man tells you to-morrow, from morning till night. When he tells you to pick up a pig and walk, you pick it up and you walk, and when he tells you to sit down and rest, you sit down. You do that right straight through the day. And what's more, no back talk. Now a high-priced man does just what he's told to do, and no back talk. Do you understand that? When this man tells you to walk, you walk; when he tells you to sit down, you sit down, and you don't talk back at him. Now you come on to work here to-morrow morning and I'll know before night whether you are really a high-priced man or not."

This seems to be rather rough talk. And indeed it would be if applied to an educated mechanic, or even an intelligent laborer. With a man of the mentally sluggish type of Schmidt it is appropriate and not unkind, since it is effective in fixing his attention on the high wages which he wants and away from what, if it were called to his attention, he probably would consider impossibly hard work.

What would Schmidt's answer be if he were talked to in a manner which is usual under the management of "initiative and incentive"? Say, as follows:

"Now, Schmidt, you are a first-class pig-iron handler and know your business well. You have been handling at the rate of 12½ tons per day. I have given considerable study to handling pig iron, and feel sure that you could do a much larger day's work than you have been doing. Now don't you think that if you really tried you could handle 47 tons of pig iron per day, instead of 12½ tons?" What do you think Schmidt's answer would be to this?

Schmidt started to work, and all day long, and at regular intervals, was told by the man who stood over him with a watch, "Now pick up a pig and walk. Now sit down and rest. Now walk—now rest," etc. He worked when he was told to work, and rested when he was told to rest, and at half past five in the afternoon had his 47½ tons loaded on the car. And he practically never failed to work at this pace and do the task that was set him during the three years that the writer was at Bethlehem. And throughout this time he averaged a little more than $1.85 per day, whereas before he had never received over $1.15 per day, which was the ruling rate of wages at that time in Bethlehem. That is, he received 60 per cent, higher wages than were paid to other men who were not working on task work. One man after another was picked out and trained to handle pig iron at the rate of 47½ tons per day until all of the pig iron was handled at this rate, and the men were receiving 60 per cent, more wages than other workmen around them.

Questions

1. Why might workers be interested in working below their full efficiency?
2. What does Taylor think is the remedy for this suboptimal output?
3. What does Taylor think of Schmidt's character? His intelligence? Do you think Taylorism is elitist?
4. Outside of ignorance, why might Schmidt work inefficiently?
5. We can infer from Taylor's dialogue that Schmidt (whether real or not) is not a native speaker of English. Why do you think this quality is part of Taylor's illustrative example?
6. Worker output went up nearly four times but wages went up only 60 percent. How could you argue that the company benefited? How could you argue that the workers benefited?

"Labor" and "Capital" Are False Terms (1922)

HENRY FORD

Henry Ford transformed the car from a rich man's plaything into a working man's everyday luxury. With his constant striving for more efficient, low-cost production, the Model T defined a new automobile age. As early as 1903, Ford believed, invoking Adam Smith, "the way to make automobiles is to make one automobile like another automobile, to make them all alike, to make them come from the factory just alike—just like one pin is like another pin when it comes from a pin factory." At the same time, Ford was astoundingly hostile to finance, seeing himself more as a mechanic—or if pressed, a manufacturer—than a businessman in capitalism. He wrote that "Business men believed that you could do anything by 'financing' it. If it did not go through on the first financing then the idea was to 'refinance.' The process of 'refinancing' was simply the game of sending good money after bad. . . . I determined absolutely that never would I join a company in which finance came before the work or in which bankers or financiers had a part." In this essay he takes pains to distinguish a hardworking manufacturer like himself from an idle finance capitalist.

Among the tools we work with are words. Words stand for ideas, but ideas are often held back for lack of words, as freight is held up for lack of cars. Many men who possess ideas are hindered because they do not possess enough words to deliver them. You may notice this in current discussions of our social problems. It sometimes happens that people who indulge in these discussions exhibit a lack of word-tools with which to complete their mental work. For example: you may hear the whole human race summed up under two heads, Labor and Capital; and you may hear serious discussions proceed on the assumption that these two "classes" comprise all the elements of the social problem.

When you take the man who works with his hands and set him on one side, and the capitalist-idler on the other side, you have not divided the human world. There are hosts of people in between. But because we are tied to the terms Labor and Capital, we go along under the notion that we have included everybody.

To speak only of Labor and Capital is to permit too much good company to surround the mere capitalist who produces nothing and who skims the cream off other men's product.

If we must divide the world into two camps, why not label them Producers and Non-Producers? That rules out the idlers of every class—and we must isolate the idlers first. When we find the producers and classify them according to their value to the productive process, then we are in a position to go on to the question of distributing the rewards of production.

In the division of humanity into "Labor" and "Capital" you may not fairly include the manufacturer with "capitalists." A manufacturer works. He has a part in the production of useful commodities. He earns his bread. But a capitalist doesn't work at all. In a false phrase, "his money works for him." Having control of capital which he did nothing to acquire he uses it to skim a heavy tax off other men's product. When you get to these idlers who gamble in money, you have reached the "capitalist," but in all fairness we ought to be careful upon whom we place that name.

Mere capitalists, men who possess money and nothing else, men who use their control of money to escape useful work—this class of "capitalists" never has ideas that help the world. It schemes to fatten on other men's ideas.

Capital that a business makes for itself, that is employed to expand the workman's opportunity and increase his comfort and prosperity, and that is used to give more and more, and ever more men work, at the same time reducing the cost of service to the public—that sort of capital, even though it be under single control, is not a menace to humanity.

Ultimately it does not matter where this surplus is held nor who controls it; it is its use that matters.

Capital that is not constantly creating more and better jobs is more useless than sand. Capital that is not constantly making the conditions of daily labor better and the reward of daily labor more just, is not fulfilling its highest function.

The highest use of capital is not to make more money, but to make money do more service for the betterment of life. Unless we in our industries are helping to solve the social problem, we are not doing our principal work.

Questions

1. Why does Ford draw a distinction between "labor and capital" and "producers and non-producers"? Do you think this distinction makes sense? Why or why not?
2. Why might someone disagree with Ford's claim that "ultimately it does not matter where this surplus is held nor who controls it; it is its use that matters"?
3. Ford, who kept his company private, was famously hostile to Wall Street financiers. How can you see this sentiment in this essay?

4. What would a nineteenth-century Populist think about Ford's position on labor and capital? What do you think the Populist would think of Ford's business? Of Ford?

5. Who do you think believed that "the highest use of capital" is to make more money? How might one of those "idle" capitalists have replied to this essay?

6. Where would Ford and a member of the IWW agree?

The Great A&P and the Struggle for Small Business in America (2011)

MARC LEVINSON

The anti–chain store movement of the 1920s and '30s can be seen as the last gasp of small business populism. In fighting the chain stores, and especially the A&P, small-town businessmen struggled to maintain local control and autonomy in an era when agriculture and manufacturing were already heavily capitalized enterprises. The chain stores, though they sent money from small towns to big cities, did provide cheaper prices. In the end, Americans got higher wages from manufacturing and lower prices from the chain stores. The debates over the A&P in the 1920s, nonetheless, eerily presage many of the arguments we continue to have today about the social value of Walmart.

Big Business Now Sweeps Retail Trade," *The New York Times* declared in a 1928 headline running the entire width of a page. "Huge Corporations, Serving the Nation Through Country-Wide Chains, Are Displacing the Neighborhood Store." Across the United States, the newspaper reported, some thirty-eight hundred retail chains were operating 100,000 stores. "Out of every dollar spent in retail stores today 17 cents goes into the treasury of chain corporations." Of course, most of those chains had only a handful of stores, but a few were quite large. Foremost among them was a single company operating twice as many stores as the next seven chains combined, with sales more than four times those of the next-largest food retailer. "By all odds the largest retail trade trust in the world is the Great Atlantic and Pacific Tea Company," the Times affirmed.

The *Times* deemed A&P an "amazing concern," but most of the 2.1 million Americans who earned their livings making and selling food had a decidedly different view. The company's headlong growth and rampant price-cutting were a threat to every part of the food distribution system. A&P's demands that suppliers slash prices and provide advertising allowances cut into grocery manufacturers' profits. Its insistence that food processors, soap makers, and fruit and vegetable growers deal with it directly, without middlemen, endangered tens of thousands of agents, jobbers, and wholesalers whose purpose was to link food suppliers with individual grocers. A&P's financial strength, giving it the ability to plant a store anywhere it chose, darkened the prospects not only of the 400,000 people who ran independent food stores and their families but of uncounted numbers of men who dreamed of someday becoming merchants and of the small-town bankers and insurance agents who counted local retailers among their clients.

Table 1: Largest U.S. Retailers, 1929

Company	Category	Sales ($m)
Great Atlantic & Pacific Tea	Grocery	$1,054
Sears, Roebuck	Department/Mail Order	$415
F. W. Woolworth	Variety	$303
Montgomery Ward	Department/Mail Order	$292
Kroger Grocery and Baking	Grocery	$287
Safeway	Grocery	$214
J. C. Penney	Dry Goods	$210
S. S. Kresge	Variety	$147

| American Stores | Grocery | $143 |
| Gimbel Brothers | Department | $125 |

Source: *New York Times,* January 12, 1930, and other reports.

The woes of small merchants were especially acute in the small towns of the South and Midwest, where farm-based economies reeled under sagging commodity prices even as the big cities prospered. Through the first half of the 1920s, wholesalers and independent shop owners in these regions pushed political leaders to act against the chains. The first success came in 1925, when the town of Danville, Kentucky, population five thousand, required an annual license fee of grocery stores, with "cash and carry" grocers—such as chain stores—required to pay several times as much as "regular service" grocers. The ordinance was quashed by a state court, but the reprieve for chain stores would prove temporary.

New fuel was added to the conflict when the two largest catalog retailers, Sears, Roebuck and Montgomery Ward, began opening retail stores in 1925 and 1926. With their vast selections and money-back guarantees, Sears and Montgomery Ward had long taken business from small-town retailers, but their appeal was constrained by the need for customers to order by mail and wait for their purchases to arrive. The prospect that Sears or Ward's might open a store on the local Main Street encouraged hardware dealers and shoe-store owners to make common cause with grocers and druggists, who had been fighting the chains for years.

A 1928 study supported by the Chamber of Commerce of the United States concluded that "the death knell has been sounded for one-third of all retail outlets in the country" due to the growth of chains. Spurred by such inflammatory reports, the FTC launched two investigations—one of chain stores in general, and one focused on A&P. In June 1928, an FTC attorney sent the company pages of questions about its purchasing, pricing, and advertising practices to find out why A&P was selling name-brand merchandise more cheaply than other grocers. A few months later, the attorney wrote to ask whether A&P "has partially abandoned cut price appeal in its advertising." Finding no wrongdoing, the commission terminated the investigation in 1929, but the reprieve would prove temporary: A&P would be under federal investigation continuously for the next quarter century.

No factual investigation, however, could quell the growing concern about chain stores, for the worry had less to do with price competition than with the survival of small-town America. The chain store altered economic geography. Thousands of towns were home to grocery warehouses or the offices of small retail companies. A chain such as A&P, on the other hand, obtained economies of scale by centralizing its warehouses and offices in regional business centers. In small towns, it had only stores, with few employees and no highly paid executives. As local competitors fell by the wayside, jobs vanished with them, destroying the social fabric and leaving communities bereft of capital and civic leadership. "If businessmen become purely representatives of a large corporation without residence, property, or direct personal interest in the local community, the significance of such a change in community life is indeed apparent," one of the earliest scholars of the chain store wrote in 1927. Agreed a Michigan newspaper, "The consumer who patronizes the chain store, instead of the regular merchant, is effectually destroying the value of any property he owns in the town in which he lives."

The reality was that small stores had become unprofitable even before the Great Depression. In 1928, A&P's 1,615 traditional grocery stores with weekly sales below $700 were money losers. The grocery departments in one-third of the combination stores lost money, as did more than half the meat departments. A&P's own accounting showed that scale was vital: combination stores with sales above $3,000 per week produced annual returns on investment above 80 percent.

For a company of A&P's size, the speed of the planned shift to bigger stores was ambitious. But those thousands of combination stores were never built. Instead, the shift to bigger stores was driven by [. . .] the supermarket.

It took a brash grocer named Michael J. Cullen to shake up the industry. Cullen, the son of Irish immigrants, had learned the grocery trade as a clerk at A&P just after the turn of the century, and later worked as a regional manager for the Kroger chain in Illinois. The store, Cullen thought, should be "monstrous," four or five times the size of the typical grocery store. It should be located not on a busy shopping street but a few blocks away, where rents were lower and parking ample. It should offer a wide variety of branded merchandise, generating massive traffic by selling three hundred items at cost and another two hundred at cost plus 5 percent and advertising those low prices heavily. Sales would exceed $600,000 per year—ten times the average of chain-owned combination stores. The store would hold operating expenses per dollar of sales to half those of the average combination store by relying on self-service and keeping the staff small. The targeted annual profit was $16,900 per store. Relative to sales, such a profit would be no larger than A&P's or Kroger's. But Cullen's large store would need far less investment per dollar of sales. He calculated that each store would require $30,000 of equipment and inventory, so a profit of $16,900 implied a stunning 56 percent return on capital. "I would lead the public out of the high-priced houses of bondage into the low prices of the house of the promised land," Cullen wrote.

Questions

1. Why did small retailers resist chain stores?
2. How was the language of chain store resistance similar to that of the Grangers and Populists of the previous century?
3. What made the lower prices of the supermarkets and chain stores possible?

4. How was the chain store similar to and different from large industrial firms like U.S. Steel?

5. Do you think that lower consumer prices justified the loss of local small businesses?

6. What kinds of analogies to today's economy do you see in the anti-chain store movement?

MODULE 16

NEW DEAL CAPITALISM

Second Fireside Chat (1933)

FRANKLIN DELANO ROOSEVELT

Franklin Roosevelt used the medium of radio to an extent that no previous president had, to communicate directly with Americans. In his fireside chats, he attempted to calm fears about the Great Depression and explain why his policies would solve the ongoing crisis. In this second Fireside Chat, FDR addressed many different aspects of the economy, from home mortgages to farm prices to industrial work. The New Deal was marked by a multipronged set of policies that did not seek out a single root cause for the Depression. As Roosevelt said in this chat, the country was "faced by a condition and not a theory."

On a Sunday night a week after my Inauguration I used the radio to tell you about the banking crisis and the measures we were taking to meet it. I think that in that way I made clear to the country various facts that might otherwise have been misunderstood and in general provided a means of understanding which did much to restore confidence.

Tonight, eight weeks later, I come for the second time to give you my report; in the same spirit and by the same means to tell you about what we have been doing and what we are planning to do.

Two months ago we were facing serious problems. The country was dying by inches. It was dying because trade and commerce had declined to dangerously low levels; prices for basic commodities were such as to destroy the value of the assets of national institutions such as banks, savings banks, insurance companies, and others. These institutions, because of their great needs, were foreclosing mortgages, calling loans, refusing credit. Thus there was actually in process of destruction the property of millions of people who had borrowed money on that property in terms of dollars which had had an entirely different value from the level of March, 1933. That situation in that crisis did not call for any complicated consideration of economic panaceas or fancy plans. We were faced by a condition and not a theory.

There were just two alternatives: The first was to allow the foreclosures to continue, credit to be withheld and money to go into hiding, thus forcing liquidation and bankruptcy of banks, railroads and insurance companies and a recapitalizing of all business and all property on a lower level. This alternative meant a continuation of what is loosely called "deflation," the net result of which would have been extraordinary hardships on all property owners and, incidentally, extraordinary hardships on all persons working for wages through an increase in unemployment and a further reduction of the wage scale.

It is easy to see that the result of this course would have not only economic effects of a very serious nature, but social results that might bring incalculable harm. Even before I was inaugurated I came to the conclusion that such a policy was too much to ask the American people to bear. It involved not only a further loss of homes, farms, savings and wages, but also a loss of spiritual values—the loss of that sense of security for the present and the future so necessary to the peace and contentment of the individual and of his family. When you destroy these things you will find it difficult to establish confidence of any sort in the future. It was clear that mere appeals from Washington for confidence and the mere lending of more money to shaky institutions could not stop this downward course. A prompt program applied as quickly as possible seemed to me not only justified but imperative to our national security. The Congress, and when

I say Congress I mean the members of both political parties, fully understood this and gave me generous and intelligent support. The members of Congress realized that the methods of normal times had to be replaced in the emergency by measures which were suited to the serious and pressing requirements of the moment. There was no actual surrender of power, Congress still retained its constitutional authority, and no one has the slightest desire to change the balance of these powers. The function of Congress is to decide what has to be done and to select the appropriate agency to carry out its will. To this policy it has strictly adhered. The only thing that has been happening has been to designate the President as the agency to carry out certain of the purposes of the Congress. This was constitutional and in keeping with the past American tradition.

The legislation which has been passed or is in the process of enactment can properly be considered as part of a well-grounded plan.

First, we are giving opportunity of employment to one-quarter of a million of the unemployed, especially the young men who have dependents, to go into the forestry and flood-prevention work. This is a big task because it means feeding, clothing and caring for nearly twice as many men as we have in the regular army itself. In creating this civilian conservation corps we are killing two birds with one stone. We are clearly enhancing the value of our natural resources, and we are relieving an appreciable amount of actual distress. This great group of men has entered upon its work on a purely voluntary basis; no military training is involved and we are conserving not only our natural resources, but our human resources. One of the great values to this work is the fact that it is direct and requires the intervention of very little machinery. [...]

Next, the Congress is about to pass legislation that will greatly ease the mortgage distress among the farmers and the home owners of the Nation, by providing for the easing of the burden of debt now bearing so heavily upon millions of our people.

Our next step in seeking immediate relief is a grant of half a billion dollars to help the States, counties and municipalities in their duty to care for those who need direct and immediate relief.

The Congress also passed legislation authorizing the sale of beer in such States as desired it. This has already resulted in considerable reemployment and incidentally has provided much needed tax revenue.

We are planning to ask the Congress for legislation to enable the Government to undertake public works, thus stimulating directly and indirectly the employment of many others in well-considered projects. [. . .]

I am certain that the people of this country understand and approve the broad purposes behind these new governmental policies relating to agriculture and industry and transportation. We found ourselves faced with more agricultural products than we could possibly consume ourselves and with surpluses which other Nations did not have the cash to buy from us except at prices ruinously low. We found our factories able to turn out more goods than we could possibly consume, and at the same time we were faced with a falling export demand. We found ourselves with more facilities to transport goods and crops than there were goods and crops to be transported. All of this has been caused in large part by a complete lack of planning and a complete failure to understand the danger signals that have been flying ever since the close of the World War. The people of this country have been erroneously encouraged to believe that they could keep on increasing the output of farm and factory indefinitely and that some magician would find ways and means for that increased output to be consumed with reasonable profit to the producer.

Today we have reason to believe that things are a little better than they were two months ago. Industry has picked up, railroads are carrying more freight, farm prices are better, but I am not going to indulge in issuing proclamations of over-enthusiastic assurance. We cannot ballyhoo ourselves back to prosperity. I am going to be honest at all times with the people of the country. I do not want the people of this country to take the foolish course of letting this improvement come back on another speculative wave. I do not want the people to believe that because of unjustified optimism we can resume the ruinous practice of increasing our crop output and our factory output in the hope that a kind Providence will find buyers at high prices. Such a course may bring us immediate and false prosperity but it will be the kind of prosperity that will lead us into another tailspin.

It is wholly wrong to call the measures that we have taken Government control of farming, industry, and transportation. It is rather a partnership between Government and farming and industry and transportation, not partnership in profits, for the profits still go to the citizens, but rather a partnership in planning, and a partnership to see that the plans are carried out. [. . .]

We are working toward a definite goal, which is to prevent the return of conditions which came very close to destroying what we call modern civilization. The actual accomplishment of our purpose cannot be attained in a day. Our policies are wholly within purposes for which our American Constitutional Government was established 150 years ago.

I know that the people of this country will understand this and will also understand the spirit in which we are undertaking this policy. I do not deny that we may make mistakes of procedure as we carry out the policy. I have no expectation of making a hit every time I come to bat. What I seek is the highest possible batting average, not only for myself but for the team. Theodore Roosevelt once said to me: "If I can be right 75 percent of the time I shall come up to the fullest measure of my hopes." [. . .]

To you, the people of this country, all of us, the members of the Congress and the members of this Administration, owe a profound debt of gratitude. Throughout the depression you have been patient. You have granted us wide powers; you have encouraged us with a widespread approval of our purposes. Every ounce of strength and every resource at our command we have devoted to the end of justifying your confidence. We are encouraged to believe that a wise and sensible beginning has been made. In the present spirit of mutual confidence and mutual encouragement we go forward.

Questions

1. What would Populists of the nineteenth century have thought about FDR's reforms?
2. Is there a meaningful difference between government "planning" and government "control"?
3. What areas of the economy did FDR intend to help?
4. How could these programs be interpreted as unconstitutional?

The Many and the Few: A Chronicle of the Dynamic Auto Workers (1985)

HENRY KRAUS

In the middle of the Great Depression, auto workers stood up to the largest corporation in the United States—and won. Henry Kraus's insider account of the Flint Strike of 1936 reveals the chaos of those days. This strike was one of the most successful in U.S. history, transforming the United Auto Workers into one of America's strongest unions. Its success depended on worker solidarity but also a keen sense of strike strategy, using the novel resistance of the sitdown strike (where workers occupy the machines). By occupying a part of the General Motors supply chain that could not be replaced, the workers forced the company to negotiate. Unlike in the nineteenth century, the state and federal authorities refused to back local police or the corporation in the strike. Worker power allowed for union success.

Bob Travis received a phone call from "Chink" Ananich, one of the Fisher One boys. "Chink" was working on the swing shift and had slipped out of the plant to make his important announcement.

"They're moving dies out, Bob!" he said excitedly. "You sure?"

"Yeah! The boys in the press room working near the doors by the railroad dock say they got crank press dies on some trucks and they're loading a flock of freight cars." Travis made his mind up instantaneously.

"Okay! They're asking for it!" he said almost gayly. "Tell the boys stewards' meeting at lunch time. Bring everybody down."

There is hardly anything about which a unionist is more sensitive than on the subject of the "runaway shop." It is one of the oldest of tactics used against organization efforts. In Travis' own experience, besides, the memory was fresh of how General Motors had slipped two-thirds of the jobs right from under his co-workers at Toledo-Chevrolet in revenge for the defeat it had sustained in May 1935. Present always to his mind were the confusion and suffering and despair that this act had caused, and the picture of fathers of families coming to the union office and pleading that the organization do something to get their jobs back. Those who were still working felt as though they were taking the bread out of the others' mouths. The role played by Travis in the Flint strike and by many volunteers who later came up from his local to engage in it was directly traceable to this tragic experience and to the desire of the victims to pay off the responsible corporation in the coin of union solidarity.

After "Chink" Ananich hung up Travis called the Fisher One union office.

"Put the flicker on," he told the girl.

There was a big red 200-watt bulb over the front of the office which was right across from the plant. The boys near the windows inside the factory had instructions to give a look over every so often. If the flicker was on that meant something was up and that there would be a meeting. At 8 p.m. the workers streamed out of the plant for "lunch hour." In four minutes the union hall was filled with an excited crowd of men. The report of the moving of the dies had evidently spread everywhere by this time. Everybody's mind seemed made up before even a word was spoken. Travis got right down to brass tacks.

"Boys, we'll make this snappy," he said. "I understand there's something happening over there on the press room dock."

"That's right," one of the men called out, "they're taking dies out of the press room. They got four or five cars lined up there."

The men from the die room substantiated this.

"Well, what are we going to do about it?" Travis asked, looking slowly about the room. There was a cold sort of pause. A chap raised his hand and stood up.

"Well, them's our jobs," he said quietly. "We want them left right here in Flint."

"That's right!" several others exclaimed.

"Boys," Travis said, still holding himself back, "I'm not going to tell you what you ought to do. That ought to be plain enough to you if you want to protect your jobs. In my plant in Toledo, General Motors walked off with 1,500 jobs a year ago and in Cleveland the Fisher Body boys struck just Monday to save theirs. What do you want to do?"

"Shut her down! Shut the goddam plant!"

The cry was taken up by the whole room till it was nothing but one big shout.

"Okay, fellows, that's what I wanted to hear you say. Now the important thing to remember from here on out is—discipline. You can't have too much of it in a strike, especially at the beginning. Roy and I will come in after you've got the plant down and help you get everything organized. Bud and the rest of the committee will be in charge. You'll have to enlarge the committee so as to get representation on it from all departments. Remember, absolutely no liquor. And tell the girls in cut-and-sew to go home and come around to the Pengelly headquarters tomorrow morning. We'll have plenty of work for them to do. Okay, good luck!"

"Everybody stays in till the warning whistle!" I yelled from the door.

"That's right," Travis said. "We don't want any stooges tipping the company off ahead of time."

The men stood still facing the door. It was like trying to chain a natural force. They couldn't hold back and began crowding forward. Then suddenly they broke through the door and made a race for the plant gates, running in every direction toward the quarter-mile building front which bordered the main highway from Detroit.

We waited outside, anxiously watching the windows. The starting whistle blew. We listened intently. There was no responsive throb. Was it right? we asked ourselves, looking at each other. Had they pulled it off?

"Here's where the fight begins," Travis said between tight lips as we stamped nervously on the cold pavement. But there was no sign of any untoward activity inside the plant. Several minutes passed. Then suddenly a third floor window was flung open and there was "Chink" Ananich waving his arms.

"Hooray, Bob! She's ours!"

Then other windows went up and smiling workers gathered about them.

"Was there any trouble?" we shouted.

"Naw!"

A little later the girls came out, wearing overalls and working caps. And there was a straggling male here and there. But the vast majority of the three thousand men remained voluntarily inside the plant that first night. [. . .]

The job of organizing the sitdown was tremendous, particularly since the great majority of the workers had had no experience with unions or with the discipline required in such crises. Many joined up only on that first night while the sudden calling of the strike had eliminated the possibility of even the most elementary preparations. The situation was pretty chaotic the first few days as a result.

One of the early steps was to confine the sitdown to one building, the north unit, as it was called, and to merely subject the south unit and press shop to a constant patrol. This cut the defense needs. But the men very quickly learned the importance of leadership and even proposed on their own measures endowing the strike committee with special powers. [...]

The committee immediately ordered all further leaves to be halted and called union headquarters for reinforcements. Perhaps the only thing that saved the strike during this period of disorganization was the revolutionary newness of the sitdown tactic which undoubtedly proved far more confusing to the company than to the union, rendering impotent the traditional strikebreaking technics.

Questions

1. What was new about the sitdown strike compared to earlier strikes?
2. What tactical advantage did the strikers possess in occupying only a small part of the factory? Why did they choose that part of the factory?
3. How did morale matter in the occupation?
4. Why did the strikers value discipline?
5. Why did the company want to move its dies under cover of darkness?

MODULE 17

CAPITALISM AT WAR

Emergency Measures (1941)

FRANKLIN DELANO ROOSEVELT

From the East Room of the White House.

MY FELLOW AMERICANS OF ALL THE AMERICAS; MY FRIENDS:

[. . .] Our future—our future independence is bound up with the future independence of all of our sister Republics.

The pressing problems that confront us are military and naval problems. We cannot afford to approach them from the point of view of wishful thinkers or sentimentalists. What we face is cold, hard fact.

The first and fundamental fact is that what started as a European war has developed, as the Nazis always intended it should develop, into a world war for world domination. Adolf Hitler never considered the domination of Europe as an end in itself. European conquest was but a step toward ultimate goals in all the other continents. It is unmistakably apparent to all of us that, unless the advance of Hitlerism is forcibly checked now, the Western Hemisphere will be within range of the Nazi weapons of destruction. [. . .]

Our whole program of aid for the democracies has been based on hard-headed concern for our own security and for the kind of safe and civilized world in which we wish to live. Every dollar of material that we send helps to keep the dictators away from our own hemisphere, and every day that they are held off gives us time to build more guns and tanks and planes and ships.

We have made no pretense about our own self-interest in this aid. Great Britain understands it—and so does Nazi Germany.

And now—after a year—Britain still fights gallantly, on a "far-flung battle line." We have doubled and redoubled our vast production, increasing, month by month, our material supply of the tools of war for ourselves and for Britain and for China—and eventually for all the democracies.

The supply of these tools will not fail—it will increase. [. . .]

To the people of the Americas, a triumphant Hitler would say, as he said after the seizure of Austria, and as he said after Munich, and as he said after the seizure of Czechoslovakia: "I am now completely satisfied. This is the last territorial readjustment I will seek." And he would of course add: "All we want is peace and friendship, and profitable trade relations with you in the New World."

[And] were any of us in the Americas so incredibly simple and forgetful as to accept those honeyed words, what would then happen?

Those in the New World who were seeking profits would be urging that all that the dictatorships desired was "peace." They would oppose toil and taxes for more American armament. And meanwhile, the dictatorships would be forcing the enslaved peoples of their Old World conquests into a system they are even now organizing—to build—to build a naval and air force intended to gain and hold and be master of the Atlantic and the Pacific as well. [. . .]

The American laborer would have to compete with slave labor in the rest of the world. Minimum wages, maximum hours? Nonsense: Wages and hours [would be] fixed by Hitler. The dignity and power and standard of living of the American worker and farmer would be gone. Trade unions would become historic[al] relics, and collective bargaining a joke. Farm income? What happens to all farm surpluses without any foreign trade? The American farmer would get for his products exactly what Hitler wanted to give. The farmer would face obvious disaster and complete regimentation. Tariff walls—Chinese walls of isolation—would be futile. Freedom to trade is essential to our economic life. We do not eat all the food we [can] produce; and we do not burn all the oil we can pump; we do not use all the goods we can manufacture. It would not be an American wall to keep Nazi goods out; it would be a Nazi wall to keep us in.

The whole fabric of working life as we know it—business and manufacturing, mining and agriculture—all would be mangled and crippled under such a system. Yet to maintain even that crippled independence would require permanent conscription of our manpower; it would curtail the funds we could spend on education, on housing, on public works, on flood control, on health and, instead, we should be permanently pouring our resources into armaments; and, year in and year out, standing day and night watch against the destruction of our cities.

Yes, even our right of worship would be threatened. The Nazi world does not recognize any God except Hitler; for the Nazis are as ruthless as the Communists in the denial of God. What place has religion which preaches the dignity of the human being, of the majesty of the human soul, in a world where moral standards are measured by treachery and bribery and Fifth Columnists? Will our children, too, wander off, goose-stepping in search of new gods?

We do not accept, [and] we will not permit, this Nazi "shape of things to come." It will never be forced upon us, if we act in this present crisis with the wisdom and the courage which have distinguished our country in all the crises of the past.

[. . .] The Axis Powers can never achieve their objective of world domination unless they first obtain control of the seas. That is their supreme purpose today, and to achieve it, they must capture Great Britain. They could then have the power to dictate to the Western Hemisphere. No spurious argument, no appeal to sentiment, [and] no false pledges like those given by Hitler at Munich, can deceive the American people into believing that he and his Axis partners would not, with Britain defeated, close in relentlessly on this hemisphere of ours.

But if the Axis Powers fail to gain control of the seas, then they are certainly defeated. Their dreams of world domination will then go by the board; and the criminal leaders who started this war will suffer inevitable disaster. [...]

The blunt truth is this—and I reveal this with the full knowledge of the British Government: the present rate of Nazi sinkings of merchant ships is more than three times as high as the capacity of British shipyards to replace them; it is more than twice the combined British and American output of merchant ships today.

We can answer this peril by two simultaneous measures: first, by speeding up and increasing our own great shipbuilding program; and second, by helping to cut down the losses on the high seas. Attacks on shipping off the very shores of land which we are determined to protect present an actual military danger to the Americas. And that danger has recently been heavily underlined by the presence in Western Hemisphere waters of a Nazi battleship of great striking power.

There are same timid ones among us who say that we must preserve peace at any price—lest we lose our liberties forever. To them I say this: never in the history of the world has a nation lost its democracy by a successful struggle to defend its democracy. We must not be defeated by the fear of the very danger which we are preparing to resist. Our freedom has shown its ability to survive war, but our freedom would never survive surrender. "The only thing we have to fear is fear itself."

There is, of course, a small group of sincere, patriotic men and women whose real passion for peace has shut their eyes to the ugly realities of international banditry and to the need to resist it at all costs. I am sure they are embarrassed by the sinister support they are receiving from the enemies of democracy in our midst—the Bundists, [and] the Fascists, and Communists, and every group devoted to bigotry and racial and religious intolerance. It is no mere coincidence that all the arguments put forward by these enemies of democracy—all their attempts to confuse and divide our people and to destroy public confidence in [our] Government—all their defeatist forebodings that Britain and democracy are already beaten—all their selfish promises that we can "do business" with Hitler—all of these are but echoes or the words that have been poured out from the Axis bureaus of propaganda. Those same words have been used before in other countries—to scare them, to divide them, to soften them up. Invariably, those same words have formed the advance guard of physical attack.

Your Government has the right to expect of all citizens that they take [loyal] part in the common work of our common defense—take loyal part from this moment forward. I have recently set up the machinery for civilian defense. It will rapidly organize, locality by locality. It will depend on the organized effort of men and women everywhere. All will have opportunities and responsibilities to fulfill. Defense today means more than merely fighting. It means morale, civilian as well as military; it means using every available resource; it means enlarging every useful plant. It means the use of a greater American common sense in discarding rumor and distorted statement. It means recognizing, for what they are, racketeers and fifth columnists, [who are] the incendiary bombs in this country of the moment.

All of us know that we have made very great social progress in recent years. We propose to maintain that progress and strengthen it. When the nation is threatened from without, however, as it is today, the actual production and transportation of the machinery of defense must not be interrupted by disputes between capital and capital, labor and labor or capital and labor. The future of all free enterprise—of capital and labor alike—is at stake. This is no time for capital to make, or be allowed to retain, excess profits. Articles of defense must have undisputed right of way in every industrial plant in the country. [. . .]

I repeat the words of the Signers of the Declaration of Independence—that little band of patriots, fighting long ago against overwhelming odds, but certain, as [are we] we are now, of ultimate victory: "With a firm reliance on the protection of Divine Providence, we mutually pledge to each other our lives, our fortunes, and our sacred honor."

Questions

1. Why did FDR think American industry was the crucial factor in defeating Nazism?
2. In FDR's view, why did some Americans not want to fight the Nazis?
3. What did it mean that FDR juxtaposed the American "minimum wage" and Nazism?
4. How would Nazi victory in Europe hurt American workers in the United States?

Executive Order to Desegregate Wartime Production (1941)

FRANKLIN DELANO ROOSEVELT

While we think of FDR as the definitive liberal president, he had a troubled and contradictory legacy regarding race relations during his administration. Most indicatively, in 1938 he did not support an antilynching bill in Congress for fear of alienating Southern Democrats. Yet a few years later, during World War II, he issued Executive Order 8802, which prohibited racial discrimination in the defense industries. FDR issued the order only under duress. The prominent African-American labor leader A. Phillip Randolph had threatened a march on Washington (two decades before Martin Luther King Jr.'s famous march) unless FDR enabled black Americans to join the surging ranks of war workers. Despite the order's realpolitik origins, it was a significant step towards the end of labor discrimination in the United States, forcing industrial workforces to integrate—just as the army did. Following the war, these interracial experiences would help shift the racial consciousness of the United States.

Reaffirming Policy Of Full Participation In The Defense
Program By All Persons, Regardless Of Race, Creed,
Color, Or National Origin, And Directing Certain Action
In Furtherance Of Said Policy

WHEREAS it is the policy of the United States to encourage full participation in the national defense program by all citizens of the

United States, regardless of race, creed, color, or national origin, in the firm belief that the democratic way of life within the Nation can be defended successfully only with the help and support of all groups within its borders; and

WHEREAS there is evidence that available and needed workers have been barred from employment in industries engaged in defense production solely because of considerations of race, creed, color, or national origin, to the detriment of workers' morale and of national unity:

NOW, THEREFORE, by virtue of the authority vested in me by the Constitution and the statutes, and as a prerequisite to the successful conduct of our national defense production effort, I do hereby reaffirm the policy of the United States that there shall be no discrimination in the employment of workers in defense industries or government because of race, creed, color, or national origin, and I do hereby declare that it is the duty of employers and of labor organizations, in furtherance of said policy and of this order, to provide for the full and equitable participation of all workers in defense industries, without discrimination because of race, creed, color, or national origin;

And it is hereby ordered as follows:

1. All departments and agencies of the Government of the United States concerned with vocational and training programs for defense production shall take special measures appropriate to assure that such programs are administered without discrimination because of race, creed, color, or national origin;

2. All contracting agencies of the Government of the United States shall include in all defense contracts hereafter negotiated by them a provision obligating the contractor not to discriminate against any worker because of race, creed, color, or national origin;

3. There is established in the Office of Production Management a Committee on Fair Employment Practice, which shall consist of a chairman and four other members to be appointed by the President. The Chairman and members of the Committee shall serve as such without compensation but shall be entitled to actual and necessary transportation, subsistence and other expenses incidental to performance of their duties. The Committee shall receive and investigate complaints of discrimination in violation of the provisions of this order and shall take appropriate steps to redress grievances which it finds to be valid. The Committee shall also recommend to the several departments and agencies of the Government of the United States and to the President all measures which may be deemed by it necessary or proper to effectuate the provisions of this order.

Franklin D. Roosevelt
June 25, 1941

Questions

1. Do you think that the U.S. government really would have canceled defense contracts in wartime if racial discrimination occurred?
2. How do you think white industrial workers responded to this executive order?
3. Why would FDR not want a march on Washington in 1941?

PART IV

MAKING AMERICAN
CAPITALISM GLOBAL

MODULE 18

AMERICAN SUPERPOWER

The Marshall Plan (1947)

GEORGE MARSHALL

The victors of World War II sought to learn from history and not repeat what they saw as the mistakes of the peace following World War I. Instead of exacting tribute from a conquered Germany, a tactic which was widely believed to have weakened the Weimar economy and enabled Hitler's rise to power, the Allied Powers instead sought to rebuild it. George Marshall's plan represents a break in military history. Japan, meanwhile, was demilitarized, but its economy exploded through the infusion of American capital.

I need not tell you gentlemen that the world situation is very serious. That must be apparent to all intelligent people. I think one difficulty is that the problem is one of such enormous complexity that the very mass of facts presented to the public by press and radio make it exceedingly difficult for the man in the street to reach a clear appraisement of the situation. Furthermore, the people of this country are distant from the troubled areas of the earth and it is hard for them to comprehend the plight and consequent reaction of the long-suffering peoples, and the effect of those reactions on their governments in connection with our efforts to promote peace in the world.

In considering the requirements for the rehabilitation of Europe the physical loss of life, the visible destruction of cities, factories, mines, and railroads was correctly estimated, but it has become obvious during recent months that this visible destruction was probably less serious than the dislocation of the entire fabric of European economy. For the past 10 years conditions have been highly abnormal. The feverish maintenance of the war effort engulfed all aspects of national economics. Machinery has fallen into disrepair or is entirely obsolete. Under the arbitrary and destructive Nazi rule, virtually every possible enterprise was geared into the German war machine. Long-standing commercial ties, private institutions, banks, insurance companies and shipping companies disappeared, through the loss of capital, absorption through nationalization or by simple destruction. In many countries, confidence in the local currency has been severely shaken. The breakdown of the business structure of Europe during the war was complete. Recovery has been seriously retarded by the fact that 2 years after the close of hostilities a peace settlement with Germany and Austria has not been agreed upon. But even given a more prompt solution of these difficult problems, the rehabilitation of the economic structure of Europe quite evidently will require a much longer time and greater effort than had been foreseen.

There is a phase of this matter which is both interesting and serious. The farmer has always produced the foodstuffs to exchange with the city dweller for the other necessities of life. This division of labor is the basis of modern civilization. At the present time it is threatened with breakdown. The town and city industries are not producing adequate goods to exchange with the food-producing farmer. Raw materials and fuel are in short supply. Machinery is lacking or worn out. The farmer or the peasant cannot find the goods for sale which he desires to purchase. So the sale of his farm produce for money which he cannot use seems to him unprofitable transaction. He, therefore, has withdrawn many fields from crop cultivation and is using them for grazing. He feeds more grain to stock and finds for himself and his family an ample supply of food, however short he may be on clothing and the other ordinary gadgets of civilization. Meanwhile people in the cities are short of food and fuel. So the governments are forced to use their foreign money and credits to procure these necessities abroad. This process exhausts funds which are urgently needed for reconstruction. Thus a very serious situation is rapidly developing which bodes no good for the world. The modern system of the division of labor upon which the exchange of products is based is in danger of breaking down.

The truth of the matter is that Europe's requirements for the next 3 or 4 years of foreign food and other essential products—principally from America—are so much greater than her present ability to pay that she must have substantial additional help, or face economic, social, and political deterioration of a very grave character.

The remedy lies in breaking the vicious circle and restoring the confidence of the European people in the economic future of their own countries and of Europe as a whole. The manufacturer and the farmer throughout wide areas must be able and willing to exchange their products for currencies the continuing value of which is not open to question.

Aside from the demoralizing effect on the world at large and the possibilities of disturbances arising as a result of the desperation of the people concerned, the consequences to the economy of the United States should be apparent to all. It is logical that the United States should do whatever it is able to do to assist in the return of normal economic health in the world, without which there can be no political stability and no assured peace. Our policy is directed not against any country or doctrine but against hunger, poverty, desperation, and chaos. Its purpose should be the revival of working economy in the world so as to permit the emergence of political and social conditions in which free institutions can exist. Such assistance, I am convinced, must not be on a piecemeal basis as various crises develop. Any assistance that this Government may render in the future should provide a cure rather than a mere palliative. Any government that is willing to assist in the task of recovery will find full cooperation, I am sure, on the part of the United States Government. Any government which maneuvers to block the recovery of other countries cannot expect help from us. Furthermore, governments, political parties, or groups which seek to perpetuate human misery in order to profit therefrom politically or otherwise will encounter the opposition of the United States.

It is already evident that, before the United States Government can proceed much further in its efforts to alleviate the situation and help start the European world on its way to recovery, there must be some agreement among the countries of Europe as to the requirements of the situation and the part those countries themselves will take in order to give proper effect to whatever action might be undertaken by this Government. It would be neither fitting nor efficacious for this Government to undertake to draw up unilaterally a program designed to place Europe on its feet economically. This is the business of the Europeans. The initiative, I think, must come from Europe. The role of this country should consist of friendly aid in the drafting of a European program so far as it may be practical for us to do so. The program should be a joint one, agreed to by a number, if not all European nations.

An essential part of any successful action on the part of the United States is an understanding on the part of the people of America of the character of the problem and the remedies to be applied. Political passion and prejudice should have no part. With foresight, and a willingness on the part of our people to face up to the vast responsibilities which history has clearly placed upon our country, the difficulties I have outlined can and will be overcome.

Questions

1. When the economies of Europe and Japan returned, American economic supremacy was threatened. Did the U.S. make the right choice in aiding its previous enemies?
2. What lessons can we take from the Marshall Plan in aiding the developing world today?
3. Was the Marshall Plan as apolitical and humanitarian as described?

The Stages of Economic Growth (1959)

WALT WHITMAN ROSTOW

An influential postwar economist, W. W. Rostow formalized economic history into a theory of development. His idea of the "take-off" period, when an economy's growth becomes self-sustaining, became the holy grail of postwar economic policy, as the IMF and the World Bank attempted to industrialize the so-called Third World. While his outline roughly fits the experience of the developed world, it was (and remains) controversial when applied to developing economies, which emerge into a world already filled with American, Japanese, and European products and capital. Rostow posits one road to industrial capitalism, demanding that we wonder if there is only one way or many ways to develop a capitalist economy.

This article summarizes a way of generalizing the sweep of modern economic history. The form of this generalization is a set of stages of growth, which can be designated as follows: the traditional society; the preconditions for take-off; the take-off; the drive to maturity; the age of high mass consumption. Beyond the age of high mass consumption lie the problems which are beginning to arise in a few societies, and which may arise generally when diminishing relative marginal utility sets in for real income itself.

A Dynamic Theory of Production

As modern economists have sought to merge classical production theory with Keynesian income analysis they have introduced the dynamic variables: population, technology, entrepreneurship, etc. But they have tended to do so in forms so rigid and general that their models cannot grip the essential phenomena of growth, as they appear to an economic historian. We require a dynamic theory of production which isolates not only the distribution of income between consumption, saving, and investment (and the balance of production between consumers and capital goods) but which focuses directly and in some detail on the composition of investment and on developments within particular sectors of the economy. The argument that follows is based on such a flexible, disaggregated theory of production.

At any period of time, the rate of growth in the sectors will vary greatly; and it is possible to isolate empirically certain leadings sectors, at early stages of their evolution, whose rapid rate of expansion plays an essential direct and indirect role in maintaining the overall momentum of the economy. For some purposes it is useful to characterize an economy in terms of its leading sectors; and a part of the technical basis for the stages of growth lies in the changing sequence of leading sectors. In essence it is the fact that sectors tend to have a rapid growth phase, early in their life, that makes it possible and useful to regard economic history as a sequence of stages rather than merely as a continuum, within which nature never makes a jump.

The stages of growth also require, however, that elasticities of demand be taken into account, and that this familiar concept be widened; for these rapid growth phases in the sectors derive not merely from the discontinuity of production functions but also from high price or income elasticities of demand. Leading sectors are determined not merely by the changing flow of technology and the changing willingness of entrepreneurs to accept available innovations: they are also partially determined by those types of demand which have exhibited high elasticity with respect to price, income, or both.

The demand for resources has resulted, however, not merely from demands set up by private taste and choice, but also from social decisions and from the policies of governments—whether democratically responsive or not. It is necessary, therefore, to look at the choices made by societies in the disposition of their resources in terms which transcend conventional market processes. It is necessary to look at their welfare functions, in the widest sense, including the non-economic processes which determined them.

The Traditional Society

The central economic fact about traditional societies is that they evolved within limited production functions. Both in the more distant past and in recent times the story of traditional societies is a story of endless change, reflected in the scale and patterns of trade, the level of agricultural output and productivity, the scale of manufactures, fluctuations in population and real income. But limitations of technology decreed a ceiling beyond which they could not penetrate. They did not lack inventiveness and innovations, some of high productivity. But they did lack a systematic understanding of their physical environment capable of making invention a more or less regular current flow, rather than a stock of ad hoc achievements inherited from the past. They lacked, in short, the tools and the outlook towards the physical world of the post-Newtonian era.

The Preconditions for Take-off

The initial preconditions for take-off were created in Western Europe out of two characteristics of the post-medieval world which interacted and reinforced each other: the gradual evolution of modern science and the modern scientific attitude; and the lateral innovation that came with the discovery of new lands and the rediscovery of old, converging with the impulse to create new technology at certain strategic points. The widening of the market—both within Europe and overseas—brought not only trade, but increased specialization of production, increased inter-regional and international dependence, enlarged institutions of finance, and increased market incentives to create new production functions. The whole process was heightened by the extension to trade and colonies of the old dynastic competition for control over European territories, inherited from the world of traditional societies.

The Take-off

As I have suggested in an earlier article, the take-off consists, in essence, of the achievement of rapid growth in a limited group of sectors, where modern industrial techniques are applied. Historically, the leading sectors in take-off have ranged from cotton textiles (Britain and New England); to railroads (the United States, France, Germany, Canada, Russia); to modern timber-cutting and railroads (Sweden). In addition, agricultural processing, oil, import substitution industries, shipbuilding, and rapid expansions in military output have helped to provide the initial industrial surge.

The take-off is distinguished from earlier industrial surges by the fact that prior and concurrent developments make the application of modern industrial techniques a self-sustained rather than an abortive process. Not only must the momentum in the three key sectors of the preconditions be maintained but the corps of entrepreneurs and technicians must be enlarged, and the sources of capital must be institutionalized in such a way as to permit the economy to suffer structural shocks; to redispose its investment resources; and to resume growth. It is the requirement that the economy exhibit this resilience that justifies defining the take-off as embracing an interval of about two decades.

The Drive to Maturity

During the drive to maturity the industrial process is differentiated, with new leading sectors gathering momentum to supplant the older leading sectors of the take-off, where deceleration has increasingly slowed the pace of expansion.

The Age of High Mass Consumption

There have been, essentially, three directions in which the mature economy could be turned once the society ceased to accept the extension of modern technology as a primary, if not over-riding objective: to offer, by public measures, increased security, welfare, and, perhaps, leisure to the working force; to provide enlarged private consumption—including single family homes and durable consumers goods and services—on a mass basis; to seek enlarged power for the mature nation on the world scene. A good deal of the history of the first half of the twentieth century can be told in terms of the pattern and succession of choices made by various mature societies as among these three alternatives.

Questions

1. What is a leading sector? Why would a new sector emerge that grows rapidly? Why is this important to Rostow's vision of capitalism?
2. For Rostow, why is economic history more useful than economic models?
3. What is the role of science in the development of capitalism?
4. Where would Rostow and Pomeranz agree or disagree? What implications do their views have for economic development of newly industrializing countries today?
5. These steps seem simple. What makes them difficult to achieve?

6. The "Age of High Mass Consumption" in mature societies appears to be the last step in capitalist development. How might other thinkers we've read consider this idea?

7. Today we live in an economy of decreased security and stagnating wages for most Americans. How might Rostow explain this development? Would it contradict his stagist model?

8. Like socialists, Rostow embraces a stagist model of history (though he is not a socialist). Do you think that history has a direction and an end?

MODULE 19

POSTWAR CAPITALISM

Budgetism: Opiate of the Middle Class (1956)

WILLIAM H. WHYTE

William Whyte is best known for his attack on corporate conformity, *The Organization Man*. Before he wrote that book, he wrote this essay attacking the use of installment credit among middle-class suburbanites. In the essay, he describes a generation that has no respect for saving and no fear of another depression. While we often hear today that debt is only a recent phenomenon, we can clearly see in this essay that in the midst of postwar prosperity Americans borrowed liberally. What made this decision different than today's, perhaps, is that while our wages have stagnated for forty years, theirs grew year after year. Borrowing today and paying back tomorrow truly was a reasonable choice. The solvency of this postwar generation, then, is due less to an aversion to borrowing than the luck of being born at just the right time. The budget might be able to discipline an individual, but it cannot discipline an economy.

Is thrift un-American? Not long ago this would have been just another of those self-answering questions—like Must Workers Be Robots?—that people set up for conferences. But the question now deserves serious consideration. As a normal part of life, thrift now is un-American. To be sure, aggregate "savings" are at a high level, but in an era when money that people are repaying on loans goes down in the statisticians' books as savings, over-all figures can be illusory.

More and more, people are saving not to accumulate but to spend; for no longer do they identify saving with morality. They save little not because they cannot save—people have never been more prosperous. They save little because they do not really believe in saving.

They have become prey to "budgetism." This does not mean that they actually keep formal budgets. Quite the contrary; the beauty of budgetism is that one doesn't have to keep a budget at all. It's done automatically. In the new middle-class rhythm of life, obligations are homogenized, for the overriding aim is to have oneself committed to regular, unvarying monthly payments on all the major items. Come the first of the month and there is practically nothing left to decide. And so it will be next month, and the month after—a smooth, almost hypnotic rhythm so compelling that suburbanites will go to great lengths to gear any expenditure to it.

They have little sense of capital. They are acquisitive, yes, but for the good life, and in the good life it is stability—or at least the illusion of it—that is all important to them. Money is secondary, and actual cash they almost fear. *Fortune* has examined the budgets of a cross section composed of eighty-three young couples in the $5,000-to-$7,500; with a few exceptions, the couples reveal themselves as so unconcerned with total cost or interest rates that they provide a veritable syllabus of ways to make two dollars do the work of one.

The optimism of the younger suburbanites is tremendous. They have in fact discounted in advance a good part of the annual increase in American productivity. In a continually expanding economy, they seem to assume future prosperity will retroactively pay for today, and so there is no sense in self-denial.

The suburbanites have an almost obsessive desire for regularity in money transactions. Two decades ago, one could divide Americans into three sizable groups: those at the lower end of the income scale who thought in terms of the week, those who thought in terms of the month, and those who thought in terms of the year. There are still many people at both ends of the scale, but with the widening of the middle class, the month has become the standard module in American budgetary thinking. Salary checks, withholding deductions, mortgage payments, are firmly geared to a thirty-day cycle, and so increasingly, are all other items.

Depression? They don't even think about it. If they are pressed into giving an opinion, their explanation would suggest that America has at least found something very close to the secret of perpetual motion. "We are all in the same boat," they observe, implying that because of this fact their great expectations will have a self-enforcing quality.

"The Depression would be a political issue," explains a twenty-eight year old clerk. "The government would certainly see to it that a depression would not take place." And if one did take place, some add, it wouldn't hurt. "It's all relative," one young husband explains. "If my salary went down, prices would be going down too, so in the end I would be just as well as I was before."

However the suburbanites finance their cars, they pay far more than they think they do. The average estimate made by couples in *Fortune*'s cross section of the interest they were paying: 5.3 percent. Actual interest exclusive of insurance: 19 percent.

One thing seems certain: whatever form the plans take, the exploitation of budgetism is going to become an increasingly vital factor in the economy. Suburbia provides only a foretaste of what can happen; our whole population is moving toward the more regularized life, and as the guaranteed annual wage becomes more of a reality, the conditions for middle-class budgetism will become more universal. And then, finally, there are the children of suburbia—a generation for whom the depression is not a father's tale but a grandfather's. As suburbanites sometimes remark, nobody is going back.

Questions

1. Why is Whyte critical of the borrowing habits of young suburbanites?

2. Why do these borrowers care more about the monthly payments than the overall cost of borrowing?

3. Whyte seems to imply that if the borrowers knew the true costs of borrowing, they would borrow less. Do you think this is true? What is at stake in believing that borrowers can be educated out of debt?

4. The young clerk believes that the government would be able to stop another Great Depression. Why is Whyte more skeptical?

5. Do you think that the borrowers believe they will lose their jobs soon? How did postwar stability affect consumer borrowing?

Rethinking the Postwar Corporation: Management, Monopolies, and Markets (2012)

LOUIS HYMAN

In this essay, Louis Hyman examines the rise and fall of the post-war conglomerate—a new form of the corporation that arose in the particular economy of the postwar United States. Whereas Alfred Chandler and similar business historians believed that corporations became ever more efficient in the twentieth century, Hyman posits a less Whiggish narrative. He also finds that while we associate the rise of finance with the 1980s, many financial practices, like the leveraged buyout, were widely used in the 1960s. Unlike those of the 1980s, however, these earlier, finance-driven conglomerates were denounced by investors and the government alike. Their fall, he argues, made possible the rise of the market-oriented lean corporations of the 1980s that focused on short-term profits and downsized workforces.

While postwar American politicians juxtaposed the free markets of the U.S. economy to the centrally planned economies of the USSR, John Kenneth Galbraith, the celebrated postwar economist and intellectual, argued in 1967 that "we have an economic system which, whatever its formal ideological billing, is in substantial part a planned economy." For his main evidence, Galbraith pointed to the operations of the five hundred largest industrial corporations that produced two-thirds of this planned-but-capitalist economy's manufactured goods. Despite free market ideology, these corporations carefully avoided market-based relationships. Managers, capital, and supply chains were all internalized rather than contracted. Through planning, Galbraith argued, corporations "minimize[d] or [got] rid of market influences" and it was this private planning by corporations, often bigger than many of the world's governments, that defined postwar American capitalism.

In Galbraith's model, big businesses—planned and inefficient—had to be big because they had to contain all the functions that they would not trust to the market. His critique of planning compared the American to the Soviet economy, where the planned economy underpinned a repressive society. Yet in the United States, the main bugbear of the misuse of economic power had always centered on monopoly, not planning. In a convoluted way, the fall of this American planned economy twenty years before the fall of the Soviet one partially resulted from the postwar attempt to restrain what was seen as a new form of monopoly, the conglomerate. While either the government or the market could have disciplined the growth of conglomerates, only the markets had any meaningful effect, despite vocal objections by regulators. This gnarly history reveals the complex transformation underway as the postwar corporation became the corporation of today.

The conglomerate was a new form of the corporation that rose in importance during the postwar period emerging from the defense economy, the rising stock market, and the strict antimonopoly laws of the period.

Americans have a long history of opposing monopolies, believing that through the power of market concentration a company could dominate an industry and thereby price gouge consumers, undermine small businesses, and subvert the political process. Postwar conglomerates, similar in size to monopolies, elicited the same level of anti-bigness resentment, yet unlike monopolies, they lacked the market power to set prices. Conglomerates contain interests in wildly dissimilar businesses. While U.S. Steel owned wire, structural, and many other forms of steel manufacturing, LTV at its apex in 1968 produced golf balls, rental cars, missiles, electronics, and packaged meat. Unlike a monopoly, which dominates a market, a conglomerate usually does not. While the advantages of price-setting are obvious, the advantages of a string of unrelated business units are not. Size does not always create pricing power. It was not a monopoly but shared the monopoly's ability to inspire a fear of economic concentration. Neither horizontally nor vertically integrated, the conglomerate corporation was a hodgepodge of different industries.

In only a few years, conglomerators like Harvard MBA Charles "Tex" Thornton of Litton Industries and James Ling of LTV assembled companies among the largest in the United States. Investors admired the "synergies" made possible by the triumph of these men who claimed that they could manage anything. At the height of the infatuation with conglomerates in 1965, *Time* magazine reported that it was the "hard-driving Litton management" that boosted the value of Thornton's acquisitions, and Litton was seen as the best place for young executives to learn the most innovative management techniques. A mystique about their management underpinned their rising values, yet it was mergers and acquisitions that enabled most conglomerate growth.

The real source of most conglomerate "value" emerged instead from financial chicanery predicated on a rising stock market that enabled aggressive mergers and acquisitions.

Reliance on finance began with the acquisition. Litton Industries, a conglomerate run by Thornton, relied on the rising stock market of the late 1950s and early 1960s to amass a sprawling empire of companies, ranging from small electronics manufacturers to colossal shipyards. Through the services of the investment bank Lehman Brothers, Thornton arranged stock swaps between his conglomerate, Litton Industries, and the acquired company.

While most postwar firms relied on retained earnings, conglomerates creatively borrowed from capital markets to finance their expansion. By 1969, these stock market darlings disappeared, as a suddenly bearish market undid their complicated financial schemes. The financial practices of the conglomerates in the 1960s inaugurated an era of financial daring more closely associated with the 1980s. While the names of many conglomerates were forgotten, their financial methods were not, and it was partially through their example that finance took a new hold on American business.

Yet the conglomerate, at the same time, came in the 1970s to represent the worst excesses of the bloated postwar corporation. The largest conglomerates of the mid-1960s, like LTV, fell apart by the mid-1970s, or, like General Electric, so totally reorganized themselves as to be celebrated as harbingers of a new kind of corporation. The new lean corporations of the post-1970s period found their intellectual and managerial roots, curiously, in the sprawling conglomerates of the postwar period. Without the failure of the conglomerate, the explanations of "how a firm should operate" that guided the post-1970s capitalism would not have been possible. Conglomerates provided the perfect narrative through which a generation of management consultants could buttress their theories of corporate organization and, in the process, help justify and implement a new form of the American corporation. In the critique of the conglomerate, a new set of financial and organizational ideas became dominant and reshaped the way business experts understood the relationship between monopolies, markets, and the corporation. Every assumption about the corporation was rethought.

Possibly more than any other man, James Ling's rise and fall exemplified the workings of the postwar conglomerate. Like many other major conglomerators, he started out with a small business in the defense- and oil-fueled economy of the Sunbelt; but through a discovery of corporate finance, he quickly transformed it into a massive conglomerate. Ling repeatedly bought and sold companies by issuing debt. Using that cash to purchase a company, he would then issue cheaper, long-term debt against the assets of this new company to retire the old debt. In this way he turned debt into defense companies, just as the federal government's contracts remade the Sunbelt into the center of the defense economy. Operational improvements were incidental to the reshuffling of debt and equity. In many ways, Ling's focus on finance presaged the "financialization" associated with the 1970s and 1980s. Before the leveraged-buyout became a household term, James Ling pioneered the practice of using debt to construct an empire.

In April 1968, James Ling thought he had it all figured out. His backers at Lehman Brothers, and then Goldman Sachs as well, had arranged a complicated plan to sell various stocks, bonds, and options of his subsidiaries as integrated "units" onto the market. With this cash, he could buy all the stock he needed to expand his empire. From electronics to meat to steel, LTV would span the entire U.S. economy. By 1969, Ling had gone from a Texas electrical contracting company with $3,000 in assets to the twenty-fifth largest company in the Fortune 500, bigger even than Lockheed, where he had, so long ago, taken a second, night-time job during World War II. Ling's triumphs strained his finances to the breaking point, but he continued to trust that he would be able to spin off portions of his acquisitions to settle his debts as he had so many times before.

With the rising percentage of conglomerate mergers and their rising importance in the economy, the Justice Department, under both Presidents Lyndon Johnson and Richard Nixon, began to take greater notice.

In 1968, the FTC announced that because of "growing concern" that conglomerates could "substantially lessen competition," closer investigations would begin. The government investigations could not have come at a worse time for the conglomerates. For the first time, a major conglomerate, Litton, reported a decline in revenues, which compelled many analysts to "wonder," as the New York Times reported, "if the interchangeability of management skills from one industry to another truly exists." Rather than miracles of management, perhaps conglomerates were only "paper pyramids" of finance. Tactical moves like LTV's splitting into separate companies undermined the "synergy" argument that justified the conglomerate. If Ling expected the three companies to succeed independently, then what had been the value of the conglomerate's management synergies?

With the end of the 1960s bull market, stocks could no longer be swapped between companies for a premium, and the merger movement was brought to an end. For Ling, the sudden shift meant that no one bought the strange "units" from Lehman or Goldman, and he found himself short on cash. A fire sale of his assets ensued, and as he sold into a declining market, LTV—and the mystique of James Ling—unraveled. In 1969, LTV operating profits fell 90 percent.

Why have we understood that the financialization of the economy began in the 1970s and not with James Ling and the conglomerates? By 1969, James Ling stood out so much that the Johnson administration launched an investigation into the complicated dealings that he and a few others undertook. Once revealed, the financial schemes of the conglomerates were denounced as aberrations within the 1960s economy, worthy of government and investors' suspicion.

By the end of the 1960s, public suspicions of these big conglomerates, whether monopolies or not, had been aroused and their stocks began to fall much faster than even the now bearish market. Between the Justice Department and the press, investors had their choice of worrying if the government would split up the conglomerates, or even worse, if conglomerates were nothing more than hype, whose growth in profits had come from acquisitions and accounting, not increased productivity. The real danger of conglomerates might not have been power, but weakness. The size of these companies might have fundamentally undermined the productivity and value of American business.

At the beginning of the 1970s, the stock market and American business began to reconsider what they thought they knew about the American corporation and the conglomerate in particular. Rather than just a clever way to use retained earnings and evade taxes, so much of the conglomerate growth was achieved through borrowed money. If the rise of the conglomerate had brought many corporations under the control of those who privileged finance above production, the demise of the conglomerates did not restore operations to the center of the economy.

The ideal corporation was now a narrow monopoly—not a sprawling empire—that relied on the market for as many goods and services as possible. This corporation reoriented itself to the market in ways that Galbraith could not have imagined only a few years earlier. The sprawl of the postwar conglomerate would disappear but Ling's aberrant financial methods, so repellant to Americans of the 1960s, would be almost normal to Americans of the 1980s, who would endlessly celebrate the debt traders and M&A experts of Wall Street. While the conglomerates fell apart in 1969, Lehman Brothers and other New York investment banks remembered their lessons in creative finance. Conglomerates like Litton and LTV may have emerged out of the postwar defense economy in the Sunbelt, but their financing came out of New York. Finance had returned. While 1968 has been noted for its many world historical events, the downfall of James Ling and his role in shaping that post-1968 world have been largely forgotten.

Questions

1. How did conglomerates use finance to quickly grow their companies?
2. We think of finance as centered in New York, but the conglomerates' financial innovations came from Texas. Why would financial innovation occur outside of the center of the finance industry?

3. What brought down the 1960s conglomerates? Federal investigations? The market?

4. Should we only be concerned about big firms if they are monopolies? In what ways, outside of pricing power, might a large firm be dangerous within American capitalism? Within American politics?

5. The breakup of the 1960s conglomerates led to the merger and acquisitions craze of the 1980s. Why do you think this moment in our business history has been erased from popular memory?

MODULE 20

AMERICAN HUBRIS

IBM Annual Report (1967)

IBM

In the postwar era, IBM defined computers. The System/360 was the first computer that could be upgraded while still maintaining compatibility in user data and software. For the first time as well, peripherals—from specialized scientific instruments to everyday printers—could be connected to the System/360's standardized ports. With these innovations, the System/360 created the first digital ecosystem—the forerunner of today's Apple/PC/Android/UNIX world.

At the same time during the 1960s, IBM developed, like many other U.S. corporations, into a multinational firm with manufacturing and distribution operations around the world. One of the reasons for the rising demand for IBM computers was the very complexity of tracking these global operations. In this selection from IBM's 1967 Annual Report, we can see these two developments come together.

During 1967, IBM's continued progress was highlighted by the strong demand for its products and services throughout the world.

Consolidated gross income from worldwide operations amounted to $5,345,290, an increase of $1,097,584 over 1966. Earnings were $651,499, 558, a $125,369, 3[00] increase over the prior year.

The 1967 results reflect the continuing high level of business volume of the Company's System/360 data processing product line, as well as a very substantially increasing level of outright sales of this equipment during the last six months of the year. As [we] have previously commented to stockholders, outright sales have the effect of realizing income currently which, on a rental basis, would be realized in future periods. Changes in the level of these sales can result in significant fluctuations in income from year to year and even wider fluctuations from quarter to quarter.

Users of IBM equipment have the choice of either renting or purchasing their equipment from IBM or procuring it from third parties who are in the business of owning equipment and leasing it to our users. While the great majority of IBM equipment users continue to buy directly from IBM, there has been an increase in the amount of data processing equipment purchased by leasing companies for lease to users. Orders for System/360 and other computer systems continued at a high level throughout the year and worldwide production exceeded 1,000 systems a month.

During 1967, IBM's worldwide employment increased by 23,000 to over 221,000 people. This increase reflects the growth of all areas of the business, including further expansion of our manufacturing and laboratory facilities. The need for new facilities and the production of data processing equipment for rental to customers required a worldwide investment this year of approximately $1.5 billion. New or enlarged facilities became operational or were started at a number of locations in the United States, as well as at 14 locations in nine countries around the world.

During the past year, IBM completed its fifteenth year of making and marketing electronic systems. The Company announced its first such system, the IBM 701, a vacuum tube computer for scientific use in 1952. At the time there was substantial opinion that no more than 50 companies would ever use such computers.

Since then the computer industry has grown from what seemed little more than a promising idea to a few companies into a major industry here and abroad. It has attracted both large and small companies and encouraged the formation of hundreds of new enterprises. It has created opportunities for thousands of suppliers and has resulted in plant and capital equipment. It has grown to a point where today there are thousands of computer installations throughout the world.

Continued Progress in Data Processing

Orders for, and installations of, IBM Data processing equipment continued at a high rate during 1967, particularly in the System/360 line. System/360 is an integrated family of computers designed for both business and scientific applications. The standard architecture of the System allows customers to move from smaller models to more powerful ones with little or no change in their programs or data processing procedures. When announced in April, 1964, System/360 consisted of six basic models and a range of 44 peripheral devices, such as card and tape readers, printers and display terminals.

Worldwide Computer Manufacturing

The production of System/360 and other IBM computers reached a new peak in 1967 as new or enlarged facilities became operational in the United States and abroad.

Production began in temporary facilities in Boca Raton, Florida, and shipments of the smallest computer in the System/360 line, the Model 20, began from there in September. Construction of a permanent manufacturing facility of 200,000 square feet will begin in 1968.

In Japan, manufacturing operations were transferred from Tokyo to a new 222,000 square-foot plant at nearby Fujisawa. The new plant produces Models 20 and 40 of System/360, and other data processing equipment for shipment to several World Trade countries.

An additional 152,000 square feet of space was added to the new IBM plant at Mainz, West Germany. The Mainz plant produces System/360 Model 30 as well as magnetic core memory units. Additional expansion was completed at IBM's Greenock, Scotland, plant, which makes units for System/360 in addition to producing much of the World Trade's punched card equipment.

In addition, expansion programs were required in San Jose, California Raleigh, North Carolina, Burlington, Vermont, and East Fishkill, New York, for System/360 manufacturing.

Questions

1. What was new about System/360? Why did it matter that the new computer technology could be "compatible" with new kinds of hardware and software?
2. What do you think changed when IBM went from an American company to a multinational? In what ways was it still an American firm?
3. What do you notice about the locations that IBM chose for its manufacturing operations? Why have multiple locations? Why those locations?

MODULE 21

CHEAPER

A One-Sided Class War: Rethinking Doug Fraser's 1978 Resignation from the Labor-Management Group (2003)

JEFFERSON COWIE

In this piece, labor historian Jefferson Cowie examines a letter written in 1978 by Douglas Fraser, the president of the UAW, in which he resigns from a committee ostensibly created to promote labor-management cooperation. By 1978, it had become apparent to labor leaders that the postwar Treaty of Detroit (the policy of cooperation between labor and management in the massive American auto industry) had long since expired, and that once again unions and management had diverging interests. Here Cowie argues that instead of the postwar being an "exceptional" period of labor-management cooperation that fell apart in the 1970s, we should see the postwar period as simply a lower-level simmering of conflict.

In July of 1978, Douglas Fraser, President of the United Auto Workers, resigned from John Dunlop's Labor-Management Group in a flurry of publicity. The committee had been set up under the Nixon administration to seek out cooperative solutions to labor-management problems and to pass advice along to the White House. Although the group was supposed to reflect the postwar consensus in labor-management relations, Fraser's public resignation and the press conference that accompanied it shredded the fiction of that consensus with brilliant rhetorical barbs that sent shudders of concern all the way to the Carter White House. "I believe leaders of the business community, with few exceptions, have chosen to wage a one-sided class war today in this country—a war against working people, the unemployed, the poor, the minorities, the very young and the very old, and even many in the middle class of our society," he declared. "The leaders of industry, commerce and finance in the United States have broken and discarded the fragile, unwritten compact previously existing during a past period of growth and progress." Promising to forge a new social movement, he explained, "I would rather sit with the rural poor, the desperate children of urban blight, the victims of racism, and working people seeking a better life than with those whose religion is the status quo, whose goal is profit and whose hearts are cold. We in the UAW intend to reforge the links with those who believe in struggle: the kind of people who sat-down in the factories in the 1930s and who marched in Selma in the 1960s," Fraser declared.

Fraser's letter, and the historic moment in which he released it, have lent themselves to two interpretations, and I would like to suggest a third. First, as the autoworkers' president intended it, the document represents an attempt (failed as it turned out) to break out of the limits of the postwar bargaining system that constrained working class politics within the Democratic Party and restricted shopfloor power to the confines of the collective bargaining system. In this case, Fraser's letter stands as the path not taken, one that might have searched for ways to throw off the shackles of business unionism and move toward a more militant and inclusive brand of social movement unionism. Second, historians, obviously aware of the fact that the revival Fraser had planned never came to fruition, have used this letter to demarcate the end of the postwar "golden age," the sunset of the "fragile, unwritten compact," as Fraser called it, which shaped over three successful decades of industrial relations. The phrase "one-sided class war" has often been cited as evidence of business abrogating its end of the deal.

In historian Nelson Lichtenstein's words, that the postwar settlement is a "suspect construct" that obfuscates as much as it illuminates.

The collapse of labor politics did not necessarily mark the end of a respected settlement between management and labor over the terms of industrial governance; rather it appears that the idea of a postwar "accord" was more of an idea created and reified in the face of the *continued* decline of organized labor that dated all the way back to the mid 1950s. It allowed for the creation of a semi-imaginary historical benchmark against which very real contemporary assaults on unions and key industrial sectors could be measured. Clearly higher levels of union density, lower rates of capital mobility, lower levels of global competition in the post war era suggest that things were different in the "golden age," but it was so uneven, and so poorly congealed that it hardly lives up to the quasi-corporatist notions that a later generation would apply to it.

From the vantage point of a new century, a different interpretation of the Fraser letter suggests itself than the "end of a golden age" narrative. Rather than the beginning of a revival or the collapse of a compromise, the document reflects, in ways that may not have been intended by the author, the historic limits of U.S. organized labor and the thematic continuities that link the "exceptional" postwar era with the rest of U.S. labor history.

If we "listen closely," as Brody suggests, we can hear more continuity than rupture in the postwar era through Fraser's letter, more confessions of weakness than assertions of power. If we read Fraser's letter closely, however, even the exceptional postwar era fits in the overarching pattern of U.S. labor history, defined by both a limited role for unions and a long and unrelenting campaign against the collective voice for American workers by business and the state.

July 17, 1978

Dear Labor-Management Group Member:

I have come to the reluctant conclusion that my participation in the Labor-Management Group cannot continue. I am therefore resigning from the Group as of July 19. You are entitled to know why I take this action and you should understand that I have the highest regard for John Dunlop, my colleagues on the labor side and, as individuals, those who represent the corporate elite in the Group.

Attractive as the personalities may be, we all sit in a representative capacity. I have concluded that participation in these meetings is no longer useful to me or to the 1.5 million workers I represent as president of the UAW.

I believe leaders of the business community, with few exceptions, have chosen to wage a one-sided class war today in this country—a war against working people, the unemployed, the poor, the minorities, the very young and the very old, and even many in the middle class of our society.

The leaders of industry, commerce and finance in the United States have broken and discarded the fragile, unwritten compact previously existing during a past period of growth and progress . . .

That system has worked best, of course, for the "haves" in our society rather than the "have-nots." Yet it survived in part because of an unspoken foundation: that when things got bad enough for a segment of society, the business elite "gave" a little bit—enabling government or interest groups to better conditions somewhat for that segment. That give usually came only after sustained struggle, such as that waged by the labor movement in the 1930s and the civil rights movement in the 1960s.

The acceptance of the labor movement, such as it has been, came because business feared the alternatives. Corporate America didn't join the fight to pass the Civil Rights Act of 1964 or the Voting Rights Act, but it eventually accepted the inevitability of that legislation. Other similar pieces of legislation aimed at the human needs of the disadvantaged have become national policy only after real struggle.

This system is not as it should be, yet progress has been

made under it. But today, I am convinced there has been a shift on the part of the business community toward confrontation, rather than cooperation. Now, business groups are tightening control over American society. As that grip tightens, it is the "have-nots" who are squeezed . . .

The new flexing of business muscle can be seen in many other areas. The rise of multinational corporations that know neither patriotism nor morality but only self-interest, has made accountability almost non-existent. At virtually every level, I discern a demand by business for docile government and unrestrained corporate individualism. Where industry once yearned for subservient unions, it now wants no unions at all.

General Motors Corp. is a specific case in point. GM, the largest manufacturing corporation in the world, has received responsibility, productivity, and cooperation from the UAW and its members. In return, GM has given us a Southern strategy designed to set-up a non-union network that threatens the hard-fought gains won by the UAW. We have given stability and have been rewarded with hostility. Overseas, it is the same. General Motors not only invests heavily in South Africa, it refuses to recognize the black unions there.

My message should be very clear: if corporations like General Motors want confrontation, they cannot expect cooperation in return from labor.

Even the very foundations of America's democratic process are threatened by the new approach of the business elite. No other democratic country in the world has lower rates of voter participation than the U.S., except Botswana. Moreover, our voting participation is class-skewed—about 50 percent more of the affluent vote than workers and 90 percent to 300 percent more of the rich vote than the poor, the black, the young and the Hispanic. Yet business groups regularly finance politicians, referenda and legislative battles to continue barriers to citizen participation in elections. In Ohio, for example, many corporations in the Fortune 500 furnished the money to repeal fair and democratic voter registration.

Even if all the barriers to such participation were removed, there would be no rush to the polls by many in our society who feel the sense of helplessness and inability to affect the system in any way. The Republican Party remains controlled by and the Democratic Party heavily influenced by business interests. The reality is that both are weak and ineffective as parties, with no visible, clear-cut ideological differences between them, because of business domination. Corporate America has more to lose by the turn off of citizens from the system than organized labor. But it is always the latter that fights to encourage participation and the former that works to stifle it.

For all these reasons, I have concluded there is no point to continue sitting down at Labor-Management Group meetings and philosophizing about the future of the country and the world when we on the labor side have so little in common with those across the table. I cannot sit there seeking unity with the leaders of American industry, while they try to destroy us and ruin the lives of the people I represent.

I would rather sit with the rural poor, the desperate children of urban blight, the victims of racism, and working people seeking a better life than with those whose religion is the status quo, whose goal is profit and whose hearts are cold. We in the UAW intend to reforge the links with those who believe in struggle: the kind of people who sat-down in the factories in the 1930s and who marched in Selma in the 1960s.

I cannot assure you that we will be successful in making new alliances and forming new coalitions to help our nation find its way. But I will assure you that we will try.

Sincerely,

Douglas A. Fraser, President

Questions

1. Do you agree or disagree with Cowie's interpretation?

2. Do you think postwar labor unions like the UAW allied themselves with the "rural poor, desperate children of urban blight, the victims of racism, and working people"? Why or why not?

3. Why does Fraser compare the labor movement with the civil rights movement in his letter? What were the similarities and differences between the two?

4. Geography plays an important role in Fraser's outrage. Companies moved to the American South and to other countries using the profits gained from UAW labor. How might you argue that this is the proper action of business? What arguments would you make that it is improper? Does it matter whether the firms moved to the South or another country?

Labor and Monopoly Capital: The Degradation of Work in the Twentieth Century (1974)

HARRY BRAVERMAN

Harry Braverman's book, *Labor and Monopoly Capital*, describes a process that began with "scientific management" and Taylorism in the late nineteenth century and never stopped. As various kinds of automation took over industrial processes, workers' work became more boring—and their individual expertise became less significant. This would only become more the case with the introduction of greater computer control of factory production processes, a process that became more and more important after the 1960s. And as this particular selection shows, the increased control, repetitiveness, measurement, and management control over work weren't just restricted to blue-collar factory jobs, but to office-based white- and pink-collar jobs as well. The scene here is that of the pre-desktop-computer era of the 1970s. Significant information processing was taking place, but it still required extensive labor in order to create the punch cards necessary for feeding into large mainframe computers. But many of the techniques described here would be used to eliminate even more jobs, and to measure and "incentivize" labor in the post-PC office.

Here is a description, reported on the occasion of the change-over from a pre-computer tabulating machine system (which also required punched cards) to a computer system: One key-puncher reported that before the installation of the computer, her work had been somewhat varied and had occasionally called for the exercise of judgment. This had made it bearable. [. . .] The new work [. . .] is more monotonous and repetitious. Since there is no variation in job content, the pace is continuous, steady, and "pressured." The most frequent comment among the girls is, "We are working for the machine now." [. . .] [All] key-punch girls [are] "nervous wrecks." "If you happen to speak to an operator while she is working, she will jump a mile. You can't help being tense. The machine makes you that way." [Another former operator] reported the same kind of tension: "If you just tap one of them on the shoulder when she is working, she'll fly through the ceiling." [. . .] Although the girls do not quit, they stay home frequently and keep supplies of tranquilizers and aspirin at their desks. The key-punchers felt that they were really doing a factory job and that they were "frozen" to their desk as though it were a spot on the assembly-line.

As in the factory, the machine-pacing of work becomes increasingly available to office management as a weapon of control. The reduction of office information to standardized "bits" and their processing by computer systems and other office equipment provides management with an automatic accounting of the size of the work load and the amount done by each operator, section, or division. [. . .] The American Management Association's [. . .] Seventh Annual Conference on Systems and Procedures in 1958 stressed that the systems profession is devoted to methods improvement or "working smarter." Implicit in this was the job of motivating the office worker to greater productivity. Henry Gunders, associate director, Management Advisory Services, Price Waterhouse and Company, Houston, Texas, maintained that in the unmeasured office the rate of clerical output is low. He estimates that such an office is operating on 50 to 60% efficiency, and that with clerical output measured, even unaccompanied by incentives, there would be a 20 to 30% increase in output. [. . .] Key-punching, in particular, lends itself to objective count. Government agencies and private business firms reported that this type of work measurement was standard procedure. [. . .] An executive of one large insurance company commented that, although it is not generally mentioned, an objective record of productivity is kept, and the operator whose output lags is fired.

[. . .] The factory atmosphere is unmistakably present. Not only are the office machine operators often required to punch a time clock, but they are not permitted to converse while at work. They are subject to dismissal with as little notice as a week or at most a month. There are few distinguishing marks between the employee in the electronic office and the factory worker in light manufacturing.

As work has been simplified, routinized, and measured, the drive for speed has come to the fore. "Everything is speed in the work now," said a woman who found herself near a nervous breakdown, and the pace is "terrific." And with the economies furnished by the computer system and the forcing of the intensity of labor come layoffs which selectively increase the tendency toward factory-like work: "With each reduction in force, the remaining workers are told to increase their output. Automation has reduced the staff in that office by more than one-third, and more mechanization is in prospect. The union spokesman said that the categories of jobs which have disappeared are those which require some skill and judgment. Those remaining are the tabulating and key-punch operations, which become even simpler, less varied, and more routinized as work is geared to the computer." The vice-president of an insurance company, pointing to a room filled with key punch operators, remarked: "All they lack is a chain," and explained himself by adding that the machines kept the "girls" at their desks punching monotonously and without cease. The workers themselves are under no illusions about their "white-collar" jobs: "This job is no different from a factory job except that I don't get paid as much," one operator in a large farm-equipment office said.

[. . .] Howard C. Carlson, a psychologist employed by General Motors, has said: "The computer may be to middle management what the assembly line is to the hourly worker." The tendency of the labor process exemplified in the various machine jobs is not confined to the workers grouped immediately around the computer. On the contrary, with the exception of a specialized minority whose technical and "systems" skills are expanded, this tendency increasingly affects all clerical workers.

In its early stages, a new division of labor may specialize men in such a way as to increase their levels of skill; but later, especially when whole operations are split and mechanized, such division develops certain faculties at the expense of others and narrows all of them. And as it comes more fully under mechanization and centralized management, it levels men off again as automatons. Then there are a few specialists and a mass of automatons; both integrated by the authority which makes them interdependent and keeps each in his own routine. Thus, in the division of labor, the open development and free exercise of skills are managed and closed.

The alienating conditions of modern work now include the salaried employees as well as the wage-workers. There are few, if any, features of wage-work (except heavy toil—which is decreasingly a factor in wage-work) that do not also characterize at least some white-collar work. [. . .] The use of automatic and semi-automatic machine systems in the office has the effect of completely reversing the traditional profile of office costs. [. . .] The cost of operating a large office consisted, almost entirely of the salaries [. . .] [now] a large investment in the purchase of expensive equipment [is the largest cost]. Past or "dead" labor in the form of machinery owned by capital, now employs living labor, in the office just as in the factory. But for the capitalist, the profitability of this employment is very much a function of time, of the rapidity with which dead labor absorbs living. The use of a great deal of expensive equipment thus leads to shift work, which is particularly characteristic of computer operations.

At the same time, the employment of machinery pushes the office installation toward the warehouse and industrial districts of the cities. This is facilitated by the development of remote terminals and other communications devices which annihilate distance and do away with almost all the inconveniences of separate installations, so that executive offices can be maintained in the more expensive and accessible locations while the mass of clerical workers can be moved into lower-rent districts, often together with warehousing or production facilities. Thus the convenience and cachet of working in the central part of town, with its greater shopping interest and more varied lunching facilities, etc., begins for many clerical workers to disappear.

At the same time, the labor market for the two chief varieties of workers, factory and office, begins to lose some of its distinctions of social stratification, education, family, and the like. Not only do clerical workers come increasingly from families of factory background, and vice-versa, but more and more they are merged within the same living family. The chief remaining distinction seems to be a division along the lines of sex. Here the distribution within the clerical and operative groups is strikingly congruent: in 1971, the category of operatives was made up of 9 million men and 4 million women, while that of clerical workers was made up of 10.1 million women and 3.3 million men. The sex barrier that assigns most office jobs to women, and that is enforced both by custom and hiring practice, has made it possible to lower wage rates in the clerical category, as we have seen, below those in any category of manual labor. The growing participation of women in employment has thus far been facilitated by the stronger demand for clerical employees and the relatively stagnating demand for operatives.

Questions

1. What recurring dynamics of capitalism can you identify in the offices that Braverman describes?

2. Braverman's book appeared in 1974. Does what it says about how work is routinized and measured apply to the present-day world of work in an office? What about what he has to say about how different kinds of work are divided up between men and women, or where work takes place?

3. If you work, is your work like this work? If your current work is not, do you remember doing a job like the ones described here?

4. Does automation and measurement improve human life? If so, how? If not, why not?

MODULE 22

INSTABILITY

Where Managers Will Go (1992)

JOHN HUEY

The recession of the early 1990s brought deindustrialization to white-collar America. Suddenly the automation that had displaced American blue-collar workers in the 1970s and '80s hit office workers and middle management. Job stability, even for the salaried employee, was gone. This "downsizing" was made possible by new information technology and by the idea of the "lean corporation," in which noncore corporation functions were outsourced to the "market." Flexible and nimble, corporations began to focus on short-term worker costs rather than long-term investment in their employees' development. In this selection from *Fortune*, Huey describes this transformation as it happened.

The great management sweep-out isn't going to stop anytime soon, forcing millions to rethink their careers. The most successful are finding new niches born of change.

For those of you who have been dutifully climbing the corporate ladder rung by rung, it's hardly news that a brave new world of corporate—and post-corporate—employment has dawned. It's safe to say that over the past decade millions of managerial jobs were "surplussed" in the flattening or restructuring of corporate America. The country's management cadre has understandably had a hard time accepting the finality of this shrinkage.

The American Management Association has the same message

for a whole class of corporate workers. "Middle managers are losing their jobs out of proportion to their place in the work force, and they continue to be a special target of downsizing," says the AMA's Eric Greenberg, who notes that this is especially true during mergers, acquisitions, and transfers of business offshore. "None of this is going to lessen in the coming decade, and these jobs are not coming back."

What's more, "the worst is yet to come," says James Swallow, a vice president specializing in manufacturing strategy at A.T. Kearney management consultants. "Based on what we're seeing, there's a lot more restructuring on the way. There are a number of companies out there with plans that haven't said a thing publicly yet." He adds, "A lot of people will walk out of these management positions and never see these kinds of jobs again—from supervisors in the $30,000 to $50,000 range to directors of manufacturing and materials making $120,000 to $150,000."

Accepting this new reality is the first and most essential step toward surviving—and then prevailing—in the brave new world. If you want to qualify as a successful manager in the 1990s, you will have to pursue at least one of several unfamiliar paths. If you remain within the corporate world, you will have to transform yourself from an overseer into a doer, from a boss into a team leader or maybe just a team player. You will be called on less to tell people what to do and more to take responsibility for the success or failure of your business. Your skills will be measured on a global scale. You will need to be computer fluent.

You can also expect further changes in the already tattered social contract between you and the corporation. "There was a time when someone would come to the front door of AT&T and see an invisible sign that said, AT&T: A JOB FOR LIFE," says Harold Burlingame, senior vice president of human resources at Ma Bell. "That's over. Now it's a shared kind of thing. Come to us. We'll invest in you, and you invest in us. Together, we'll face the market, and the degree to which we succeed will determine how things work out."

Meet Bill Wendell. After a 19-year corporate marketing career, including a stint at Textron's Sheaffer Eaton division and then with Gillette's Papermate unit, the 43-year-old marketing manager saw his opportunities running out fast. He had soaked up Gillette's legendary consumer products discipline as European marketing manager for stationery products in the Eighties. But when he returned to Boston, he found that Gillette—battered by two hostile takeover attempts—had restructuring on its mind. So in early 1991, Wendell began looking in earnest for alternatives.

What he found was a personal shock, because it required uprooting his family from New England, where his son left seven cousins, to Milwaukee, where they knew no one. But he also discovered the professional challenge he realized he had been craving. As VP of marketing and sales for Success Business Industries—a 130-year-old maker of desk calendars and such—he landed in the middle of a turnaround attempt, one that required radical updating of the company's product line.

"The major difference day to day is how much more I have to do myself," says Wendell. "At the old Gillette there were all these layers of support staff—market research, customer service, advertising, packaging, product design. Here the marketing department is my marketing director and me. Yet the tasks and issues are no fewer. There're just fewer zeros on the ends of the numbers."

An obvious alternative is to start your own business, which is what Michael Bressler, 46, a veteran of several big ad agencies, did when the big Richmond printing company he worked for as VP of marketing, sales, and customer service went out of business. He explains, "After eight months of looking for a job [in the $75,000-plus range to which he was accustomed], I made a decision that I didn't want anybody else telling me when I could or couldn't work. So I set out to develop a business plan and execute it." What he came up with was Affiliated Graphics, which basically brokers printing services to clients, aiming to improve the service and quality they receive while lowering their costs. It has four employees and turns a modest profit, but only after "making some terrible mistakes along the way," says Bressler, "like not realizing that you can run a business without profits, but you can't run one without cash flow."

The new shape of corporate America will present all kinds of opportunities for consulting, temporary management, and new business niches. "What we call a corporation will change," says Steve Weiss, who runs Quest, a futurist laboratory that helps a group of top FORTUNE 500 clients look ahead. "The great redundancy is going to shrink: If a company has a core competency, its management can go to a variety of organizations and select the very best that money can buy—marketing, design, finance, human relations, whatever is needed." Anticipating and gearing up to fill these ever-changing needs of the downsized corporate world presents a vast new sphere of opportunity.

There's no denying the bad news, especially for managers who have become overly comfortable in the corporate womb, not keeping their skills updated and honed to a competitive edge. The good news is that the brave new world will place a renewed premium on such qualities as initiative, creativity, and the mastery of technology. The survivors will be those who—if necessary—take a moment to lick their wounds and dust themselves off, then collect their talents, steel their confidence, and strike out looking for challenging new opportunities in a restructured world.

Questions

1. Who did this restructuring benefit?
2. Do you think that these white collar workers fared better in this "new shape" than blue collar workers? Why or why not?

3. What did corporations lose and gain by abandoning the long-term "social compact" with their employees? How do you think it affected American business?

4. Do you think this "new shape of corporate America" was an opportunity or a tragedy?

Not Just a Mortgage Crisis: How Finance Maimed Society (2010)

GERALD F. DAVIS

The mortgage meltdown that began in 2007 quickly transformed into a credit crisis, and then into a broader economic crisis. The dramatic rise in home prices over the previous decade was unprecedented in American history, as during the century prior to 1998 house prices had merely kept pace with inflation (Shiller, 2006). Yet the expectations of homeowners and their creditors reflected a view of homes as investments that never lost value. Through serial refinancing and lines of credit, families extracted equity at a rate of $800 billion per year, much of which funded consumer spending that outpaced Americans' stagnant employment income (Greenspan and Kennedy, 2008). Industries from mortgage brokerage and granite-countertop installation to vacation travel and consumer electronics benefited from the bubble. Roughly one-quarter of the jobs created during the Bush years were in housing-related industries, and at the peak of the bubble there were more real estate agents than farmers in the US. When prices experienced their inevitable reversal, the seeming prosperity of the bubble years was quickly revealed to be an illusion. Around the globe, investors who relied on American homeowners to make their mortgage payments, and producers who relied on American consumers to buy their goods, were caught short. Back in the US, rates of foreclosure reached unthinkable levels, as millions of "homeowners" found that they owed more on their mortgage than their house was worth. The innovations flowing from the creative genius of Wall Street turned out to be not entirely benign.

Things are worse than we think. The mortgage bubble was just one part of a broader shift in the economy toward a finance-centered system that ties the fates of households, businesses, and governments to the vagaries of financial markets through the device of securitization—packaging capital assets (essentially any claim on future cash flows) into tradable securities. Mortgage-backed bonds are the most mundane and, generally, low-risk form of securitization, but we have recently witnessed the unanticipated consequences of mortgage securitization. Wall Street constructed an infrastructure for securitization transactions that created wildly innovative products, from bonds backed by lawsuit settlements owed by tobacco companies to state governments, to those backed by the life insurance settlements of elderly retirees in Florida (Quinn, 2008). Advances in information and communication technologies allowed the creation and valuation of increasingly exotic instruments (although the precision of the "valuation" of these securities is debatable). One result is that investors and issuers occasionally faced some rather malign incentives. Buying a second house as an investment, with a low-documentation, no-money-down mortgage, was like being awarded a stock option: if the house's value went up, the buyer profited; if it went down, then the buyer could walk away with a minimal loss, while the mortgage issuer (and the house's neighborhood) suffered the consequences. And a hurricane that wiped out Palm Beach would be a bonanza for purchasers of "life settlement" bonds.

In this essay, I describe two related changes associated with widespread securitization. The first is changes in the nature and organization of the financial services industry, which has seen a paradoxical increase in concentration among the biggest banks in the US, yet a disaggregation of finance across the value chain. The second is changes in household ties to financial markets and in the worldviews of Americans. The financial crisis has temporarily stilled the manic pace of securitization of the previous two decades. But securitization is not going to disappear due to the mortgage meltdown, any more than the World Wide Web disappeared due to the collapse of the dot-com bubble. The cost advantages of the technology are far too compelling to go back. What we might hope for going forward is not to put the genie back in the bottle, but to grapple intelligently with the organizational and policy implications of securitization.

[. . .] The wellspring of this transformation is securitization. Thanks to the law of large numbers, bundling together thousands of mortgages creates a pool that is fairly predictable even if the individual constituents are highly variable. And while a pool of mortgages from the same town in Oregon or Michigan might be somewhat risky—imagine if the local factory burned down, or the new housing development turned out to be built on a toxic waste dump—a geographically diverse pool is not, because housing market downturns were (until recently) localized. As a result, securitization initially made mortgages cheaper for home buyers and safer for investors. Moreover, by allowing banks to move assets (loans) off their balance sheet, securitization frees up capital for other loans.

The rationale for securitization is unimpeachable. Clearly, if it worked for mortgages, it could work for other kinds of loans. Given that commercial banks and other financial institutions had incentives to move loans off their books, and investment banks earned fees from underwriting these transactions, securitization spread like the swine flu across the balance sheets of American banks. Mortgage-backed bonds were followed by auto loans, student loans and credit card receivables. If you have a balance outstanding on your Visa card, it is highly likely that your expected payment stream is now owned by a bondholder somewhere in the world. Business receivables are also regularly securitized: even a company in bankruptcy can issue a highly rated bond if the buyers that owe it money are themselves creditworthy.

Because of the high fixed costs associated with the infrastructure for securitization, and strong demand from global investors for their product, investment banks had good reasons to keep the deals flowing. As economist James Mason put it, "Once you get into it, it's a bit like heroin." Corporate loans, royalties from album sales and television show syndications, property liens, veteran's pensions, social security payments to the elderly and infirm—name the cash flow, and it's a good bet that a banker somewhere has tried to securitize it. And the basic idea could be expanded to include blends of prior securitizations, not just "single malts." Collateralized debt obligations are the best-known example, consisting of a mix of prior asset-backed securities.

[. . .] Thanks to securitization and deregulation, the financial services industry looks almost nothing like it did 30 years ago. Commercial banks underwent a massive consolidation movement after the geographic restrictions on banking were removed, leading to an hourglass-shaped industry structure in which a handful of national-scale behemoths (J. P. Morgan Chase, Citigroup, Bank of America and now Wells Fargo) were complemented by an array of relatively tiny local banks (Marquis and Lounsbury, 2007). Five of the 10 biggest banks in 1989 are now combined in J. P. Morgan Chase. Meanwhile, nearly all the mid-sized urban banks that were the stalwarts of local communities were gobbled up. The biggest banks in San Francisco, Los Angeles, St. Louis, Boston, Jacksonville and dozens of other cities now report to B of A's corporate headquarters in Charlottesville, North Carolina, and seven of the 10 largest US cities no longer host a major local bank (see Davis, 2009: Ch. 4).

At the same time, securitization encouraged the disaggregation of the value chain in finance, as Palmer and Maher (2010, this issue) describe. At the height of the bubble, there were 50,000 free-standing mortgage brokerage firms, as home buyers (and refinancers) turned to brokers rather than banks for their loans. The loans themselves were frequently originated by "non-bank" specialists such as Countrywide and New Century, which could avoid the need for depositors by reselling the loans they originated to Wall Street banks. By the same token, business loans made by commercial banks were routinely securitized, rendering the old distinction between commercial banking and investment banking largely obsolete: if debt was going to end up trading on markets rather than held on the balance sheet, then the Glass–Steagall Act was largely beside the point. An entire "shadow banking" system, comprised of players ranging from asset finance firms to hedge funds, arose in parallel to the traditional banking system, leaving our old maps of the banking industry deceptive.

One result of the changing terrain of financial services was that the US ended up with a complete mismatch between its federal regulatory system and the players in the industry (see Hirsch and Morris, 2010, this issue). Regulatory agencies benefit from having large territories, and state governments can benefit from fostering local industries (e.g. mortgage banking in California; industrial banking in Utah; consumer credit in Delaware). As a result, some regulatory agencies and states competed to provide the most hospitable regulatory frameworks for their "customers," that is, the financial institutions they nominally regulated. Customers among the financial services industry were, of course, sophisticated shoppers, as indicated by the fact the top-level regulator for AIG—America's largest insurance company—was the Office of Thrift Supervision (OTS), created in the wake of the savings and loan crisis of the late 1980s to regulate thrifts. AIG had purchased a small savings and loan a few years before its downfall, which allowed it to be regulated by a federal agency intended to oversee small-town thrifts—hardly a match for AIG's high-flying London-based derivatives business. (OTS also oversaw Washington Mutual, the largest bank failure in US history, and IndyMac, another failed giant, and it appeared to be the preferred regulator for the more "creative" players in finance.) It is as if by buying a steam engine, a nuclear power plant could thereby choose to be regulated by the county steam commissioner rather than the Nuclear Regulatory Commission. [. . .]

The most salient example of this shift in sensibilities, of course, is the US housing market. Enabled by the securitization of mortgages, and encouraged by rapid price increases and the relatively modest returns available from other asset classes, buyers turned homes into stock options. Over one-quarter of the houses sold in 2005 were purchased as investments, which their buyers intended to turn over for a profit. Houses were listed for sale on eBay, with many bought and sold sight unseen. Entrepreneurial brokers went door to door encouraging home owners—even those whose mortgages had long since been paid off—to take out new loans, either to invest in home improvements or to pay off other loans and gain the tax advantages of mortgage debt. Internet-savvy home owners who needed cash could check out their house's imputed value, their credit rating, and mortgage interest rates daily on the Web, just as they checked out the value of their 401(k) before deciding whether to buy a new car (Davis, 2009: Ch. 6). [. . .]

The mortgage crisis was the culmination of a larger transformation in the American economy toward a finance-centered model. From corporations operated exclusively to create shareholder value, to banks that had become façades fronting for financial markets, to households tied in myriad ways to the markets, finance came to permeate American life to a degree that would have been hard to imagine a generation ago. Moreover, it was not just a change in the economy, but a change in society. A financial sensibility helped transform a nation of ants into a nation of grasshoppers, and turned most families' major savings vehicle—their home—into a liability, with consequences to be felt for years to come. (At this writing, projections indicate that one-third of mortgages will be underwater within months.)

Questions

1. After studying repeated bubbles and crashes in the history of American capitalism, what do you see that is new about this crisis? What is not?

2. Was this financial crisis a failure of regulation? Why does Davis think the regulators failed?
3. How does Davis think securitization changed the behavior of lenders and investors?
4. Does this narrative, written in the middle of the crisis, still ring true today?

Bibliography

Adam Smith, *An Inquiry into the Nature and Causes of the Wealth of Nations*, 1776.

Karl Marx and Friedrich Engels, *Manifesto of the Communist Party*, 1848.

Gregory Clark, *A Farewell to Alms: A Brief Economic History of the World*, Princeton: Princeton University Press, 2007.

King James I, *The Charter of the Virginia Company*, 1606.

Mayflower Compact, 1620: Agreement Between the Settlers at New Plymouth.

John Locke, *Second Treatise of Civil Government*, 1690.

William Waller Hening, *Statutes at Large; Being a Collection of all the Laws of Virginia*, Richmond: Samuel Pleasants, 1809–1823, II, 170, 260, 266, 270.

Sidney Mintz, *Sweetness and Power: The Place of Sugar in Modern History*, New York: Penguin Books, 1986.

Benjamin Franklin, *The Autobiography of Benjamin Franklin*, 1791.

James Madison, *Federalist 10*, November 22, 1787.

James Madison, *Federalist 51*, February 8, 1788.

Sections from *The Constitution of the United States*, 1787, and Amendments thereto.

Alexander Hamilton, *Reports of the Secretary of the Treasury of the United States on Public Credit*, 1790.

Alexander Hamilton, *Report on a National Bank*, 1790.

Alexander Hamilton, *Report on Manufactures*, 1791.

James K. Paulding, *Letters from the South*, vol. 2.

Vincent Nolte, *The Memoirs of Vincent Nolte*, New York: G. H. Watt, 1934.

Henry Clay, "The American System," speech to the Senate of the United States, February 2, 3, and 6, 1832.

Charles Ball, *Slavery in the United States*, New York: John S. Taylor, 1837.

Kenneth Pomeranz, *The Great Divergence: China, Europe, and the Making of the Modern World Economy*, Princeton: Princeton University Press, 2001.

Sean Wilentz, *Chants Democratic: New York City and the Rise of the American Working Class, 1788–1850*, New York: Oxford University Press, 1984.

"The Bay State Strike," *The New York Times*, February 29, 1860.

President Andrew Jackson, *Veto Message Regarding the Bank of the United States*, July 10, 1832.

Edward E. Baptist, "Toxic Debt, Liar Loans, and Securitized Human Beings," from Michael Zakim and Gary Kornblith, eds., *Capitalism Take Command*, Chicago: University of Chicago Press, 2011.

"Atrocious Murder of Helen Jewett," *Spirit of the Times* [newspaper], April 16, 1836.

Joshua Leavitt, *The Financial Power of Slavery*, 1840.

Abraham Lincoln, *Address before the Wisconsin State Agricultural Society*, September 30, 1859.

William Cronon, *Nature's Metropolis: Chicago and the Great West*, New York: W. W. Norton, 1991.

Sven Beckert, *The Monied Metropolis: New York City and the Consolidation of the American Bourgeoisie, 1850–1896*, Cambridge: Cambridge University Press, 2001.

Richard White, *Railroaded: The Transcontinentals and the Making of Modern America*, New York: W. W. Norton, 2011.

Jacob Riis, *How the Other Half Lives: Studies Among the Tenements of New York*, New York: Charles Scribners' Sons, 1890.

National People's Party Platform, 1892.

Charles Postel, *The Populist Vision*, New York: Oxford University Press, 2007.

Andrew Carnegie, *The Gospel of Wealth*, New York: The Century Co., 1901.

Jane Addams, *Twenty Years at Hull-House with Autobiographical Notes*, New York: The MacMillan Company, 1910.

W. E. B. DuBois, *The Souls of Black Folk*, Chicago: A. C. McClurg & Co., 1903.

"Jim Crow Laws," National Park Service, accessed February 10, 2017. http://www.nps.gov/malu/learn/education/jim_crow_laws.htm.

Eugene V. Debs, *Opening Speech Delivered as Candidate of the Socialist Party for President at Indianapolis*, September 1, 1904.

Industrial Workers of the World, *Preamble to the IWW Constitution*, July 7, 1905.

William Z. Foster, *Syndicalism*, Chicago: 1913.

Joe Hill, *I.W.W. Songs To Fan the Flames of Discontent*, Joe Hill Memorial Edition, (Chicago: I.W.W. Publishing Bureau), 1917.

Frederick Taylor, *The Principles of Scientific Management*, New York: Harper & Brothers, 1913.

Henry Ford, "Ford Ideals: Being a Selection from 'Mr. Ford's Page'" in *The Dearborn Independent*, Dearborn, MI: Dearborn Pub. Co, 1922, 87, 89–93.

Marc Levinson, *The Great A&P and the Struggle for Small Business in America*, New York: Hill & Wang, 2011.

Franklin Roosevelt, *Second Fireside Chat*, May 7, 1933.

Henry Kraus, *The Many and the Few: A Chronicle of the Dynamic Auto Workers*, Urbana: University of Illinois Press, 1985.

Franklin Roosevelt, *Radio Address of the President Announcing Unlimited National Emergency*, May 27, 1941.

Franklin Roosevelt, *Executive Order 8802: Prohibition of Discrimination in the Defense Industry*, June 25, 1941.

George Marshall, *Speech at Harvard University on the European Aid Program*, June 5, 1947.

Walt Whitman Rostow, "The Stages of Economic Growth," *Economic History Review* (1959): 1, 2, 4, 7, 8, 11.

William Whyte, Jr., "Budgetism: Opiate of the Middle Class," *Fortune*, Volume 53, June 1, 1956, 133–34, 137.

Louis Hyman, "Rethinking the Postwar Corporation: Management, Monopolies, and Markets" in *What's Good for Business: Business and American Politics since World War II*, New York: Oxford University Press, 2012, 195–97, 199–204, 209.

IBM, *Annual Report*, 1967.

Jefferson Cowie, "'A One-Sided Class War': Rethinking Doug Fraser's 1978 Resignation from the Labor-Management Group," *Labor History*, 2003, 307–309, 311–14.

Harry Braverman, *Labor and Monopoly Capital: The Degradation of Work in the Twentieth Century*, Monthly Review, New York, 1974.

John Huey, "Where Managers Will Go," *Fortune* 125, no. 2 (January 27, 1992): 50.

Gerald F. Davis, "Not Just a Mortgage Crisis: How Finance Maimed Society," *Strategic Organization*, February 2010.

Permissions

The First Charter of Virginia
Courtesy of the Lillian Goldman Law Library's Avalon Project, Yale Law School

The Mayflower Compact
Courtesy of the Lillian Goldman Law Library's Avalon Project, Yale Law School

Sweetness and Power
From *Sweetness and Power* by Sidney W. Mintz, copyright © 1985 by Sidney W. Mintz. Used by permission of Viking Penguin, a division of Penguin Group (USA) LLC.

The Great Divergence
Kenneth Pomeranz, *The Great Divergence*, Princeton University Press. Reprinted by permission of Princeton University Press.

Chants Democratic
Chants Democratic: New York City and the Rise of the American Working Class, 1788–1850, by Sean Wilentz, 101–103, 119–24. By permission of Oxford University Press, USA.

Veto Message Regarding the Bank of the United States
Courtesy of the Lillian Goldman Law Library's Avalon Project, Yale Law School

Toxic Debt, Liar Loans, and Securitized Human Beings
Excerpts from "Toxic Debt, Liar Loans, Collateralized and Securitized Human Beings, and the Panic of 1873" by Edward E. Baptist from *Capitalism Takes Command*, edited by Michael Zakim and Gary J. Kornblith © 2012 by The University of Chicago. Reprinted by permission of the University of Chicago Press.

Nature's Metropolis
From *Nature's Metropolis: Chicago and the Great West* by William Cronon. Copyright © 1991 by William Cronon. Used by permission of W. W. Norton & Company, Inc.

The Monied Metropolis
The Monied Metropolis: New York City and the Consolidation of the American Bourgeoisie, 1850–1896 by Sven Beckert © Cambridge University Press 1993. Reprinted with permission of Cambridge University Press.

Railroaded
From *Railroaded: The Transcontinental and the Making of Modern America* by Richard White. Copyright © 2011 by Richard White. Used by permission of W. W. Norton & Company, Inc.

The Populist Vision
The Populist Vision by Charles Postel (2009), 3–5, 9–10. By permission of Oxford University Press, USA.

The Great A&P and the Struggle for Small Business in America
Excerpts from "Minute Men and Tax Men" and "The Supermarket" from *The Great A&P and the Struggle for Small Business in America* by Marc Levinson. Copyright © 2011 by Marc Levinson. Reprinted by permission of Hill and Wang, a division of Farrar, Straus and Giroux, LLC.

The Many and the Few
From *The Many and the Few: A Chronicle of the Dynamic Auto Workers*, by Henry Kraus. Used by permission of University of Illinois Press.

The Stages of Economic Growth
Copyright © 2008, John Wiley and Sons.

Budgetism
Excerpted from *Fortune* magazine, May 1, 1956, copyright © 1956 Time Inc. Used under license.

IBM Annual Report
Reprint Courtesy of International Business Machines Corporation, copyright © 1967 International Business Machines Corporation.

Where Managers Will Go
From *Fortune* magazine, January 27, 1992, copyright © 1992 Time Inc. Used under license.

Not Just a Mortgage Crisis
Reproduced by permission of SAGE Publications Ltd., London, Los Angeles, New Delhi, Singapore and Washington, DC, from Gerald F. Davis, "Not Just a Mortgage Crisis: How Finance Maimed Society," *Strategic Organization*, copyright © Gerald F. Davis, 2010.